6 GO

# Private Voluntary Organizations
# As Agents of Development

D0587584

# Westview Replica Editions

The concept of Westview Replica Editions is a response to the continuing crisis in academic and informational publishing. Library budgets for books have been severely curtailed. Ever larger portions of general library budgets are being diverted from the purchase of books and used for data banks, computers, micromedia, and other methods of information retrieval. Interlibrary loan structures further reduce the edition sizes required to satisfy the needs of the scholarly community. Economic pressures on the university presses and the few private scholarly publishing companies have severely limited the capacity of the industry to properly serve the academic and research communities. As a result, many manuscripts dealing with important subjects, often representing the highest level of scholarship, are no longer economically viable publishing projects--or, if accepted for publication, are typically subject to lead times ranging from one to three years.

Westview Replica Editions are our practical solution to the problem. We accept a manuscript in camera-ready form, typed according to our specifications, and move it immediately into the production process. As always, the selection criteria include the importance of the subject, the work's contribution to scholarship, and its insight, originality of thought, and excellence of exposition. The responsibility for editing and proofreading lies with the author or sponsoring institution. We prepare chapter headings and display pages, file for copyright, and obtain Library of Congress Cataloging in Publication Data. A detailed manual contains simple instructions for preparing the final typescript, and our editorial staff is always available to answer questions.

The end result is a book printed on acid-free paper and bound in sturdy library-quality soft covers. We manufacture these books ourselves using equipment that does not require a lengthy make-ready process and that allows us to publish first editions of 300 to 600 copies and to reprint even smaller quantities as needed. Thus, we can produce Replica Editions quickly and can keep even very specialized books in print as long as there is a demand for them.

# About the Book and Editor

## *Private Voluntary Organizations As Agents of Development*
### edited by Robert F. Gorman

Private voluntary organizations have an increasingly important
role to play in the provision of development assistance, either as
alternative forms of resource flow or as channels of aid that are
systematically integrated into the official intergovernmental aid
system.  This book explores the practical and theoretical aspects
of PVOs, including the nature of and prospects for PVO/government
ties, the role of PVOs as facilitators of small enterprise, PVO
relationships with indigenous voluntary agencies, and the need for
careful evaluation of PVO projects from the standpoint of cost-
effectiveness and replicability.  The role of PVOs as advocates
of development educators is also discussed.

Dr. Robert F. Gorman is assistant professor of Political
Science at Southwest Texas State University. He recently served as
a  fellow on the Council on Foreign Relations in the Bureau for
Refugee Programs in the U.S Department of State.  He is currently
a visiting scholar at Africare, a Washington D.C.-based private
voluntary organization, where he is conducting research on refugee-
related development assistance under a Ford Foundation grant.  He
is author of *Political Conflict in the Horn of Africa* and numerous
articles on political and economic issues in Africa.

# Private Voluntary Organizations As Agents of Development

edited by Robert F. Gorman

Westview Press / Boulder and London

*A Westview Replica Edition*

Published in the United States of America by
   Westview Press, Inc.
   5500 Central Avenue
   Boulder, Colorado 80301
   Frederick A. Praeger, Publisher

Library of Congress Cataloging in Publication Data
Main entry under title:
Private voluntary organizations as agents of development.
   (A Westview replica edition)
   1. Economic assistance. 2. Technical assistance.
I. Gorman, Robert, 1950-      .
HC60.P722 1985      361.7'6      83-23325
ISBN 0-86531-997-9

Printed and bound in the United States of America
10 9 8 7 6 5 4 3 2 '

# Contents

# Tables

# Figures

# Preface

Over the past decade, interest in the nature and role of Private Voluntary Organizations (PVOs) as potential agents of development has increased. Still, the literature on this subject is surprisingly thin. The systematic and scholarly study and evaluation of PVOs is long overdue and merits ever greater attention. It is in such a spirit, and with the knowledge that systematic analysis of PVOs has only recently begun, that this volume was conceived. Because of the largely exploratory nature of the existing knowledge about PVOs, we do not claim to have compiled a definitive work in this volume. However, it is our belief that we have addressed and, perhaps, clarified some of the more important questions about PVOs as agents of development. We hope that this book will stimulate further study of this important subject.

At one level this book represents evidence of the growing interest among scholars and practitioners alike in the role of PVOs as agents of development. Most of the contributions to this volume are revised versions of papers presented at the 24th annual International Studies Association (ISA) meetings held in Mexico City in April of 1983. At no previous ISA Conference were so many papers dealing with various aspects of PVOs in evidence. The appearance of this volume underscores our belief that scholarly interest in PVOs is on the upswing and that future research on PVOs can be enhanced by collaborative efforts.

We also believe that in order to understand both the theoretical and practical concerns that arise from PVO activities, it is necessary to approach such inquiries from a variety of perspectives. Hence, it is appropriate to note that among the contributors to this volume are several political scientists, an economist and an anthropologist. The contributors include scholars, as well as former and active government and PVO officials. The perspectives and the views of the various contributors are not always in complete concert, nor was there any intention that they should be so. Nevertheless, it is the common belief of the contributors that PVOs constitute an increasingly important avenue for development and that their role must be carefully studied and understood to ensure that it will remain a productive and beneficial one.

The editor wishes to thank both the Council on Foreign Relations and Southwest Texas State University for the assistance that made the timely appearance of this volume possible.

*Robert F. Gorman*
*Washington, D.C.*

# 1
# Introduction

*Robert F. Gorman*

Over roughly the past three decades, there have been literally thousands of volumes that have addressed innumerable issues and concerns surrounding the processes of economic and political development in poor countries. Development has been variously conceived of as a goal, an end product, a set of policies, and as a process. Advice on how to achieve development has run the gamut from advocacy of bilateral and multilateral aid, trade, and investment to socialist revolution, self-reliance, and autarky—to name but a few of the more obvious prescriptions. Students of development have included economists, psychologists, sociologists, anthropologists, historians, theologians, politicians, technicians, administrators, and political scientists. In short, many words written by people with different perspectives have described what development is and how it can be best achieved.

In such a context, this volume represents but a modest effort to study the role of private voluntary organizations (PVOs) in the development process. Admittedly, PVOs provide only a small segment of the globe's development assistance. But it has been frequently observed that, however modest their relative overall contribution, PVOs have performed a vital role in targeting assistance for the emergency relief needs of refugees from natural disasters and man-made cataclysms, as well as in servicing the longer-term development needs of the world's poor. PVOs have often been characterized as efficient vehicles through which resources can be channelled across national borders directly to the poor, with a minimum of the diversion and dilution that often accompanies aid flows through multilateral and national bureaucracies. These and other aspects of PVOs will be explored further in the following pages.

What are PVOs? The various studies that are included in this volume have provided a number of useful definitions, from which some general features of a

catholic definition of PVOs emerges. Those PVOs which
will comprise the focus of this study are
nongovernmental (private), tax-exempt, nonprofit
agencies engaged in overseas provision of services for
relief and development purposes. They also derive at
least a portion of their funds from private, charitable
contributions. This encompasses a wide variety of
organizations but suggests some parameters. Excluded
from our analysis are the thousands of voluntary
agencies which are engaged primarily in local or
domestic pursuits that have little or no international
impact. Nevertheless, these groups represent a
potential population of agencies which could be tapped
by their foreign-service-oriented brethren to broaden
the constituency for international development
activities.

Also excluded from this analysis are those agencies
that are officially responsible to governments or
international organizations (IOs), as well as those that
receive virtually all of their resources from
governments and IOs. Although it is conceivable that a
100 percent governmentally funded organization which is
not statutorily responsible to a government could
function as an independent agent, and not as a mere
appendage of a government, the voluntary character of
such an organization is still absent.

Apart from groups fully funded by governments, a
real question exists regarding how voluntary an agency
must be to qualify for consideration as a PVO. In other
words, what mix of government versus voluntary,
charitable contributions must an agency maintain to
qualify as a PVO? Some organizations such as Catholic
Relief Services (CRS) and CARE, for instance, receive as
much as 80 percent of their revenue from U.S. government
sources. On the other hand, the remaining funds that
each of these organizations secures through private
sources exceeds entire budgets of many, indeed most,
other PVOs. The matter of private versus public funding
is one which will be addressed in much greater detail in
the following pages. It is enough to observe here, that
those organizations which continue to solicit even a
small portion of their resources through private
sources, are treated as PVOs in this study.

Also excluded from our analysis are all
profit-making organizations. While these may make
considerable contributions to development through
investment activities and through donations to private
charities, their primary purpose does not lie in the
direction of philanthropy. By contrast, PVOs have as
their raison d'etre the provision of resources and
services to others without profit as a motive.

Beyond the general nature of PVOs discussed above,
there is great diversity in their operating styles,
management practices, and development philosophies.

Rather than limit the definition of PVOs any further
than has been suggested above, we believe it best to
recognize the diversity of the PVO community as a fact,
and, perhaps, as a strength. We will take note of the
wide diversity of PVOs by distinguishing between those
that are heavily financed by governments and those which
are not; between those that are secular and those that
are religious in orientation; and between those that are
large in terms of personnel, budget, and scope of
operations and those that are smaller in size and more
limited in scope. In the chapters that follow
distinctions of this sort are analyzed in greater depth.

In addition to understanding what a PVO is, it is
also useful to consider where PVOs have an impact. Put
simply, PVOs have an impact everywhere. There is hardly
a corner of the globe that does not in some fashion or
another show evidence of the activities of PVOs, whether
in the developed world as a result of the widespread
fund raising and educational efforts of PVOs, or in the
developing world where thousands of PVO personnel engage
in grass-roots efforts to promote human development. A
brief perusal of the Organization for Economic
Cooperation and Development (OECD) directory of
nongovernmental organizations will attest to the global
scope of PVO activities.[1] Most PVOs are headquartered
in the developed world, primarily in Europe and North
America. However, hundreds of indigenous PVOs (IPVOs)
have emerged in the developing world itself--some as
affiliates of foreign-based PVOs, others as autonomous
local entities. These groups are of considerable
potential importance, particularly if, as students of
development have claimed, development cannot in the
final analysis be imported, but must be nurtured
domestically through the development of indigenous
institutions. Hence, the emergence of IPVOs may be a
harbinger of genuine, self-reliant development in the
Third World and thus may merit encouragement and support.

Using a broad definition of PVOs involved in
overseas service, the United States alone serves as
headquarters for over four hundred PVOs.[2] This
represents the largest single concentration of PVOs in
any single country. Only seven of the contiguous
forty-eight states have no PVOs headquartered within
their geographical bounds. The largest concentrations
of PVOs are in the Midwest, the Northeast, and
California. New York serves as the headquarters for 111
PVOs. Sixty-eight are headquartered in Washington D.C.,
thirty-eight in California, thirty-two in Illinois and
thirty-one in Pennsylvania. But the reach of PVOs goes
beyond major population centers. Church-based PVOs, for
instance, can reach even the most remote congregations.
Moreover, given the use of the modern electronic media
by many PVOs for promotional purposes, few Americans
remain completely unexposed to the development and

relief activities of PVOs.

In addition to their pervasiveness in the United States, U.S.-based PVOs carry out relief and development activities in almost every corner of the globe. They act as linkages between the U.S. public as potential donors and the vast numbers of poor recipients of PVO development and relief assistance. The reach of the U.S. PVOs is truly global in character and effect, and touches the lives of people in countless ways and innumerable places. It is instructive, for instance, to look at each developing country and count the number of U.S.-based PVOs that operate programs in each one. Using the Technical Assistance Information Clearinghouse (TAICH) Directory of nonprofit organizations that engage in overseas development activities, one gets a sense of the global involvement of PVOs.[3] In the case of Africa, one finds that there are ninety-two U.S.-based PVOs operating programs in Kenya, fifty-six in Zaire, fifty-five in Tanzania, fifty-one in Nigeria, forty-nine in Uganda and thirty-eight in Sudan. A total of fifty-one African countries host one or more U.S.-based PVOs. Indeed, if one were to add together the number of PVOs that operate programs in each of these countries, the total would reach about 1,060, for a regional average of roughly twenty PVOs per country. Of course, many U.S.-based PVOs operate programs in more than one African country, which accounts for this rather large figure. Church World Service (CWS) assists thirty-eight African nations, and CRS thirty-one, to give but two examples.

In Latin America there are thirty-nine countries that host U.S.-based PVOs. Mexico, alone, hosts ninety-four U.S. PVOs. Brazil hosts eighty-five, Peru eighty-one, and Colombia sixty--to give only a few examples. There is an average of fifty PVOs operating programs per Latin American country. In East Asia and the island nations of the Pacific, there are about thirty-two nations that host a total of six-hundred U.S. PVOs, the largest concentrations being in the Philippines with 109 and in Indonesia with eighty-two. Finally, looking at the Near East and South Asia, a total of twenty-three countries host 515 U.S. based PVOs, for a regional average of twenty-two PVOs per country. India, alone, boasts a total of 115 U.S. PVOs. Looking at the global picture, a total of 145 countries and territories host nearly 3,450 U.S.-based PVOs. Using such a measure, it is obvious that PVOs are a pervasive phenomenon throughout the Third World. Taken individually, the impact of any one PVO may be rather small and, perhaps, even unnoticeable. Indeed, the presence of some PVOs in Third World countries consists of only a few missionaries involved in educational or health activities. In many cases, however, PVOs have numerous projects within a country,

employing substantial numbers of expatriate and
indigenous staff persons.  They are involved in every
conceivable aspect of development; education, technology
transfer, income generation, credit extension,
agricultural development, water projects, reforestation
schemes, and community health programs.

Whether PVOs perform the varied tasks they pursue
in the developing world effectively is another
question.  What can be said, however, is that U.S. PVOs
have carved out for themselves an important and probably
permanent place in the global effort to promote
development among the countries of the Third World.

As noted above, PVOs operate not only out of the
United States, but from a number of other developed
countries as well.  Still, as Table 1.1 indicates, the
United States leads the OECD both in the number of PVOs
and in the amount of development assistance provided by
PVOs.  Excluding those PVOs that are classified in the
OECD Directory as being international in character (that
is, as being organizations which cannot be attributed to
a particular nation) the United States accounts for over
one-fourth of the total (428 of 1602 PVOs).[4]  U.S.
PVOs also rank first in the amount of development
assistance they provide, which exceeds $1,300 million.
The PVOs from the Federal Republic of Germany (FRG)
follow with $420.7 million, the United Kingdom (UK) with
$104.7 million and Canada with $102 million.  However,
it should be noted that substantial percentages of PVO
disbursements from all developed countries represent
official government funds channelled through PVOs.
Typically, government contributions to PVOs exceed 50
percent of all PVO disbursements.

While the United States leads in the number of PVOs
and the amount of PVO assistance, table 1.2 illustrates
that U.S. PVO contributions, as measured by percentage
of Gross National Product (GNP) and on a per capita
basis, lag somewhat behind those of a number of
Development Assistance Countries (DAC) in Europe.  In
terms of PVO contributions as a percentage of GNP, the
United States ranks sixth, behind Norway, the FRG,
Switzerland, Belgium and Sweden.  Based on the per
capita measure it ranks fifth behind Switzerland,
Norway, Sweden and the FRG, respectively.  Americans
contribute nearly six dollars per person to PVOs, while
the Swiss contribute ten, the Norwegians about eight,
and the Swedes and West Germans about seven each.
Still, when compared with the even weaker showing of
official U.S. bilateral and multilateral assistance on
the same measures with other DAC countries, U.S. PVOs
can be said to be reasonably energetic.  Indeed, if only
in terms of the sheer size of their contribution, the
role of U.S. PVOs in development activities cannot be
discounted, even if other indicators show them lagging
somewhat behind their counterparts in Europe.

TABLE 1.1
PVOs by Number in OECD Countries and by Volume
of Development Assistance

| Country | Number of PVOs | Rank | PVO Development Assistance (1980, in U.S. Millions of Dollars) | Rank |
|---|---|---|---|---|
| Australia | 24 | 16 | 39.8 | 9 |
| Austria | 39 | 13 | 23.5 | 13 |
| Belgium | 93 | 6 | 45.0 | 8 |
| Canada | 150 | 2 | 102.0 | 4 |
| Denmark | 50 | 11 | 12.9 | 15 |
| FRG | 111 | 5 | 420.7 | 2 |
| France | 120 | 3 | 35.7 | 10 |
| Finland | 49 | 12 | 15.5 | 14 |
| Iceland | 1 | 22 | -- | -- |
| Ireland | 16 | 17 | -- | -- |
| Italy | 64 | 10 | 3.1 | 17 |
| Japan | 36 | 14 | 26.4 | 12 |
| Luxembourg | 15 | 19 | -- | -- |
| Netherlands | 78 | 8 | 78.7 | 5 |
| New Zealand | 16 | 17 | 6.8 | 16 |
| Norway | 34 | 15 | 33.0 | 11 |
| Portugal | 3 | 21 | -- | -- |
| Spain | 9 | 20 | -- | -- |
| Sweden | 85 | 7 | 59.0 | 7 |
| Switzerland | 69 | 9 | 63.2 | 6 |
| UK | 112 | 4 | 104.7 | 3 |
| USA | 428 | 1 | 1,301.0 | 1 |

Source: OECD, Directory of Non-Governmental Organizations in OECD
Member Countries Active in Development Cooperation, volume 1,
(Paris, 1980). This source includes only those groups involved, at
least in part, in development education and/or development aid.
Groups which are exclusively involved in relief work are excluded.
Data on 1980 PVO development assistance is adapted from the Develop-
ment Assistance Countries Review, Table A 10, Flows of Financial
Resources to Developing Countries and Multilateral Agencies.

TABLE 1.2
PVO Contributions as a Percentage of GNP
and on a Per Capita Basis

| Country | PVO Contribution as a Percentage of GNP | Rank | Per Capita Contribution (in U.S. dollars) | Rank |
|---------|------------------------------------------|------|--------------------------------------------|------|
| Australia | .035 | 12 | 2.80 | 11 |
| Austria | .040 | 10 | 3.10 | 10 |
| Belgium | .070 | 4 | 4.60 | 7 |
| Canada | .050 | 8 | 4.30 | 8 |
| Denmark | .025 | 14 | 2.50 | 12 |
| FRG | .080 | 2 | 6.90 | 4 |
| France | .006 | 15 | .70 | 15 |
| Finland | .047 | 9 | 3.20 | 9 |
| Italy | .001 | 17 | .05 | 17 |
| Japan | .003 | 16 | .23 | 16 |
| Netherlands | .060 | 6 | 5.70 | 6 |
| New Zealand | .038 | 11 | 2.20 | 13 |
| Norway | .085 | 1 | 8.10 | 2 |
| Sweden | .068 | 5 | 7.10 | 3 |
| Switzerland | .072 | 3 | 10.00 | 1 |
| UK | .034 | 13 | 1.90 | 14 |
| USA | .060 | 6 | 5.90 | 5 |

Sources: Data on population and GNP are adapted from Ruth Leger
Sivard, World Military and Social Expenditures (Leesburg, Virginia:
World Priorities, 1981). Data on GNP and Population are based on
1978 figures, while data on PVO contributions are based upon 1980
figures obtained from the DAC Review for 1980. Hence, the figures
in this table should be interpreted only as approximations.

What should be quite clear from the above tables,
is that PVOs are quite active not only within the United
States but in other developed countries. This should be
borne in mind as we turn our attention in this volume to
a more explicit analysis of U.S., and to a lesser
extent, Canadian PVOs. While ample justification exists
to study U.S.-based PVOs, as the above data demonstrate,
it should not be assumed by the reader that U.S. PVOs
have a monopoly on development assistance monies,
strategies, and programs. We have chosen the largely
American context as the focus of this book not merely
because of its objective importance in global PVO
activities, but also because it is within the realm of
the experience and expertise of the contributors to this
volume.
Having defined the nature of PVOs and examined the
scope of their activity, it is appropriate that we turn
now to a brief discussion of the recent emergence of

PVOs as agents of relief and development. Although this volume is not intended to be a comprehensive history of PVOs in development assistance, it is important to note that PVOs have played an important part historically in the provision of assistance to the poor, particularly after World War II (WWII). PVOs, along with governments and the nascent machinery of the United Nations (U.N.) system, were heavily involved in the provision of emergency relief assistance programs to cope with the devastating refugee problems and economic dislocations that occurred in the wake of WWII. Even before WWII, missionary organizations, while pursuing their own religious goals, provided education and material resources to poor regions of the globe. As the decolonization of the international system proceeded and as the post-independence problems of the newly emerging nations grew, PVOs expanded their services to the Third World.

Throughout the post-WWII period, PVOs provided modest but important emergency relief assistance to refugees, while contributing as well to the physical needs of nonrefugees in developing countries. An important distinction should be made here between emergency refugee relief assistance and development assistance. Although PVOs have historically engaged in both, the primary focus until the mid-1960s was a welfare dominated one. That is, food, health benefits, etc., were supplied without systematically attempting to create a self-reliant capability among the indigenous poor or to promote long-term development. The welfare orientation began to shift in the late 1960s and with even greater emphasis in the 1970s to a recognition among many PVOs that genuine development would be generated only if a more self-reliant approach were adopted by local institutions. During this period, however, the emergency relief needs of the poorest of the poor grew rather than diminished, so that many of the resources PVOs had at their disposal were funneled into refugee and emergency relief rather than long-term development efforts. Indeed, as PVOs attempted to cope with the refugee problems of Asia and Africa in the 1970s, it became clear that a focus on long-term development would be essential to ameliorate the future problems of refugees. With this objective in mind many of them began to spend a larger amount of time and energy promoting long-term development and not simply short-term refugee relief.

The focus of this book will be primarily on the more recent development activities of PVOs, while recognizing that many of the lessons learned from evaluating those activities will be of relevance to the refugee relief side of PVO programs. The fact that the development aspect of the PVO mission is emphasized here, should not in any way be taken as a diminution of

the important role PVOs play in refugee relief
activities.  Rather, it should be seen as an attempt to
demonstrate that refugee relief problems must be
ultimately addressed in the broader context of
development.

ORGANIZATION OF THE VOLUME

Although there is no formal division of this book
into sections, those contributions which consist in the
main of reviews of specific bodies of literature as they
apply to PVOs, and those which are of a more theoretical
or conceptual nature are among the earlier chapters.
The later chapters tend to evaluate and examine specific
activities of PVOs.

Based on extensive experience in the private
voluntary sector, Minear leads off with an inquiry into
the role of PVOs as agents of development.  He examines
a series of philosophical and policy-oriented questions
that thoughtful persons from the voluntary sector and
others will find refreshingly candid.  In so doing, he
reviews a substantial body of literature on development
assistance, and suggests several ways that PVOs can
rethink their role as assistance agencies.

Gorman follows with a review of the Basic Human
Needs (BHN) literature and a discussion of how PVOs can
fit into the institutional arrangements that currently
exist and/or could be developed to further promote the
achievement of BHN objectives.

Blaser then reviews several bodies of literature
which have been until now, largely ignored as being
applicable to PVOs, namely, the literature on theories
of organization and public choice.  He demonstrates how
PVOs can be analyzed in much the same way as other
organizational entities.  He explores the role of
incentives and disincentives in group participation,
coalition-building, and in inter-organizational behavior.

In the chapters that follow, a more explicit
emphasis is placed on evaluating PVO performance in
particular contexts.  Roberts, for instance, examines
specific nongovernmental and governmental pressures that
arise from the PVOs' domestic environment.  He observes
that these may often affect programmatic decisions of
PVOs more than the needs to be found in the field itself.

Smith follows with a comparative discussion of
several key characteristics of PVOs based on interviews
with officials from both U.S. and Canadian PVOs.  He
examines the views of these officials about the mission,
effectiveness, governance, and political character of
the PVOs they represent.  The observations that flow
from these interviews are informative and insightful.

Hunt then examines the role of PVOs in the
important area of Small Enterprise Development.  After

an exhaustive review of evaluation literature on
enterprise development and credit schemes for small
entrepreneurs, Hunt suggests several conclusions about
how PVOs engaged in this sector can avoid pitfalls and
promote small enterprises in a way that will enhance
rather than detract from efforts to promote general
development--including efforts to alleviate the
condition of poorer segments of Third World countries.

Ellis follows with an evaluation of PVOs as
disseminators of appropriate technologies. He finds
that PVOs have in this particular respect not performed
as well as they might have been expected to. He calls
into question the cost-effectiveness and replicability
of many PVO projects in this area, but suggests that
performance could be improved, primarily through more
careful economic costing of projects and by designing
and identifying programs in keeping with local needs.
His proposal for a computerized information network for
program identification, economic costing, generation of
local price information on commodities and manufactures,
holds promise as one way to improve project success in
terms of cost-effectiveness.

Calavan closes the list of contributions with an
imaginative examination of what may be refered to as the
fundamentals of appropriate administration. He provides
a series of recommendations on how administrators of all
kinds, whether with PVOs, central, or local governments,
can work in ways that will create room for the
development of local initiatives. Development
administrators should find in Calavan's chapter ample
food for thought on how to pursue such a development
strategy.

Finally, in a brief concluding chapter, several of
the major themes that recur throughout the volume are
briefly identified and summarized.

NOTES

1. See, for instance, the OECD, Directory of
Non-governmental Organizations in OECD Member Countries
Active in Development Cooperation, v. 1, (Paris, 1981).

2. See Wynta Boynes, ed., U.S. Non-Profit
Organizations in Development Assistance Abroad, TAICH
1983 Directory. This Directory, compiled by the
Technical Assistance Information Clearinghouse of the
American Council of Voluntary Agencies for Foreign
Service, is the most comprehensive listing available of
U.S. PVOs, their programs, and activities. Although the
Directory draws a distinction between voluntary

agencies, missions, and foundations, the term PVO can be generally understood to encompass them all. The key commonalities are that voluntary agencies, missions and foundations are private, nonprofit, nongovernmental organizations involved in overseas development activities.

3. Ibid.

4. See OECD, <u>Directory of Non-governmental Organizations</u>, for profiles on individual organizations.

# 2
# Reflections on Development Policy: A View from the Private Voluntary Sector

*Larry Minear*

Issues of development policy have taken on new importance in recent years. Growing public skepticism about whether development programs really benefit the poor has combined with reappraisals by development professionals themselves to lead the three major providers of external development assistance--multilateral institutions, bilateral agencies, and PVOs--to raise fundamental questions about the development enterprise itself.

This essay grew out of reading and reflection about some of those questions during a sabbatical in late 1980 at the International Food Policy Research Institute in Washington, D.C. It was initially an attempt to clarify some key issues for myself and to stimulate discussion of them within the development agencies for which I work. I welcome the opportunity to have my thoughts circulate more widely, now in somewhat revised and updated form.

## DEVELOPMENT AND POWER RELATIONS

All development agencies, governmental and private alike, need a clear philosophy of development. From that philosophy will flow resource allocations and program activities.

According to one philosophy, articulated by Arnold Tolen, a church leader from Cameroon, development is "the struggle against the system of exploitation," a battle to create "self-sufficient and self-reliant societies and communities able to contribute freely and in their own right to the world community."[1] From this vantage point, activities which work to adjust existing inequities in favor of the poor would have a special claim on resources, while those which leave current power relationships unaltered would not. Priority would be given, for example, to what one economist has

13

called the "apparently 'safe' microlevel programmes [which can become] seed-beds of social struggle."[2]

If social change is viewed in less conflictual terms, development activities might take quite a different form. Organizations might seek, for example, to assist low income people and the agencies which serve them to improve the quality and range of services delivered and received. A third approach might be more contextual, based on the view that development takes different forms and has different dynamics in various communities, countries, and regions, with program activities adapted accordingly.

Whether development practitioners view the development process in revolutionary or evolutionary terms, whether it is seen as liberation from oppressive power structures or as a gradual shift to the more equitable distribution of resources, power relationships need to be taken more seriously as factors which facilitate, or obstruct, changes in the status quo. If development efforts are to improve the quality of life of the poor--and that is a theme common to most definitions--such efforts should be informed by a philosophy of social change which takes seriously the structural nature of poverty.

In his exhaustive analysis almost a decade ago of Patterns of Poverty in the Third World, Charles Elliott concluded that there are structures of enrichment and impoverishment in every society. He reviewed the interaction of such structures with the development process in thirteen countries, some of which have chosen development strategies based on economic growth and others on equity and redistribution. Elliott's rather stark conclusion was that while some countries and strategies have been more successful than others, most countries--and the international community itself--are fighting a losing battle against both urban and rural poverty. There is little to suggest that the outcomes are significantly different a decade later.

The moral of the tale is not that entrenched political inequities doom to failure from the outset all externally assisted development efforts, as some writers have sought to demonstrate. The point is rather that such inequities make some kinds of assistance to the poor more appropriate than others. For example, rather than assuming that "all the administrative structures serve only the interests of the privileged and that 'mere reformism' can never achieve anything for the excluded,"[3] outside aid can indeed help the more progressive elements in government bureaucracies do better by the poor. Government administrative bureaucracies may in fact be manipulated in favor of the poor through carefully directed external assistance.

The concern for who benefits from development aid

needs also to inform the choice of development interventions. Elliott encourages the development of "poor-biased" technology such as improvements in dryland farming and in the nutritional value of the food crops of the poor. Such technology can "actually construct an equity dynamic in favor of the excluded" by benefiting the poor disproportionately despite the fact that "any technical change is likely to bring benefits that are easily subverted by existing privileged groups."[4]

Elliott also recommends "a reorientation of international interests" to secure both greater access to and improved distribution of benefits for those otherwise excluded from the development process. "Foreign funding agencies, from the World Bank to nongovernment organizations, can increasingly put pressure on planning bureaus at least to abandon the assumption that all income streams are equally important, regardless of who owns them...The incorporation of the excluded themselves into the process of poverty planning is a necessary precondition of its success."[5]

Pressure in these areas, he concludes, offers "the best, though meagre" hope of effective social change using outside resources in favor of the poor. On the other hand, the failure to take power relations into account or the assumption that governmentally channelled aid cannot help the poor squanders opportunities for equity-oriented social change and exacerbates the situation of the poor.

## POWER RELATIONS AND PROJECTS

The international development community as a whole should be deeply troubled by Elliott's well-documented pessimism about the overall development prospect. So, too, by his skepticism that the sum total of all governmental and private development efforts, however exemplary and self-critical, will ever succeed in liberating the poor from their impoverishment. Leaving aside for the moment the larger question of whether the development enterprise can help secure justice for the poor, we need to ask whether other country and project experience confirms Elliott's thesis that there are structures of enrichment and impoverishment that resist well-meaning efforts at social change, on occasion even making such efforts counterproductive.

A range of studies suggests that it does. A Swedish report on Rural Development Research--The Role of Power Relations cites "ample evidence that rapid growth in societies with unchanged institutional structures will not have any importance for (those) individuals without access to productive resources."[6]

Various reports in the Project Impact Evaluation Series
of the U.S. Agency for International Development (AID)
also provide corroborating evidence. One such report
on a small-scale irrigation project in the Philippines
concludes that because of unsupportive government
policies in areas such as pricing, credit, marketing,
exports, and land tenure (few of which were adequately
taken into account in AID's project design), "the
farmer's contribution to development outweighs the
benefits he is reaping."[7]

An exhaustive 1979 World Bank review of
internationally supported agricultural research
concludes that while such research has lowered the real
prices of food consumed by the poor, "widely adopted
agricultural technologies will at best leave relative
income distribution unchanged among producers, but will
widen absolute income disparities when productive
assets are inequitably distributed."[8]  Another study
has found that one of the major lessons of the World
Bank's African experience is that the effectiveness of
the Bank's projects has been limited by "poor
knowledge" of sociocultural, institutional, political,
and economic realities.  The experience of numerous
countries, in Africa and beyond, confirms the study's
probably understated conclusion that "if the land
tenure situation precludes participation of the lowest
income groups in rural development programs, land
reform may be essential for realizing the potential of
a particular program."[9]

In the face of observations such as these, it is
tempting to adopt the popular Aid as Obstacle view that
virtually all government-to-government aid, channelled
through structures that for the most part reflect
inequitable power relationships, will necessarily
reinforce rather than relieve such inequalities.[10]
While such has indeed been the result of much external
aid in the past, the opposite conclusion is at least
equally valid:  that efforts need to be redoubled to
design programs that take into account and seek to
offset such outcomes.

For example, a realistic assessment of inequitable
power relationships in a given country or community
would caution an aid agency, whether governmental or
private, against seeking simply to expand existing
social services, even though this would clearly benefit
some who are poor. As Elliott points out, "the
expansion of social services does not automatically
reduce the relative or even the absolute impoverishment
of deprived groups.  Insofar as the provision of these
services tends to be biased in the direction of the
privileged,...the expansion of the services tends to
reinforce the relative deprivation of the excluded."[11]
Rather than scrapping all development assistance, more
careful design and monitoring is needed to ensure that

most of the benefits go to the poor.

An illustration of the right and wrong approaches to the issue of power relations and projects is provided by the rural roads projects evaluations in the AID series mentioned earlier. In two of the eight projects reviewed, the distribution of benefits favored the poor disproportionately. One involved the construction of "pick and shovel" roads in a mountainous area in Colombia where most of the residents were subsistence farmers. The other was the construction of similar roads in Honduras in support of small-farm cooperatives set up under an agrarian reform program. Two other rural roads projects brought benefits to both poor and rich, though the rich benefited disproportionately. The final four projects involved impacts on the poor which were ultimately more negative than positive.

The results of these eight projects suggest not that development assistance is somehow inherently counterproductive for the poor but rather that special precautions must be taken to assure that the distribution of benefits favors them. The results also suggest to the equity-minded observer that the number of situations in which constructing rural roads will empower the poor may be more limited than has been acknowledged in the past. The assumption simply does not hold that stepped up road-building efforts in remote rural areas throughout the Third World will necessarily have value to the poor or advance broadly based development.

Similarly, it would be tempting to conclude--as indeed some among the equity-minded have--that support of Third World agricultural research as currently practiced is incompatible with a concern for helping the poor. Again, the reverse conclusion is also possible: that safeguards can and must be built into research, extension, and technology transfer activities to offset their natural bias toward the more advantaged.

The Consultative Group on International Agricultural Research (CGIAR), whose various research institutes brought forth the miracle seeds of the Green Revolution, should, along with its parent organizations, the World Bank, the United Nations Development Program (UNDP), and the Food and Agriculture Organization (FAO), take much more seriously the equity assumptions and impacts of its work. More attention needs to be given to the food and agricultural requirements of subsistence and tenant farmers, along with more labor-intensive alternative technologies and more recognition of the need for what the Bank review itself calls the "widespread and effective redistribution of productive factors."[12]

Equity-sensitive research could be a key element in the larger rural development research enterprise

called for by the Swedish report, the overall purpose
of which would be "to increase the bargaining power of
the poor."[13]  Such an approach would accept what Alain
de Janvry calls "one of the most challenging aspects of
rural development...diffusing new technological options
in such a fashion as to mobilize peasants to press
toward social and structural change that will ultimately liberate them from the process of poverty to
which they are bound."[14]  As in the case of rural road
construction, however, internationally supported
agricultural research along traditional lines may not
prove to be a policy instrument suited to the empowerment of the poor.  It would thereby warrant less
support in the portfolio of measures advocated by those
concerned to challenge the structures of impoverishment.


PREFERRED EQUITY INVESTMENTS

     It is disconcerting to conclude that neither of
these two examples of major development interventions--
rural road building or agricultural research and
technology--emerges with accomplishments sufficient to
justify strong support from an equity vantage point.
Proponents of such activities, however, still find them
worthy of continued support.  "Is it fair to even
expect," asks agricultural economist Grant Scobie,
"that technological change should be the vehicle for
arresting and redirecting a set of political forces
with two or three centuries of accumulated momentum?"[15]
     The question is a reasonable one.  Can those who
provide external interventions into the development
process be held accountable for the fact that the
process has a dynamic of its own over which they have
very little control?  Even though they cannot control
the process, it seems reasonable that they should be
expected to be realistic about the effects that it will
have on their interventions.  Quite possibly Scobie's
rhetorical statement should be taken as a serious
limitation on development interventions:  "Perhaps we
are designing technology for such a hostile environment
(physically and, more importantly, sociopolitically)
that a prerequisite is a change in that sociopolitical
structure; without it, the potential recipients of the
technology may continue to either never receive it or
never capture its bounty."[16]
     Given the problems encountered in rural road
building and agricultural research and technology, what
form of development assistance is likely to prove particularly attractive to those concerned about equity?
Or is development aid a shell game with equity gains
never quite present where and when they are sought?
     The review of World Bank projects in Africa cited

earlier found modest--though since 1973 improved--
equity gains in a range of sectors.  They included
projects involving the production of tea, cotton,
tobacco, livestock and groundnuts, as well as land
settlement and increased social services.  However,
that positive finding is coupled with the unsettling
caveat that there are severe limits to the extent that
such assistance really can be expected to empower the
poor.

Noting that "increased consciousness of the equity
issue and the perceived impotency of the donors to deal
with it" has led to rising criticism of the international financial institutions and especially the
World Bank, the author counters with the observation
that such criticism is misdirected.  The Bank has never
viewed improvement of the incomes of the very poor and
the landless as a major objective.

> The Bank's emphasis on raising productivity
> of small farmers rather than redistributing
> income has also meant directing investments
> toward those who have access to some pro-
> ductive assets such as land, even if only as
> tenants, and not necessarily the poorest of
> the poor.  Much of the outside criticism of
> the Bank projects is, however, geared to the
> Bank's inability to improve incomes of the
> very poor and the landless through its
> projects.[17]

The author also notes the limits on what can be
expected of external aid, citing a 1973 speech by then
President Robert McNamara which stressed that "unless
national governments redirect their policies toward
better income distribution, there is very little that
international agencies such as the World Bank can do to
accomplish this objective."[18]

Just as World Bank officials concede their limited
effectiveness in helping those who need assistance
most, AID has taken pains to maintain that even in its
New Directions mode, its efforts are directed in the
first instance toward not the poorest of the poor but
the poor majority.  Both the World Bank under A.W.
Clausen and AID during the Reagan Administration are
showing more interest in the use of external resources
to seek changes in Third World government policies.
However, the prime beneficiaries of these recent
efforts have been, if anything, less clearly than in
earlier days the poorest.

It would be helpful for governmental external aid
agencies--and the observation applies with equal force
to PVOs--to match their greater clarity about whom they
are seeking to assist with a greater willingness to
pursue only those activities which do not further

disadvantage the very poor.  This would mean acting on
a recommendation from one of the AID project impact
evaluations to the effect that "A focused concern for
the empowerment of the poor, and a willingness to
desist from programs where these concerns cannot be
accommodated, is well within the range of options open
to development institutions such as AID."[19]
     It would also mean building equity objectives into
all development activities--into production as well as
distribution policies, into funding for transport and
power as well as for nutrition and health.  Equity
would then not be a free-standing objective but a key
dimension of all development interventions.  Agencies
which acquit themselves well in this respect--the
International Fund for Agricultural Development (IFAD),
UNICEF, and the Inter-American Foundation come to
mind--would then become increasingly the focal point of
support by those committed to advance the cause of
equitable development.


THE AMBIGUITIES OF SOCIAL CHANGE

     This discussion of power relations and development
activities highlights the complex nature of development itself.  At root we are dealing with the double-
edged nature of social change.  Change can bring
benefits for the poor:  access to new markets, new
technology, and new health and educational opportunities, for example.  But it can also reinforce old
obstacles and introduce new difficulties such as
dependence on middlemen and on imports.  It can render
social services more readily available but at the same
time undermine traditional value systems.
     A conceptual framework for the experience of
various communities and nations with development is
provided by Denis Goulet's view of modern technology as
a two-edged sword which functions both as "the bearer
and the destroyer of precious human values."  In
addition to introducing into premodern societies the
indisputable boons of modernity, modern technology also
serves as "the vector of the virus of acquisitiveness,
thereby shattering the delicate balance between social
restraints on desire and effectively available
resources."  While it brings freedom from old
constraints, technology also brings new determinisms,
not the least of which is technology itself.  With
aspirations fueled more quickly than new resources can
be expanded, "surviving social institutions and
normative structures can no longer assure that
increases are not appropriated by a few at the expense
of the many."[20]
     The ambiguities of social change run so deep that
it is small wonder that many in the development debate

reach for simplistic answers. On the one hand, there
are those who argue that since the development process
has undeniably ambiguous and often devastating results
for the poor, persons concerned about equity should
withdraw their support altogether from development
assistance programs. While their questions are
legitimate and their frustrations understandable,
neither the debate nor the cause of the poor is
furthered by the mentality which holds, as Richard
Dickinson describes it, that "governmental and
intergovernmental agencies are suspect, <u>always</u>
manipulated by leaders eager for their own power and
affluence, <u>always</u> inefficient and/or corrupt, <u>always</u>
oppressive of the poor."[21]

There are, on the other hand, those who resolve
the troubling ambiguities by ignoring questions of
empowerment altogether. The casualties from the
development process among the chronically poor and
newly marginalized are, they hold, the costs of long
overdue economic growth and social change. While
regrettable, the casualties do not make generally
rising standards of living and economic opportunity in
the Third World undesirable. Rather than seeking to
moderate the pace and direction of the development
process while issues of benefits and beneficiaries are
reviewed--the argument goes--the process of economic
growth needs instead to be hastened with increased
transfers of funds, technical assistance, technology,
and private investment.

These two opposite reactions to the ambiguities of
social change do not themselves account for the erosion
of consensus in the Congress and the country about the
effectiveness and supportability of foreign aid.
However, they represent a danger to achieving a better
understanding of the policy issues involved and to
building a broader base of support for development
assistance. Restraint and better listening are
urgently needed by both camps in the debate.

As members of the equity culture, many PVOs need
to avoid writing their own values and objectives too
large over the entire development process. Harry
Walters of the World Bank, commenting on an earlier
draft of this essay, offered the following well-placed
caution:

> You and I, and some others, may believe that one
> purpose of, even the means to, development is to
> 'empower the poor.' But this is not, nor has it
> ever been, as far as I know, the reason why
> people, societies or countries have developed...
> Some approaches to development involved greater
> equity than others...(yet which approach) will
> produce the highest form of equity in the long
> run, and the least amount of 'impoverishment' in

the process, is not obvious to me. What is
obvious is that most societies have become more
rather than less equitable after the development
process has gone on quite a while. And the poor
have eventually achieved greater power. But never
as much as those who are not poor, and never as
much as those who rule.[22]

Similar comments from John Mellor, Director of the
International Food Policy Research Institute, caution
against assuming that the only programs which benefit
the poor are those which benefit them directly.

I don't for a moment want to imply that the
natural course of events will allow
production increases in any sector to trickle
down to the poor. My point is, however, that
it is not only direct action programs [such
as those of PVOs] that can be valuable to
[the poor;...they] may reap even greater
benefits in the indirect effects of more
[food] production oriented efforts...For
example, in a country like India, if indirect
effects could take care of half of the poor,
leaving 'only' 30 percent of the population
for direct action programs, that would
relieve the burden considerably.[23]

Yet if it is inappropriate to assume that the poor
should be both the engine and the primary beneficiaries
of all social change, it is equally inappropriate to
place them at the periphery of development planning.
Many governmental aid agencies and officials treat
development as growth oriented pure and simple, with
equity an afterthought. Year after year AID seeks to
sell its program to Congress and the public by high-
lighting the fact that 75 percent of its budget is
spent on U.S. goods and services. The UNDP and the
World Bank also emphasize the value of their procurement to the industrialized countries. Ignored entirely
is the serious development policy question of the
degree to which such direct benefits to richer nations
come at the expense of human capital development in the
Third World.
    A similarly cavalier approach to equity issues
characterizes the work of the Carlucci Commission on
Security and Economic Assistance, appointed by
Secretary of State George Shultz in 1983 to recommend
ways to enlarge the constituency for U.S. foreign aid.
The Commission approached its task not by examining the
extent to which the current foreign aid program merits
the support of Americans concerned to alleviate hunger
and poverty. Rather it assumed that simply more
information about current U.S. aid efforts would be

sufficient to win broader support for the existing
program. In point of fact, those who currently hedge
their support for U.S. foreign assistance because of
the lack of importance among U.S. foreign policy
objectives attached to Third World development in its
own right are unlikely to be won over until the program
itself adopts a more thoroughgoing equity dimension.

DEVELOPMENT POLICY AND THE MAJOR PARTICIPANTS

Perplexing and complex issues of development
policy such as those discussed above have several
bearings on PVOs. PVO development support activities
need to fit within a clear understanding of the
dynamics of social transformation. Their resources
need to be used in the service of their own particular
philosophy of development and to be informed by the
division of labor, such as it is, among institutional
participants in the development process. PVO advocacy
efforts need to be grounded in careful analysis of
those public policies that can most effectively change
the structures of impoverishment.
It is widely assumed that there is an accepted
division of labor among the three major channels of
development assistance: multilateral, bilateral, and
PVO. For reasons of institutional makeup, scale of
resources, competence, and influence, it would seem
logical that multilateral agencies would concentrate on
macroresource transfers while bilateral agencies would
focus on program lending to selected sectors and PVOs
on individual project activities at the local level.
The greater resources at their disposal would enable
the multilateral development banks to exercise the most
significant leverage on government policy. PVOs would
make their distinctive contribution in working with the
poor in selected communities at the grass-roots level.
Bilateral agencies would operate somewhere in between.
Such a division of labor, however real it may have
been in earlier days, no longer reflects current
reality. During the past decade the World Bank has
taken a greater interest in those in absolute poverty
and since 1973 AID has had a "New Directions" mandate
to relate its efforts more explicitly to the poor.
Earlier distinctions between the Bank and the
International Monetary Fund (IMF) have also eroded as
the Bank has taken on lending for structural adjustment
assistance and as the frequently negative impacts of
the IMF's policies on broad-based development and the
poor have become better understood. Some PVOs, too,
have branched out well beyond operational development
activities at the grass-roots level. Some have chosen
not to work with indigenous PVO counterparts but
instead to provide technical assistance and even

second staff, in UNDP or World Bank fashion, directly
to government ministries.

Nor do the presumed differences in scale always
hold. PVOs in some countries have more resources
available than certain government aid agencies. AID
now asks selected PVOs to function as surrogate AID
missions in countries where it is not economical or
feasible to maintain a direct AID presence. Many PVO
activities are now carried out with bilateral aid
agency funds and with resources from UN specialized
agencies. Despite serious reservations by some U.S.
and Third World PVOs, AID is moving to expand its
direct funding of indigenous private agencies. Even
the World Bank is now stepping up its courtship of
PVOs. Many PVOs are themselves increasingly
uncomfortable with being expected to reach the poorest
of the poor while governmental aid agencies content
themselves with concentrating on the poor majority.

In short, there seems to be no clear-cut division
of labor among the three major channels of development
assistance. All are concerned to one degree or another
with the poor. All are somehow involved in activities
at the project level. All seek in one way or another
to influence government policy. While some have more
resources than others, none have as many resources as
they would like. More and more, they share resources
with each other.

Because of this blurring of roles, questions of
comparative advantage need review. There is probably
nothing inherently wrong in the fact that Pakistan's
rolling stock several years ago included 200 cars paid
for with World Bank funds, 330 with British
bilateral aid funds, and 50 with Pakistan government
funds--but on the surface this seems questionable.
There is perhaps more logic in the Pakistan power
generation project in which, complementing basic World
Bank financing, the transformers came from the British
aid program, the switches from the Canadians. When the
FAO takes its East Africa visitors to see a PVO dairy
project rather than one of its own efforts, it may be
acknowledging its own difficulties in small-scale,
local community activities. A more appropriate use of
FAO/UNDP resources may be reflected in a project in
Pakistan that helps the government provide technical
assistance in production, marketing, and veterinary
medicine to poultry co-ops that include six thousand
small farmers in one thousand villages, each of whom
was started off, PVO-scale, with five hens and a
rooster.

In India--hardly a typical developing nation but
still one from which much can be learned about division
of labor questions--all multilateral, bilateral, and
private aid resources combined recently commanded only
about 5 percent of India's annual development budget.

Paradoxically, agencies with smaller resource levels
are in such a situation less disadvantaged than might
be expected. UNICEF, with far fewer funds than the
World Bank's IDA, is somewhat less captive to the
central and state government planning processes and
more free to be creative. PVOs, smaller still, are
less constrained than the multilaterals to undertake
certain high visibility projects in many different
states and districts. In a country whose size,
complexity, and diversity make national schemes
difficult, PVOs are more able to focus on the poorest
states and the most serious human problems. AID, with
a shaky mandate from Congress for a revived program in
India and even more uncertain credibility with the
Indian government, has to develop its activities within
its own set of distinctive constraints.

Moreover, simply because an aid agency has more
resources, it is not necessarily more capable of
influencing Indian development at the village level.
The importance of reaching the poor, whether rural or
urban, and the difficulty of measuring the effects that
various programs have on them, create a hard task for
one and all, the larger agencies being vulnerable to
larger failures. While the PVO preoccupation with
projects has been viewed by some observers as a
liability, even the bilateral and multilateral agencies
now see projects as an important way to establish
credibility and as a virtual prerequisite for
influencing policy. Conversely, PVO activities have
influenced how Indian and external and social welfare
development agencies now proceed.


DISTINCTIVE DEVELOPMENT ROLES FOR PVOS

Whether the reference point is India or another
country, it is imperative for PVOs to give careful
thought to the activities through which they can make a
distinctive contribution. Two examples from the AID
Project Impact Evaluation Series shed light on what
that contribution should--and should not--be.

One AID report assesses the results of a Catholic
Relief Services (CRS) nutrition education project in
Morocco.[24] To a CRS feeding project of the early
1970s, an education component was added in 1975 which
combined food distribution with new attention to issues
of nutrition, sanitation, personal hygiene, and
treatment of childhood diseases. Comparisons of the
children enrolled before 1975 (when the PL 480 food had
no such education component) with their siblings who
participated after 1975 showed that given comparable
time in the programs, the number of malnourished
children in the latter group was more than halved, with
severe malnutrition eliminated altogether. The effects

on the women involved after 1975 were also demonstrably positive. Following the termination of the AID grant (the food continues), the Moroccan government, with some local beneficiary support, has maintained and expanded the program. According to the AID evaluation, the program was a success after 1975; an effective division of labor was established among CRS, AID, the Moroccan government, and local communities.

A second report in the same AID series examines CARE's involvement in the construction of rural penetration roads in Sierra Leone. CARE received an AID grant to construct 1,300 miles of roads, part of a mammoth integrated agricultural development project in which the World Bank, the Peace Corps, the British Volunteer Service Organization, and the Government of Sierra Leone were also involved. The overall socio-economic impact of the CARE roads was positive. Educational and health opportunities were improved and access was provided to a wider range of consumer goods and to agricultural inputs and markets. CARE is credited with having involved local villagers in road construction and maintenance and with having helped bring about the less political siting of road projects.

On the other hand, the roads encouraged a major shift from rice production for consumption within Sierra Leone to the production for export of cocoa, oil palm, peanuts, and livestock. Villages served by CARE roads experienced more severe rice shortages than did other villages. Changes in cultivation patterns, with rice production relegated to swamps, were linked to "declining soil fertility, deforestation, increased soil erosion, and increased exposure of swamp rice farmers to waterborne diseases."[25] CARE was caught between the government of Sierra Leone, which insisted on roads of a certain quality, and the World Bank, which wanted more miles constructed. The evaluation report suggested that CARE would have been better advised to limit itself to "certain development functions" rather than also serving as construction contractor. Lack of clarity about a workable division of labor in this instance led to a multiplication of functions for the one institutional participant probably least able to assume additional duties of this type.

Many development practitioners now view PVOs as participants in the development process with a distinctive contribution to make. There are, of course, still many frictions with the governmental aid establishment, but by and large PVOs are accepted as legitimate development agents. AID's 1982 policy paper, AID Partnership in International Development with Private and Voluntary Organizations, notable as the first unified and comprehensive AID policy toward PVOs, also acknowledges a legitimate role for private development agencies. AID policy now views PVOs as both "independent (development) entities in their own right" and as "intermediaries in conducting AID programs."[26]

AID's new policy acknowledges that "AID, by its very nature as a government development agency, operates very differently from (PVOs). AID, as the official arm of the U.S. government responsible for economic development support to Third World countries, is an instrument of our total foreign policy."[27] The paper, however, seriously underestimates the extent to which AID's active pursuit of an intermediary relationship with PVOs, as legitimized by its new policy paper and framed by current U.S. foreign policy, may undermine the private and voluntary character of many such organizations.


RELIGIOUS PVOS AND DEVELOPMENT

If clarity of understanding about its distinctive development role is necessary for the PVO community, it is even more necessary for PVOs of a religious orientation.

Of course, "religious PVOs"--themselves a heterogeneous group--share many of the comparative advantages of PVOs generally. However, as Dickinson points out, churches and their development agencies differ not only from international organizations and governments but also from other voluntary groups. "They operate by different values, have different functions, possess fewer resources, have different kinds of responsibilities. Those differences constitute both liabilities and assets for promoting development."[28]

At least four elements in the religious community's involvement in development issues deserve mention. While other development participants share these to some degree, these four characteristics, taken together, suggest a distinctive contribution to the development process.

First, religious PVOs are committed to viewing poverty and underdevelopment in structural terms. They see the chronic malnutrition of more than half a billion people and the human suffering and deprivation of countless others as evidence not of natural forces but of human choices, reinforced by human institutions. "There is something seriously askew," observes the Indian economist S.L. Parmar, "in an international economic system where agricultural societies have to rely on industrial societies to meet their food needs."[29] Underlying the global imbalances in the world's system of food production and distribution are the same issues of power relations that affect the development process.

In the arena of world economic systems and
political power, of governments, intergovernmental
organizations, and multinational corporations, the
religious community of course needs to move with care.
However, it can certainly affirm with the World Council
of Churches' Central Committee that "there can be no
justice in our world without a transfer of resources to
undergird the redistribution of political power and to
make cultural self-determination meaningful.  In the
transfer of resources a corporate act by the ecumenical
fellowship of churches can provide a significant moral
lead."  The religious community, based on its
understanding of "the nature and causes of poverty of
the many and prosperity of the few," can work for a
"new alignment of power relationships geared to the
interests of the less privileged.  That is tantamount
to saying that development must begin by structural
change."30

Second, a well-informed understanding of the seat
of underdevelopment in current economic and political
systems should lead the religious community to view the
dispossessed as key actors in the development process.
Since development is not change from without but rather
empowerment of the poor to change the structures of
impoverishment from within, there is really no
substitute for involving the poor at every step along
the way.

Government aid agencies also value popular
participation highly and sometimes even relate failures
of individual programs and projects to its absence.
The study of the World Bank's African projects referred
to earlier defines rural development as "improving
living standards of the mass of the low-income
population residing in rural areas and making the
process of their development self-sustaining."  The
author notes that "nearly 90 percent of the projects
are having a slower impact output than had been
anticipated" and relates this to "problems of
mobilizing farmers under conditions of poor communications and serious staffing and institutional
constraints."  However, development is presented as an
activity essentially done _for_ the poor, involving them
on a selective basis as one of many factors in the
process, and as a means to an end.  "Given the extreme
constraints of trained manpower...mass participation
rarely seems feasible in the short run through delivery
systems (of agricultural inputs and services) oriented
toward individual farmers.  Therefore, some delegation
of responsibility to the rural people is necessary."31

The World Bank itself, in a recent report on its
poverty-related development activities, takes a
similarly instrumental approach.  The report concedes
that "success in poverty-oriented projects depends,
much more often than in the traditional sectors of Bank

lending, on sociological, cultural and political factors,...difficult areas (which) deserve much more attention." However, rather than viewing popular participation as valuable in its own right, the report observes only that "Close attention should be paid, especially in projects addressing the needs of poor people, to institution building; sociological and cultural factors; deficiencies in administration and management; the development of efficient 'technical packages'; and the need for technical assistance."[32] AID's rural roads evaluations, too, tend to treat popular participation as a necessary ingredient in road maintenance rather than as a <u>sine qua non</u> of the development process itself.

Many religious organizations involved in overseas development activities attach more fundamental importance to participation of the poor. Most would affirm with Peter Dorner of the University of Wisconsin that:

> The energizing force in the development process is not provided solely or even primarily by the investment plans and projects of administrators and entrepreneurs. The informed self-interest of farmers and urban workers and their creative human energies are strategic to any long-term development effort. While authoritarian measures can carry development to a certain stage, it is the voluntary effort of the mass of common people that must provide the energy and the markets to keep the process going. Continued progress requires widely shared economic and political citizenship, which can often be realized only through basic reforms and the reallocation of power.[33]

The centrality of people's participation in development as an end in itself was stressed by Maxime Rafransoa of the World Council of Churches in his remarks to the World Conference on Agrarian Reform and Rural Development in July, 1979. Speaking on behalf of a consortium of PVOs bound by a common "perception of development...which differs significantly from that of many governments and international agencies," Rafransoa rejected the view held by many in the aid establishment of "the rural poor as 'target groups'...the object of someone else's actions, rather than the principal actors in their own development." He challenged the international community to make the Third Development Decade "the Decade of People's Participation," embracing new models of rural development centering around "a substantial transfer of power to the rural poor." New approaches are needed, he said, to address the "root causes of underdevelopment and poverty (which) demand a radical rethinking of policies and a radical reorganization of the power structure that impoverishes these poor."[34]

Lest the empowerment of the poor be viewed as the exclusive preserve of religious PVOs, the AID evaluation of a rural roads project in Liberia cited earlier contains a helpful observation.

> Programs for community participation, now commonly accepted at least tacitly by governments of developing nations as integral parts of their development strategy, could legitimately be used to justify structuring the project environment so as to provide collective and individual benefits to the poorest, while reducing their risks of economic disaster and of confrontation with elites. Such a balancing of costs and benefits is more a function of time and sensitivity than of money and political leverage.[35]

It is noteworthy that IFAD, the newest multilateral development agency, was created to address the needs of small farmers and landless laborers and now works energetically to structure its project activities so as to facilitate their participation in the development process. IFAD's success contains valuable lessons for governmental and private development practitioners.

A structural view of poverty and a basic commitment to the key role of the poor leads to a third distinctive element in the development activities of religious PVOs: a commitment to global education. Many PVOs and AID itself have recently begun to take great interest in global or development education. For many PVOs, this implies dramatizing the plight of the poor, with particular attention to generating funds to meet their urgent needs. For AID, the promotional element is also strong, the presumption being that if the needs of the poor are better understood, increased support for the foreign aid program will be forthcoming.

For agencies with a deeply rooted theological perspective, global education presses beyond the effort to help people in the industrialized countries better understand Third World needs. On world hunger matters, for example, it probes beneath and beyond recurring food crises such as those of 1973-75 and 1983-84 to underlying structural dysfunctions in the world's food system. Discussions of poor country problems and rich country solutions give way to exploration of "local/ global connections" and "the dynamic relationship between enrichment and impoverishment."[36] Global education from a religious base thus involves a strong

critique of current economic and political arrangements, institutions and systems, both here and abroad.
Whether global education efforts can be carried out
with integrity by the U.S. government or by PVOs using
U.S. government funds remains an open question.

With the complexity of development issues as a
backdrop and given a growing awareness of the limited
role that government and private development agencies
play in the development process itself, such
educational efforts are unlikely in the first instance
to generate more funds for PVOs or more support for the
aid establishment. Yet a well-conceived educational
strategy is no less necessary than are a clear
conception of how social transformations in favor of
the poor happen and a series of well-designed
activities to advance such changes. Global education
can provide illuminating and liberating insights to the
rich now facing for the first time "the prospect of
scarcity because the poor are demanding a different
division of the pie."37

Fourth, and implied in any serious commitment to
global education, is a commitment to public policy
advocacy. Religious PVOs have a special obligation to
be concerned, beyond their own overseas projects, about
the influences that governments and aid agencies have
on the poor. In the earlier example involving CARE's
road-building project in Sierra Leone, it was not just
CARE's involvement as a road contractor that was
ill-conceived but also the AID and World Bank project
of which CARE's work was a part. Even if not
operationally involved, PVOs--particularly those with a
religious orientation--should be concerned about an
export-cropping scheme which under the guise of
development makes small farmers in Sierra Leone
vulnerable to the fluctuations of international
commodity prices. Responsible advocacy would call into
question the AID and Bank development strategy involved
and would support international efforts to assure more
dependable producer prices through commodity agreements
or other means.

If religious PVOs take too simplistic a view of
the development process when they limit their concern
to their own overseas projects, they would also be well
advised to be clear about the content of their advocacy
as it relates to public policy. A PVO which supports
everything that passes for development assistance or
foreign aid is probably as unhelpful to the poor as one
which remains aloof from public policy advocacy
altogether.

In the absence of understanding the comparative
advantages of different sorts of aid institutions in
different aspects of development, it is also tempting
for the PVOs, and perhaps for religious PVOs in
particular, to assume that multilateral and bilateral

aid agencies should be like PVOs themselves.  It makes
good sense for PVOs to want government aid programs to
respect and even to take on characteristics that PVOs
themselves seek to embrace:  a focus on the basic human
needs of the poor, a sensitivity to the perceived needs
and cultural traditions of local communities, a
facilitation of participation of the poor and of more
fulfilling roles for women, and attention to appropriateness in local institution building and in choices of
technology and procurement methods.

But the development process is far too complex for
multilateral and bilateral aid organizations to
function effectively simply as large-sized PVOs or for
all government aid funds to be channelled through PVOs.
Moreover, greater stability in commodity prices,
broadened access to developed country markets, an
improved balance of payments ledger in favor of
developing countries, a more manageable external debt,
reduced Third World unemployment--all these are issues
beyond the specific operational ken of PVOs even though
they have direct bearing on the development context in
which PVO activities are set.  Nevertheless, religious
PVOs have a responsibility to become knowledgeable
about appropriate international and national economic
policies and supportive of appropriate activities of
government aid organizations.

A negative example may give some concreteness to
this point.  A regional representative of a major U.S.
religious PVO in India, when asked how much development
policy expertise he had on staff for his multimillion
dollar PL 480 program, replied, "Try zero."  Meanwhile,
his organization in the United States has traditionally
not lobbied for any subventions other than those it
will itself administer directly (e.g., Title II food
aid, ocean freight reimbursement funds, AID grants to
PVOs).   Would it not be more in order to recognize
that a commitment by a PVO to alleviate poverty in
developing countries requires support for a broad array
of policies and programs, only some of which can be
implemented by PVOs?  "The problems of development,"
writes Dickinson, "are too urgent, too complex, too
important for the churches not to seek allies, and to
be an ally.  It is possible to be a partner in
development with governments and international
organizations.  Some of the most important work that
churches can do to promote development and justice will
be the way they, with limited resources, enable those
with more resources to move ahead with the job."[38]

Religious and other PVOs that venture into the
broader advocacy arena face a complex array not only of
issues but also of interests and organizations.
Influencing the formation and implementation of public
policy, particularly for those groups viewed as basing
their advocacy on pleas to humanitarian generosity,

generally necessitates the building of coalitions with
other groups that have different and sometimes even
conflicting approaches to development.

Most coalitions assume a harmony of interests--or
at least a lowest common denominator of shared
concerns--as a unifying factor. In view of the
understanding of development by those within the equity
culture, there is some question about the extent to
which joint advocacy with others is possible. The U.S.
Chamber of Commerce supports foreign aid but not
because of its potential for institution building,
procurement, or job generating capability in the Third
World. The financial community supports substantial
U.S. contributions to the multilateral development
banks but not because of its interest in low-cost loans
to small business ventures in the Third World. Farming
and agribusiness groups support PL 480 not, in the
first instance, because of what food aid can do to
encourage food self-sufficiency in developing
countries.

Religious PVOs which accept the challenge to
involve themselves in advocacy must learn to live with
multiple ambiguities. They need to be prepared to join
coalitions where appropriate but also to articulate
their own special understanding of development and of
the appropriate roles of outside assistance. They need
to live with the multiplicity of interests and purposes
that most government policies reflect, working wherever
possible to reinforce those which are most
constructive. They need to look for areas where
objectives converge but at the same time remain alert
to the desires of other groups to grace their
multifarious efforts with the participation of the
religious community. They need also--and here again
they have a unique contribution to make--to ground
their advocacy in a solid understanding of development
issues and to see that such an understanding becomes
reflected in the activities of concerned citizens in
states and congressional districts throughout the land.


ILLUSTRATIVE ACTIVITIES

If it is appropriate to highlight the distinctive
nature and philosophy of religious PVOs, then some
discussion of the kinds of programmatic activities that
such organizations should be engaged in may also be
helpful. The following examples, drawn largely from
the experience of Church World Service (CWS) and
Lutheran World Relief (LWR), are presented not to imply
that other religious PVOs do not have exemplary
activities of their own but because they grow out of
the author's personal experience.

In the village of Mulegon in rural Maharashtra

State, a Harijan (or "untouchables") community has transformed barren into productive land using PL 480 Title II food aid from CWS and LWR made available through an Indian ecumenical partner agency. Outside technical assistance also helped construct a well. The poorest of the Indian poor have become self-sustaining through a combination of community organization and hard work on their part and support of various sorts from local and national Indian PVOs, two U.S. PVOs, and AID. CWS/LWR advocacy efforts in Washington have helped to secure enactment of supportive legislative improvements in PL 480, including more continuity of supply for the grant programs of Title II.

The Pakistani Technical Services Agency, with support from half a dozen private outside sources, operates an experimental farm just outside Lahore. Research and field testing have focused on improving local varieties of legumes, the food crops of subsistence farmers that have not been the subject of much research by the CGIAR's network of research institutions. Improved local varieties of peas and beans have been developed and tested on nearby farmers' fields. ("Everybody believes in agricultural extension," remarks the farm's director, "but the unanswered question is what to extend.") The farm's entire annual budget several years ago of $80,000 (far less than the annual cost of a single AID or UN technician) has accomplished a great deal, although widespread use of the newly developed strains will require supportive seed multiplication and commodity pricing policies by the Pakistan government and the private sector.

A CWS-supported project in northeastern Pakistan involved an apple production survey carried out by semi-literate farmers. The initiative became the basis for a better understanding of the apple production cycle, the formation by farmers of apple production and marketing cooperatives, and the recommendation by the Pakistan Agricultural Research Council to the government and aid donor agencies for increased storage facilities in the area. The training and use of such farmers in survey techniques has since been adopted in some Pakistan projects by FAO and the AID.

A national ecumenical development commission in Cameroon has successfully worked with small maize-growing farmers in the organization of production, marketing, and storage cooperatives. Despite the active opposition of maize dealers, who traditionally charge heavily for marketing and resale of maize to producers in the off-season, the farmers' association has prevailed. However, now it is being pressed to sell maize for a higher price outside Cameroon, leading one of its architects to observe that the association,

> which came into being as a reaction against
> the practices of some dealers motivated by a
> drive for maximum profit, seems to be in
> danger of itself pursuing the same
> objectives...If the peasants are to avoid the
> temptations of the profit motive, they will
> have to adopt a new system of values. They
> must come to see that it is a vital priority
> for Cameroon and their own region to be able
> to produce their own food supply...(and) that
> their self-reliance and the absence of
> foreign domination are more valuable than a
> little extra money.[39]

In early 1978 CWS took the lead, with support from its member denominations and from LWR, in sending Vietnam its first direct food shipment from the United States after the war. The 10,000 tons of wheat, some of it donated from U.S. farmers, represented resources totaling almost $2 million in value. The wheat was consigned to the Vietnamese Committee for Friendship and Solidarity with the American People for milling into bread and noodles and distribution through schools, orphanages, and hospitals. While the United States had a bumper wheat crop, Vietnam at the time faced food deficits of about 1.2 million tons because of drought, flooding, unusually cold weather, two typhoons, and still unrepaired war damage.

The CWS initiative provided an occasion for nationwide global education efforts. These pointed out that the United States (which pressed on Vietnam and Cambodia two-thirds of all U.S. food aid in the early 1970s) had not only refused to assist in Vietnam's postwar reconstruction but had also declined to provide CWS the normal ocean freight reimbursement. The wheat shipment, which drew statements of support from numerous members of Congress, also built on earlier CWS Washington advocacy efforts geared toward lifting the embargo on aid and trade with Vietnam. (The prohibition still stands.) One Senator congratulated an initiative that "moved beyond the broken pride of a tragic war to make possible this historic people-to-people food aid campaign." The scale of the shipment, while modest, was large enough to have practical as well as symbolic value.

Finally, CWS and LWR participate in Interfaith Action for Economic Justice (formerly the Inter-religious Taskforce on U.S. Food Policy), an ecumenical advocacy group in Washington, D.C. Born at the time of the World Food Conference out of the religious community's world hunger concern, the group has addressed hunger and development policy issues from a global perspective. It has recommended not only food

aid for hungry people in the Third World but also
expanded nutrition programs for low-income Americans.
It has worked to improve U.S. domestic agriculture,
international development assistance, and global
economic policies.  Because of the increasing
militarization and politicization of the U.S. foreign
aid program, the group has found it necessary first to
seek to change, and then to oppose, the enactment of
the U.S. foreign aid legislation as reported to the
House and Senate in recent years.

While other PVOs and groups of PVOs have advocated
a better balance within the foreign aid program between
development aid and security assistance, many have
stopped short of working to defeat the final passage of
such legislation.  Indeed, the fact that the increasing
politicization of U.S. aid has not been matched by
noticeably more reluctance within the PVO community to
accept U.S. government subventions may be undercutting
the ability of PVOs to function as serious development
agencies.  An absence of attention to key development
policy questions may turn the "P" in PVO from "Private"
to "Parastatal."


THE CHALLENGE TO PVOS

The new-found prominence PVOs now enjoy carries
with it several challenges.  First, are PVOs as good at
empowering the poor as their reputations imply?
Inattentiveness over the years to development policy
and evaluation issues makes this a difficult question
to answer.  A recent AID volume which attempts to
assess PVOs' vaunted strengths and comparative
advantage through reviewing available evaluation
literature bears the suggestive title, Turning PVOs
into Development Agencies: Questions for Evaluation.[40]
Moreover, as PVOs subject their own activities to more
careful scrutiny on development policy grounds, they
will need to pass beyond easy generalizations about
their superiority to governmental aid efforts to make
dispassionate judgments about the effectiveness of PVO
programs in their own right.

Second, PVOs as professional development agencies
will need to become more knowledgeable about
development policy questions themselves.  The new AID
policy paper on PVOs invites them into discussions on
AID's development priorities in individual Third World
countries.  The only group to be thus invited, PVOs
stand to benefit both from the expertise which this
would encourage in their own staffs and from the
opportunity it would provide to help governmental aid
programs to become more beneficial to the poor.  The
challenge is worth accepting whether or not a PVO seeks
AID funds in a given country.

Third, PVOs both individually and jointly have a
far-flung network of contacts around the world, in
industrialized and Third World countries alike. Yet
they have yet to make very creative or systematic use
of that network, either to inform their project
activities or to provide themselves with better
resources for global education and advocacy work.
While such relationships--particularly those involving
the poor themselves in development discussions--
undoubtedly complicate planning, execution, and
evaluation of PVO activities, they may also prove
enriching. PVOs need to shape their total programs
more fully in response to insights gained from such
partners and in turn to encourage them to be more
attentive to broader development policy issues.

## NOTES

1. Aaron Tolen, "The end of all pretences: an
African perspective," in Richard D.N. Dickenson, To Set
At Liberty the Oppressed: Towards an Understanding of
Christian Responsibilities for Development/Liberation
(Geneva, Switzerland: The World Council of Churches,
1975), 156, 159.
2. S.L. Parmar, "Issues in the Development
Debate" in Dickinson, To Set At Liberty, 165.
3. Charles Elliott, Patterns of Poverty in the
Third World (New York: Praeger Publishers, 1975), 395.
4. Ibid., 396.
5. Ibid., 397-8.
6. Bo Bengtsson, ed., Rural Development Research:
The Role of Power Relations (Stockholm: Swedish Agency
for Research Cooperation with Developing Countries,
1979), 24.
7. David I. Steinberg, Philippine Small Scale
Irrigation, Project Impact Evaluation No. 4. (Washington, D.C.: AID, 1980), A-1.
8. World Bank, Investment in International
Agricultural Research: Some Economic Dimensions, Staff
Working Paper No. 361 (Washington, D.C.: 1979).
9. Uma Lele, The Design of Rural Development:
Lessons from Africa (Baltimore: Johns Hopkins
University Press, 1975), 176.
10. Frances Moore Lappe, Joseph Collins, and
David Kinley, Aid As Obstacle: Twenty Questions About
Our Foreign Aid and the Hungry (San Francisco: The
Institute for Food and Development Policy, 1980).
11. Elliott, 389.
12. World Bank, Investment in Agricultural
Research, 23.

13. Bengtsson, 78.

14. Alain de Janvry, "Nature of Rural Development Programs: Implications for Technology Design," in Alberto Valdes, Grant Scobie, and John L. Dillon, eds., Economics and the Design of Small Farmer Technology (Ames, Iowa: Iowa State University Press, 1979).

15. Grant Scobie in Valdes, et al., Economics, 195.

16. Ibid., 195 (emphasis in original).

17. Lele, 241.

18. Ibid., 241.

19. Richard Cobb, Liberia: Rural Roads, Project Impact Evaluation No. 6, (Washington, D.C.: AID, 1980), A-5.

20. Denis Goulet, The Uncertain Promise: Value Conflicts in Technology Transfer (New York: International Documentation in the Contemporary Church, 1976), 23.

21. Dickinson, 122 (emphasis in original).

22. Harry E. Walters, letter to the author dated May 21, 1981.

23. John W. Mellor, letter to the author dated December 3, 1981.

24. Judith W. Gilmore, Morocco: Food Aid and Nutrition Education, Project Impact Evaluation Report No. 8, (Washington, D.C.: AID, 1980).

25. G. William Anderson, Effectiveness and Impact of the CARE/Sierra Leone Rural Penetration Roads Projects, Project Impact Evaluation Report No. 7, (Washington, D.C.: AID, 1980), 9.

26. U.S. AID, A.I.D. Partnership in International Development with Private and Voluntary Organizations (Washington, D.C.: 1982), 2.

27. Ibid., 2.

28. Dickinson, 115.

29. S.L. Parmar, "Issues," 180.

30. World Council of Churches Central Committee Statement of August, 1969, in Dickinson, To Set At Liberty, 85.

31. Lele, 192.

32. World Bank, Focus on Poverty: A Report by a Task Force (Washington, D.C.: 1982), 9, ii.

33. Peter Dorner, "Problems and Prospects of Multi- and Bilateral Assistance for Agricultural Development," Reprint No. 81 (Madison, Wisconsin: Land Tenure Center, University of Wisconsin, 1972).

34. Maxime Rafransoa, Statement of the Consortium on Non-Governmental Organizations Attending the World Conference on Agrarian Reform and Rural Development (Rome: 1979, unpublished).

35. U.S. AID, Liberia, A 5-6.

36. Richard D.N. Dickinson, Poor, Yet Making Many Rich: The Poor as Agents of Creative Justice (Geneva, Switzerland: World Council of Churches, 1983), 93.

37.  Richard Barnet, The Lean Years:  Politics in the Age of Scarcity (New York:  Simon and Schuster, 1980), 295.

38.  Dickinson, 122-3 (emphasis in original).

39.  Aaron Tolen, "The end of all pretences," 158.

40.  Judith Tendler, Turning Private Voluntary Organizations into Development Agencies:  Questions for Evaluation, Evaluation Discussion Paper No. 12, (Washington, D.C.: AID, 1982).

# 3
# PVOs and Development Through Basic Human Needs

*Robert F. Gorman*

An age-old Christian aphorism says that the poor will always be with us. Presumably, as applied to the realm of international politics, this suggests that poverty will always exist between and within states. While one can admit that relative poverty is probably a permanent condition of human existence, many challenge the notion that abject poverty and utter deprivation are necessary conditions of human experience. In recent years, the World Bank, the International Labor Organization (ILO), several other international organizations (IOs), and governments have begun to focus development assistance upon the problems of the absolute poor in an effort to relieve and, perhaps, to eradicate the harsher aspects of their predicament. This chapter will focus on the Basic Human Needs (BHN) development approach that has emerged to address these issues. It will also examine how BHN resources can best be channelled to meet the development needs of the poor and the very poor. In so doing it will be argued that Private Voluntary Organizations (PVOs) are particularly appropriate vehicles through which to achieve BHN objectives.

At a general level, PVOs and BHN advocates agree that the eradication of absolute--if not relative-- poverty is within the reach of human endeavor. While differences arise over how this goal can be achieved, the international development establishment has become increasingly concerned about the inability of conventional, macrolevel aid policies to reduce the number of the world's absolute poor and to ameliorate the plight of those among that number whose most basic needs have not been met. The assumption, still held strongly by some, had always been that aid policies aimed at generating national income and increasing the GNP of Third World countries would create trickle-down effects that would in the long run ameliorate poverty. Despite the fact that spectacular growth has been registered as measured by GNPs, in many Third World nations the position of the absolutely poor has not

41

improved, and has in extreme cases actually
deteriorated. By the mid-1970s somewhere between .7 and
1.2 billion people subsisted under conditions of extreme
poverty. The reasons for this are well known and
require only brief mention here.[1] Spectacular GNP
growth rates were often matched by equally spectacular
population growth rates, thus largely washing out the
potentially positive effects of the former. Moreover,
the additional income accrued by economic growth was
typically unevenly distributed, with elites  enjoying
many if not most of the fruits of that growth. The
emergence of dualistic, enclave economies, and
rural/urban dichotomies ensured that the positive
effects of income generation would not be felt in the
rural, often subsistence economies--isolated as they are
from the more dynamic urban ones.

For these reasons and others, some students and
practitioners of development began to reassess how
assistance should be channelled in order to ensure that
the poorest of the poor would not be left even further
behind in Third World development efforts. The upshot
has been the BHN strategy of development, which has
received a great deal of attention since its initial
formulation in the Aspen Institute's Program on
International Affairs report of 1975 and in the ILO
final report of the 1976 World Employment Conference.[2] Yet for all the attention this strategy has
received, it is surprising how little the role of PVOs
as a vehicle for BHN assistance has been assessed in the
scholarly literature. This is surprising if for no
other reason than that PVOs have been providing such
assistance to the world's poorest inhabitants for
years. Moreover, although PVOs are engaged daily in the
provision of such assistance in cooperation with
governments and IOs, the general orientation of discussions about BHN assistance strategies has remained
largely at the state-centric level, with very little
attention paid to the potential for expansion of the PVO
sector as a means of BHN delivery.[3] In the Final
Resolution of the ILO World Employment Conference, PVOs
were unmentioned as potential vehicles for BHN
assistance. Similarly, in the Brandt Commission Report,
North-South--A Program for Survival, which deals
extensively with BHN themes, only one scant, almost
offhand reference to PVOs can be found.[4] Indeed, in
some ways the actual practice of PVOs has advanced far
more rapidly than has conceptual and theoretical
assessment of their role in development assistance in
general and BHN assistance in particular. PVOs are
oriented toward action rather than toward abstraction,
and hence have not been inclined to undertake such
scholarly exercises. Scholars and BHN theorists have
less of an excuse for having ignored this potential area
for BHN development. It is all the more remarkable that

this lack of scholarly and theoretical attention to PVOs
as purveyors of BHN assistance has persisted despite the
fact that, as Elliott Schwartz has noted in an internal
U.S. government report:

> Consensus today would rate the PVOs as excel-
> lent practitioners of the basic human needs
> strategy at the grass-roots level. In fact,
> they have been the leaders and innovators of
> this approach, and it is there that they have a
> comparative advantage. There is widespread
> respect within the development community for
> the work that PVOs are doing.[5]

If the consensus Schwartz refers to actually exists, the
question arises as to why PVOs have not received much
greater scrutiny in the existing literature on BHN
strategies and approaches. The answer lies, I believe,
in the fact that PVOs currently provide only a small
portion of overall development resource flows, even
though these often constitute genuinely BHN-oriented
contributions. Furthermore, the rather low magnitude of
these funds does not excite attention due to an inherent
tendency among students of foreign aid to see states,
the U.N., and its related agencies as the primary and
dominant actors in the aid process. PVOs, then, often
get lost in the world of aid giants where scholars still
tend to see the aid process as an interstate rather than
as a transnational activity.
    The purpose of this chapter, then, is to examine
more closely the role of PVOs in BHN strategies for
development and to focus more forthrightly on the
potential contributions PVOs could make to expanded BHN
approaches. In order to do so, it will be necessary
first to discuss the nature and purpose of the BHN
strategy as well as the nature and functions of PVOs as
vehicles for development aid. It will then be possible
to consider how PVOs could be utilized more
systematically in various strategies of BHN assistance.


THE BHN CONCEPT

    As defined by the ILO Report of 1976, basic human
needs include two different but hardly distinct
elements. The first focuses on individuals as members
of families and households who require certain minimum
standards for private, material consumption of food,
shelter, and clothing. These are the most basic of all
needs, but cannot be entirely divorced from a second
level of needs that includes the provision of essential
services such as potable water supplies, sanitation,
public transportation, and facilities for the promotion
of health and education. The latter are seen as public

goods which must exist in order to ensure the
maintenance of the individual's private basic needs.
Whether public or private, all of the needs just
enumerated can be seen, using the terminology of the
Aspen Institute's 'Planetary Bargain' report, as
first-floor needs that should be met as a precondition
for meeting other needs of a population.[6] The Aspen
study suggests that such first-floor needs should be met
for all people even if this requires substantial
intervention between states. Beyond this first floor of
needs is a second floor which, the Aspen report
suggests, should be nationally defined over time to
reflect the higher aspirations of a country's
population. Here it is argued, the state must respond
largely within the limits of its own domestic resources
and capacities to the prioritization of needs with
little expectation of external intervention.

An integral part of the BHN strategy of
development--and one that sets it apart from similar
previous aid policies--is its insistence that the people
affected by BHN policies should participate in their
making.[7] The emphasis here is that development
eventually must become autonomous and self-reliant in
focus. To the extent that a local population is the
mere passive recipient of externally concocted programs,
it will not acquire the skills necessary to give the
program vitality as external participation declines.
Moreover, such programs run the risk of fostering
welfare syndromes. Hence, BHN theorists emphasize the
need for genuine local and decentralized participation
to ensure the longevity and vitality of BHN programs.
This, of course, is easier said than done, even where a
commitment to BHN policies exists among governments.[8]

Another important feature of BHN thinking is that
development strategies that do not focus upon the
improvement of the status and well-being of women are
unlikely to succeed.[9] Studies show that improvement
in the status of women is highly correlated with the
decline of population growth rates. This is significant
because it can take pressure off Third World countries
whose economies rarely grow fast enough to offset
population increases. Moreover, where women are healthy
and literate, so too are children--with obvious salutary
consequences for the future of a society. However, a
strategy that improves the status and well-being of
women and children can cause substantial cultural
turmoil. Hence, it is one that certain nations
undertake at some initial risk. Nevertheless, BHN
theorists believe that gradual improvement in the
well-being of women and children is essential to
widespread attainment of BHN objectives.

The BHN approach insists that the basic needs of
all individuals should be met both as a normative
question of ethics and as a pragmatic strategy of future

societal growth. This should lead to the ultimate
fulfillment of still higher, more subtle human needs.
The approach assumes that certain targets, or minimum
needs standards must be set which governments will
direct their energies and resources toward. It also
assumes that the ultimate development of a society
hinges on its ability to reduce the magnitude of abject
poverty, which in turn should remove some of the future
drag such poverty would otherwise impose on economic
growth. There is probably less controversy concerning
the first assumption than the second--although it is
clearly easier to set targets or minimum basic needs
standards than it is to meet them. However, in both
scholarly treatises and practical situations, target-
setting issues have been dealt with comprehensively.[10]

Regarding the second assumption on the necessity of
meeting basic needs as a precondition of genuine and
productive future growth, there is considerable debate.
BHN theorists argue that such a strategy would have
clear long-term benefits with regard to productivity and
national income growth, while admitting that certain
short-term, transitional economic shocks would be
felt.[11] Indeed, the _prima facie_ case that the BHN
strategy--far from being a drag on growth--would
actually promote more evenly paced, broad-based, and
long-term growth is quite compelling. Regardless of
whether one accepts this proposition, BHN theorists will
quickly observe that previous aid strategies have had a
singular lack of success in reaching the world's
poorest, and that the BHN strategy should be given a
fair trial before it is rejected as an unpromising
development approach.[12]

The main actors in the BHN approach, at least as
indicated in the existing literature on the subject, are
the recipient governments, donor governments, and
multilateral aid-giving agencies. Although not always
acknowledged as such, PVOs are also an important
component of such a strategy. BHN theorists are in
universal agreement that the most important actor in any
successful BHN strategy is the government of the country
with the poverty problem. Without the commitment of
recipient governments to a BHN strategy, no amount of
external assistance can ensure the gradual improvement
of conditions of life for the abjectly poor. However,
BHN theorists also note that most recipient govern-
ments--even where committed to a BHN approach--lack the
requisite domestic resources to successfully accomplish
a BHN program without in some cases substantial external
assistance. Thus, donor governments and multilateral
aid-giving institutions are seen as essential secondary
actors in the process of implementing successful BHN
strategies.

This is where the consensus ends, particularly with
regard to how donor governments and IOs should become

engaged in the BHN approach. For the most part, recipient governments would prefer to see BHN assistance funneled directly to them for internal redistribution. Moreover, to the extent that such resources are channelled directly to the poorest segments of their population beyond their own control, governments of recipient states would prefer the funds to be multilateral as opposed to bilateral in character, so as to avoid the political problems that might be associated with the latter. However, donor governments--whether they provide bilateral or multilateral assistance for BHN purposes--in many cases would prefer to see the funds going directly to the needy rather than being squandered by what they often perceive as corrupt and inefficient Third World governments. In short, there are sovereignty and accountability issues which inevitably arise as one moves to a consideration of how BHN assistance should be administered.

A related issue of concern to both potential donors and recipients is the relationship between the BHN strategy, and efforts by the Third World to promote negotiations on a New International Economic Order (NIEO). A detailed analysis of the various linkages, problems, and dilemmas associated with the BHN strategy and the NIEO negotiations is beyond the scope of this chapter. Indeed, a number of excellent treatments on this subject are available.[13] It will be useful, nonetheless, to briefly highlight some of the issues surrounding this debate since they are of considerable relevance to the role of PVOs as prospective vehicles for BHN assistance.

In the final analysis, the NIEO and BHN strategy have different equity concerns. The NIEO focuses on international inequities, while the BHN strategy focuses on intranational ones. Because of this fundamental difference of focus, problems have arisen among rich and poor nations about motivations behind the BHN strategy. Poor countries have insisted that an international redistribution of wealth through the NIEO will be required to ensure their future development. But, because Third World countries are jealous of their sovereignty, they see this redistribution as an interstate problem. They perceive the BHN strategy as a Trojan horse--a negotiating ploy by the rich states to sidetrack the NIEO and undercut the sovereignty of poor states by exposing them to external intervention. Moreover, the BHN strategy is seen by poor countries as an effort by rich states to enlarge potential markets, slow the rate of growth of Third World nations, and reduce the availability of high technology to them.[14] From this perspective, the BHN strategy is seen as being only secondarily concerned with intranational inequities. Indeed, there remains the lurking suspicion among Third World nations that the BHN strategy will ultimately redound to the benefit of the already powerful and wealthy nations. Of course, the concern of Third World governments is not entirely without justification, but it is also exaggerated. Still, just as rich nations will want to see evidence that BHN strategies are not being diluted by Third World bureaucratic leakage, so must the sovereignty and territorial integrity concerns of Third World governments be assuaged before substantial and effective BHN strategies can be implemented. Indeed, it is in this area that PVOs hold considerable promise as vehicles of development assistance that both rich and poor nations can accept.

Some have suggested that a 'planetary bargain' may be required to resolve many of the differences that separate rich northern countries from poor southern ones. One often-cited element of such a bargain would be that the poor nations be given the NIEO as a means of rectifying international inequities in return for their agreement to a genuine BHN strategy that would address the domestic inequities so typical of Third World nations.[15]

Such an outcome is not only unlikely but probably unnecessary as well. First of all, the NIEO and BHN are not mutually contradictory. Nor does the success or failure of one guarantee the success or failure of the other. They are two different approaches to resolving equity problems--each of which can be considered on the basis of its own merits. Of course, the political perceptions of many nations suggest linkages between the two approaches, and these perceptions cannot be simply ignored. However, because global bargaining of this kind is unlikely to bear any immediate fruit, and because the problems of the globe's absolute poor require immediate attention, a 'planetary bargain' is not feasible. More appropriate would be a series of minibargains between nations experiencing acute poverty problems, and other nations, IOs, and PVOs that are in a position to respond. Something akin to what the Aspen study refers to as a 'global bazaar' is likely to be the most effective negotiating strategy.[16] Such an approach would emphasize an incremental, regionally, and locally oriented strategy to cope with specific problems. As we will see later, this approach might lead to widely adopted practices and larger institutional networks of BHN development delivery. Indeed, this would be more easily and efficiently achieved as a result of actual practice than as a grand design or global regime conceived first in plenary sessions of international conferences, without the benefit of practical experience. The institutional machinery to accomplish BHN strategies in such a decentralized manner is already available. However, the crucial variable remains the will to implement such strategies in a manner that will assuage the political sensitivities of the involved parties.

There is in the BHN approach a sense of urgency--a sense of urgency that is not so apparent in the NIEO debate--which insists that the needs of the absolute poor must be met within a relatively short period of time in order to avoid further human suffering and economic deterioration within Third World nations. Generally, the timetable presented is one that foresees a basic floor being built under international poverty by the year 2000.[17]  A number of studies have also concluded that a sum of $10-15 billion a year would be required in order to finance a twenty year global BHN strategy, which, as Roger Hansen has noted, is a sum that could easily be reached if the DAC nations increased their aid donations to a level of about 0.45 to 0.5 percent of their GNPs--assuming that the increase were allocated to a BHN regime.[18]  This rather arbitrary and absolute goal of establishing a floor underneath global poverty with the expenditure of $10-15 billion is admirable but unrealistic.  Indeed, a realist would be obliged to observe that even a reversal of the trend in the growing numbers of absolute poor and a modest improvement in the lot of even a fraction of the world's poorest would be a laudable achievement. Clearly, the greater the number of the poor whose lives can be made more comfortable and whose basic needs can be met, the better.  But one should bear in mind that absolute goals are usually only relatively achieved. With this dose of realism in mind, it is important to consider how any level of available BHN funds might be efficiently channelled in the service of the destitute. Before we do so, however, it will be useful to examine more closely the role and function of PVOs as purveyors of development assistance and expertise.

THE NATURE AND FUNCTIONS OF PVOS

PVOs may be defined as nongovernmental, nonprofit, tax-exempt organizations whose primary purpose is to provide material assistance, and administrative and technical services at little or no cost to the needy.[19]  As nongovernmental agencies, PVOs have no official relationship with governments, although they often have dealings with their parent state's government as well as specific agreements with host governments that provide them access to needy populations.  As a general rule, PVOs attempt to maintain a scrupulous, nonpolitical image so as to retain the good faith and confidence of foreign governments.  Indeed, this is one advantage that PVOs enjoy as potential vehicles for BHN assistance.  However, the world is a very politically oriented one, and it is often most difficult for PVOs to steer clear of politically charged atmospheres.

In addition to the advantages that PVOs enjoy owing to their nonpolitical character, they also enjoy tax-exempt status as nonprofit organizations. This, combined with the fact that their overhead costs are generally quite low, means that PVOs as a group constitute one of the more efficient vehicles of development assistance.[20]

Beyond satisfying the elements of the above definition, PVOs differ substantially in terms of size, administrative style, and affiliation. Some PVOs, like Catholic Relief Services (CRS) and CARE, are large and well-established in terms of personnel, budget, and the global scope of their operations. CRS, for instance, has been in the relief and development business for nearly forty years and had a 1981 budget in excess of $356 million. Other PVOs are smaller in size and in many cases more regional in their scope of operations. An example would be Africare, a Washington D.C.-based PVO which operates exclusively in Africa and which had a budget in 1983 of $4.7 million.[21] Many smaller PVOs have no actual overseas programs but often donate supplies or financial resources to other PVOs that do.

From an operational standpoint, many PVOs like to maintain direct administrative control over their overseas programs. Others, like Africare, often make their development expertise and assistance available to the local government to be utilized in ways that the latter sees as complementing its own development objectives. The administrative autonomy issue is one about which there is some controversy. Obviously, from a host government standpoint, the Africare approach is preferable in many ways. Yet most PVOs prefer to maintain as much autonomy as they can, and it is often advantageous for a government to seek their assistance despite its loss of administrative control. Indeed, there is a strong demand for PVO services in the Third World. As long as a seller's market exists PVOs will be in a position to maintain a fair amount of internal program autonomy. Of course governments conclude agreements with PVOs to specify the kinds of program activities PVOs are permitted to undertake within their boundaries. Once established, however, PVOs are typically in control of the disbursement of funds and services, and, although they clearly attempt to maintain a working, cooperative relationship with the host government, they constitute a vehicle through which development assistance can be channelled while essentially bypassing the local government. Hence, in those cases where host governments have not assiduously promoted the basic needs of their poorest people through domestic remedies, PVOs are in a position to ensure that some resources are channelled into areas previously ignored by governments.

PVOs also differ in terms of their affiliation and

philosophical orientation, although they all share a
basic concern for ameliorating global poverty. Many
PVOs are religiously affiliated, notable examples being
CRS, Church World Service (CWS), Lutheran World Relief
(LWR), the American Friends Service Committee, the
Mennonite Central Committee, World Vision, International
Christian Aid, and World Concern, to name but a few. Of
those PVOs that are religiously based, some have purely
programmatic concerns, while others combine relief and
development activities with a strong sense of missionary
evangelism. Obviously, in certain situations,
governments may be reluctant to work with the latter if
the evangelistic aspect is seen to be the primary
motivation. In most cases, governments will seek
assistance from such PVOs with the understanding that
the primary aim is to provide assistance. In other
cases, governments may be unconcerned about the
proselytization aspect of evangelically oriented PVOs.
The fact that many religiously oriented PVOs work
directly through their indigenous counterparts minimizes
the perception of external intervention. Moreover,
because many of the missions established by churches are
in remote areas, they are rarely seen as a threat and,
in fact, are often viewed as a positive source of rural
development assistance that may reduce pressures on the
government to reallocate its own domestic resources. Of
course, to the extent that such an attitude exists among
governments, it needs to be overcome if a genuine BHN
program is to succeed.

A large number of nonreligious, more secularly
oriented PVOs also exists. They, too, have humanitarian
motives, but lack a denominational or religious
affiliation.[22] Among these are CARE, Africare, Save
the Children, and various national committees of UNICEF,
to give a few examples. These groups tend to view
relief and development situations as technical and
material enterprises aimed at alleviating suffering.
The spiritual needs of recipient populations are left to
others.[23] This philosophical orientation has
advantages in those cases where governments may be
sensitive to cultural intervention or religious
interference. On the other hand, secular PVOs lack the
built-in constituencies that church-based PVOs have for
soliciting resources. While differences between secular
and religious PVOs do exist, it should be emphasized
that they need not overshadow the common concerns and
values that PVOs share.

For a variety of budgetary and practical reasons,
many PVOs have focused both on refugee relief and on
long-term development projects. For purposes of this
analysis, the focus will be more on the latter than the
former, although clearly in both cases PVOs have worked
to meet BHN objectives. Disaster and refugee relief
projects are seen as temporary and emergency operations,

the crisis proportions of which ultimately diminish leaving the host country and PVOs with long-term questions of development. It might be noted, parenthetically, that refugee and disaster relief operations make headlines, thus easing the task PVOs face in earning aid dollars from what is a more typically inattentive public in regard to longer term development issues. For this reason, many PVOs are reluctant to get into the development business to the exclusion of relief. Nevertheless, many PVOs have come to realize that by focusing on long-term development issues, they might help to eradicate the underlying conditions of poverty which in turn often exacerbate relief situations when they do occur.

For several years PVOs have been engaging in efforts to promote rural development through the use of appropriate and usually small-scale technologies. Sensitive to the fact that self-reliant development is in the long run more beneficial than high-profile, external interventions, some PVOs have attempted to incorporate indigenous organizations as active participants in the process of program development. For instance, rather than teach health techniques to a large population using expatriate staff, PVOs find it more appropriate to train indigenous health workers how to teach their conationals certain health practices. Such efforts are intended to promote the development of local expertise. In this sense, PVOs have been in the forefront of assistance agencies in the effort to promote the self-participation aspect that the BHN strategy emphasizes. Clearly, PVO efforts have not always been so enlightened, but there has been a clear emphasis on their part away from heavy-handed, culturally insensitive development projects concocted in Western capitals without adequate field assessment and sensitivity to BHN objectives.


PVOS AND THE BHN STRATEGY

As we have already noted, PVOs have for some time engaged in informal BHN strategies. Several questions arise in this connection regarding the potential of PVOs as a future vehicle for BHN assistance. Where do they stand currently relative to governments and international agencies as contributors of foreign aid? What proportion of foreign assistance do they account for, and could that proportion be potentially increased? Tables 3.1 and 3.2 help to illustrate the relative size of PVO contributions to development assistance. Several conclusions can be drawn from them.

Table 3.1 illustrates flows of financial resources from DAC countries to developing countries. It demonstrates that private resource flows through banks

TABLE 3.1

Resource Flows from DAC Countries to Developing Countries and PVO Percentage Participation (in U.S. millions of dollars)

| | Resource Flows in U.S. Millions of Dollars by Year | | | | | | | | |
|---|---|---|---|---|---|---|---|---|---|
| | 1970 | 1973 | 1974 | 1975 | 1976 | 1977 | 1978 | 1979 | 1980 |
| Official Development Assistance (ODA -- bilateral & multilateral) | 6,790 | 9,351 | 11,317 | 13,585 | 13,665 | 15,745 | 19,995 | 22,419 | 26,776 |
| Other Official Flows (OOF, bilateral and multilateral) | 1,139 | 2,427 | 2,183 | 3,024 | 3,305 | 3,442 | 5,495 | 2,753 | 5,280 |
| Private Flows | 6,875 | 11,449 | 13,266 | 21,962 | 22,417 | 31,324 | 44,018 | 48,527 | 40,634 |
| Grants by PVOs | 857 | 1,364 | 1,217 | 1,342 | 1,355 | 1,489 | 1,675 | 1,997 | 2,371 |
| Total Official and Private | 15,661 | 24,611 | 27,983 | 39,913 | 40,742 | 52,000 | 71,183 | 75,696 | 75,061 |
| PVO % of Total | 5.5 | 5.5 | 4.3 | 3.4 | 3.3 | 2.9 | 2.4 | 2.6 | 3.2 |
| PVO % of ODA + OOF | 9.7 | 10.3 | 8.3 | 7.5 | 7.4 | 7.2 | 6.2 | 7.3 | 6.9 |

Source: Adapted from the Organization for Economic Co-operation and Development's Development Cooperation Efforts and Policies of the Members of the Development Assistance Committee, 1976–1981 Reviews.

TABLE 3.2
Resource Flows from the U.S. to Developing Countries
and PVO Percentage Participation

| | Resource Flows in U.S. Millions of Dollars by Year | | | | | | | | |
|---|---|---|---|---|---|---|---|---|---|
| | 1970 | 1973 | 1974 | 1975 | 1976 | 1977 | 1978 | 1979 | 1980 |
| Official Development Assistance (ODA -- bilateral & multilateral) | 3,050 | 2,968 | 3,439 | 4,007 | 4,254 | 4,682 | 5,663 | 4,684 | 7,138 |
| Other Official Flows (OOF, bilateral and multilateral) | 168 | 477 | 823 | 920 | 882 | 752 | 1,288 | 953 | 1,112 |
| Private Flows | 2,395 | 3,996 | 5,273 | 11,635 | 6,399 | 6,159 | 8,287 | 12,008 | 4,301 |
| Grants by PVOs | 598 | 905 | 735 | 804 | 789 | 840 | 931 | 1,029 | 1,301 |
| Total Official and Private | 6,211 | 8,346 | 10,270 | 17,336 | 12,324 | 12,433 | 16,169 | 18,674 | 13,852 |
| PVO % of Total | 9.6 | 10.8 | 7.1 | 4.6 | 6.4 | 6.8 | 5.8 | 5.5 | 9.4 |
| PVO % of ODA + OOF | 15.7 | 20.8 | 14.7 | 14.0 | 13.3 | 13.4 | 11.8 | 15.4 | 13.6 |

Source: Adapted from the Organization for Economic Co-opération and Development's Development Cooperation Efforts and Policies of the Members of the Development Assistance Committee, 1976-1981 Reviews.

and multinational corporations are, in terms of size, the most significant means by which resources are transferred to the Third World. It should be noted, however, that these resources are typically focused on the urban, growth-oriented sectors of Third World economies and rarely concentrate on BHN objectives. Multilateral and bilateral Official Development Assistance (ODA) combined with Other Official Flows (OOF), constitute about one-quarter to one-third of all resource flows to developing countries. Recently, a larger portion of such resources have been committed toward BHN objectives. PVOs, by comparison, contribute typically between 2.4 to 5.5 percent of total resource flows to developing countries. In 1980, for instance, PVOs contributed about $2.4 billion in development assistance, while private corporate flows accounted for $40.6 billion and all official (governmental) flows for about $32 billion. As a percentage of ODA and OOF, PVOs have accounted typically for between 6.2 to 10.4 percent of development assistance flows. This is a better measure of PVO activity because it discounts the largely non-BHN funding of private banks and corporations. Still, it must be noted that, even based on this measure, PVOs rarely account for more than 10 percent of the total. Indeed, there has been some slippage that has been only slightly recouped in the past decade regarding PVO percentage participation in development assistance. In 1973, PVOs accounted for 10.3 percent of ODA/OOF/PVO development funds compared to 6.9 percent in 1980. While contributions by PVOs are rather modest in percentage terms, it should be noted that PVO funds are typically directed to the more needy people and to the more remote areas of Third World countries, making their impact in BHN terms more significant than would otherwise appear to be the case.

Table 3.2, which illustrates flows of resources from the United States (which is the largest DAC aid-giver) to developing countries, confirms most of the trends apparent in Table 3.1. Private (non-PVO) flows tend to exceed governmental aid allocations, but not by as much as is apparent for all DAC countries combined. In the past decade, PVOs have accounted for between 12 and 21 percent of U.S. aid allocations when private (non-PVO) flows are discounted, suggesting that U.S. PVOs, at least by this measure, considerably outdistance their counterparts elsewhere in the developed world. Indeed, U.S. PVOs typically account for about half of all PVO assistance worldwide. The U.S. government, by contrast, typically contributes only a quarter of all official development assistance, and this percentage declined over the past decade.

An analysis of U.S.-based PVO budgets reveals interesting patterns of American government ties to the private voluntary sector. Of the 315 PVOs listed in the

1978 TAICH Directory that reported budgetary sources and
were actually engaged in foreign development assistance
activities, eighty-three--or roughly 26 percent--had
received some assistance from the U.S. government.[24]
Furthermore, a content analysis of the budgets of these
organizations for the year 1976 shows that, while PVOs
raised $548.7 million (or about 56 percent of their
revenue) from private sources, $436.9 million (or about
44 percent) of their funds came from U.S. government
sources.[25]  Seventy-nine per cent of all U.S.
government funds granted to PVOs in 1976, i.e. $346.9
million, were channelled through two agencies, CRS and
CARE.  These two agencies also account for about 10
percent of all private funds raised by PVOs.  The U.S.
government clearly prefers to use experienced and
well-established agencies such as these (as well as a
number of others that receive smaller but still
substantial sums of government money) as development
assistance vehicles.  Many PVOs, on the other hand, are
reluctant to seek or accept government funds, preferring
instead to work entirely through the private sector.
This avoids problems associated with both the loss of
charitable contribution identity amid large amounts of
government funds, and the tied aid problem which many
PVOs have in the past found to be contrary to their
philosophy of voluntarism.

However, there are certain limits in the
availability of private funds and in the ability of PVOs
to tap them.  Indeed, many PVOs compete for the same aid
dollars, particularly nonreligious PVOs who do not have
built-in, church-based constituencies.  Moreover, while
PVOs have been remarkably successful in accelerating the
level of private contributions and appealing to the
eleemosynary instincts of the public in the developed
world over the past decade, they rely on charitable
instincts alone at risk.  Thus, should they desire to
expand their future operations, PVOs will be faced
increasingly with the prospect of seeking government
grants, if only for such items as overseas freight
subsidies.  This realization by PVOs comes at a time
when governments, too, have sought to funnel larger
amounts of development resources through such private
channels in order to achieve BHN objectives, as
reflected in the "New Directions" legislation of the
U.S. Congress in the mid-1970s.

Clearly, the figures in Tables 3.1 and 3.2 suggest
that the U.S. government and other DAC countries could
channel even larger sums of money through PVOs in order
to meet basic human needs.[26]  Indeed, the prospects
for broadened ties between governments and PVOs, for the
purpose of BHN assistance delivery are reasonably good
based on the progress that has been made over the past
decade.

It is possible, given available data, to compare

the overall magnitude of PVO resource flows with
bilateral and multilateral and corporate flows to the
developing world in general.  However, it is much more
difficult to compare the actual direction and targets of
such flows to specific countries of the developing world
in particular.  Unfortunately, data are not available
which make it possible to know, for instance, whether
PVOs tend to focus greater proportions of their
resources on countries categorized in the Less Developed
Country (LDC) category, than do governments or corporate
entities.  Data are readily available regarding flows of
official and corporate resources to specific recipient
countries, but systematic records on PVO resource flows
to LDC countries are not available.[27]  Hence, it is
not currently possible to judge whether PVOs are any
more likely than governments to focus resources on the
poorest countries.  Even if it were possible to
determine comparative directions of resource flows to
countries at varying per capita income levels, it would
still be necessary to identify how those resources were
distributed within the recipient country to determine
the actual impact of external aid on the poor in BHN
terms.  While insufficient data are available to allow
definitive comparisons, given the general approaches,
attitudes, and program activities of various donors, it
is probably fair to say that PVOs focus their resources
in a more direct way on the specific needs of the poor
and very poor, than do governments or corporations.

One could conclude that PVOs are a potentially
useful vehicle for broadened BHN assistance delivery by
virtue of the simple fact that they exist, and that they
are already in the development assistance business.  But
the case for the utilization of PVOs in such a manner
goes beyond these basic considerations.  Based upon
several evaluation criteria identified by Elliot
Schwartz, PVOs rate reasonably well as efficient
vehicles of development assistance.[28]  Schwartz
identifies nine criteria by which PVOs can be
evaluated.  They are enumerated below with discussion
about how PVOs measure up to them.

Fostering self-help initiative among the poorest of
the poor.  Promotion of self-help initiatives is a
primary concern of the BHN strategy.  For their part,
PVOs have moved from relief and welfare modes of
assistance, to self-help initiatives during the last
decade.  Indeed, some PVOs have done so more speedily
and perhaps more effectively than have governments or
IOs.  Others, ironically, have done so at the
encouragement of the U.S. Agency for International
Development (AID).  In any case, it is important to
understand both that the former emphasis of PVOs on
relief was not entirely without positive developmental

impact on the poorest, and that self-help initiatives
now being emphasized may be of greater immediate value
to upper rather than lower strata of the poor.  As PVOs
move toward a development mode, they should be even more
careful not to discard existing efforts that effectively
reach the poorest of the poor.[29]

Mobilizing U.S. private and human resources.  PVOs
provide a significant amount of development assistance
much of which is from private sources that would
otherwise go untapped.  What is often ignored is that,
although the professional staffs of PVOs are remunerated
for their services--it might be added at a much more
modest level than their counterparts in governments and
IOs--PVOs also moblilize substantial numbers of
volunteers.  This is particularly true of the
religiously based PVOs and missionary groups.

Stimulating innovative projects.  PVOs have a good
reputation as innovators of development projects which
can be subsequently replicated.  To the extent that they
operate beyond donor government regulations, PVO
personnel may be much freer to experiment with untried
but promising initiatives.  Unfortunately, innovation
does not always go hand in hand with replication.  Not
all replicated projects are innovative, nor are all
innovative projects readily replicable.  In addition, as
has been noted by Tendler and Kramer, PVOs may act more
often than not as efficient vehicles for expanded or
improved use of existing program approaches or services
than as actual innovators of such approaches.[30]
Whether they operate as actual innovators or as
effective modelers of existing methods, the less rigidly
bureaucratic nature of PVOs may give them advantages
over governmental agencies as initiators of BHN-oriented
programs.

Strengthening people-to-people contact.  One of the
major strengths of PVOs has been their ability to
maintain a largely apolitical focus on the human needs
of prospective aid recipients.  Although no hard data
exist, there is impressionistic evidence that PVOs tend
to enhance international good will.  Certainly, PVOs
have made an especially concerted effort to educate
their own aid-giving constituencies about the
development problems experienced in the Third World,
thus heightening public awareness to those difficulties
and no doubt contributing to the continued flow of
charitable resources into PVO coffers.  It is equally
clear that PVO work among the world's destitute is
appreciated both by the poor themselves and by the vast
majority of host governments that continue to solicit
PVO services.

Encouraging the establishment of indigenous
participatory private sector institutions. PVOs tend to
focus more closely on development of community-oriented
institutions than do IOs and governmental donors. This
does not imply that all such efforts succeed or that all
PVO programs are so structured. Indeed, PVOs can be as
guilty as other donors in the top-down creation,
articulation, and implementation of programs, as Tendler
has noted in her penetrating analysis of PVO devlopment
activities.[31] However, to the extent that PVOs focus
on developing community-based institutions for projects
in such areas as sanitation, health, transportation and
education, they make an important contribution to the
BHN development process.

Promotion of self-sustaining development. Evidence
that PVOs promote self-sustaining development is quite
spotty. PVOs are often reluctant to commit funding for
development projects beyond a year or so unless they get
substantial external funding. Where outside support is
not secured, they often find themselves abandoning what
might be promising projects to the local administration
of an indigenously affiliated group. Even in cases
where the latter may have adequate managerial know-how,
they may lack sufficient resources to meet the recurrent
costs of many development programs. In some cases, the
recipient government may initially promise support, but,
given the competing claims against its scarce resources,
may find it easy to ignore, reduce, or cut funds
previously allocated to PVO-sponsored programs. Unless
PVOs can find means to promote income-generating
activities, or to substantially bolster their own
budgetary receipts to meet recurrent costs, they will
continue to face the problem of program failure as they
phase out their own monetary involvement.

Increasing LDC capacity to absorb outside capital.
A key economic argument behind the BHN strategy for
development is that by bettering the health and
increasing the levels of literacy and skill among a
country's poorest people, the overall absorptive
capacity of the country for outside capital is
increased.[32] To the extent that this is so, PVOs may
contribute to such an outcome, given their tendency to
focus on development activities that promote such ends.

Demand for PVO services. As has been noted
previously, PVO services, expertise, and assistance are
highly sought after by developing countries. Although
the motives may vary, developing countries clearly see
PVOs as an attractive development alternative. One
might assume that this is because PVOs provide valuable
services in an efficient and professional manner that
does not involve the same kinds of politically

distasteful and sometimes economically painful side
effects that accompany official multilateral and
bilateral assistance to Third World governments.  Unlike
the World Bank, PVOs do not demand that a government
undertake painful deflationary policies to acquire a
loan.  Unlike governments, PVOs typically do not tie
their aid to the purchase of donor country products.  Of
course, PVOs are not in a position to do such things.
Nor is it likely that they would have any inclination to
dictate terms to a host country.  Indeed, their
long-standing apolitical stance and BHN style has won a
great deal of respect and enhanced their reputation
among Third World governments.

Costs of services.  Finally, as has been noted
earlier, PVOs typically operate with a streamlined,
modestly paid, and in many cases volunteer staff, thus
reducing their administrative costs to a rather low
level by comparison to the rather bulky and expensive
U.N. and governmental bureaucracies.  PVOs can typically
make an aid dollar stretch much further than bilateral
and multilateral agencies can, while focusing those
dollars directly upon the needs of the poor.

Further Considerations.  Based upon the nine
aforementioned evaluation criteria, PVOs fare reasonably
well compared to major donors, although there is no
doubt room for improvement.  In addition to these
criteria, one may assess how PVOs respond to specific
problems associated with the implementation of BHN
assistance.  For instance, Paul Streeten, a prominent
BHN theorist, has observed that BHN programs face
several problems including; the remoteness of target
populations; the problem of adapting technologies to the
needs of a particular group; social and linguistic
differences of target populations from the population of
a country as a whole; the political weakness of target
groups which have little influence on domestic
allocation of resources; and the isolation of target
populations from the cash economy and the economic
progress experienced there.[33]
Streeten suggests that these and other problems
create enormous difficulties in reaching the lowest 20
percent of income earners in developing countries.  He
notes that, "Most delivery systems do not reach these
people because of existing power structures, market
imperfections or cost considerations."[34]  However,
because of the state-centric orientation of Streeten's
analysis, the potential role of PVOs in overcoming such
administrative dilemmas is not fully appreciated or
discussed.  PVOs are certainly not immune from the
temptation to target funding at levels other than the
poorest 20 percent of a population.  Indeed, in sectors
such as agricultural development, the temptation exists

to fund programs for those farmers who are known to be
capable of capitalizing on the assistance, and putting
it into productive use.  In such cases, the poorest
individuals and families in rural areas may be ignored.
As a general rule, however, PVOs are more likely to be
sensitive to the basic needs of the very poor than are
the larger and more productivity-oriented official aid
programs.  Hence, they constitute one of the more
flexible and potentially useful means by which to reach
the bottom 20 percent of income earners in developing
countries.

Based on most of the evaluation criteria discussed
above, one can conclude that PVOs are in an advantageous
position as vehicles for BHN assistance delivery.  Donor
governments and U.N. agencies seem to have become aware
of this in recent years, and a variety of cooperative
ventures between governments, IOs, and PVOs have been
attempted.[35]  There are certain obvious structural and
political obstacles to such joint ventures, but it
appears that the successful implementation of BHN
strategies will require even more systematic and
comprehensive cooperation between recipient countries
and the donor community.  This gives rise to a number of
important questions regarding both the flow of resources
between and among various actors in the BHN strategy,
and the role each actor will play in the implementation
of such a strategy.  It is to a consideration of such
issues that we now turn.


MODELS OF BHN RESOURCE FLOWS

An analysis of PVO participation in a BHN regime
would be remiss if it did not address the question of

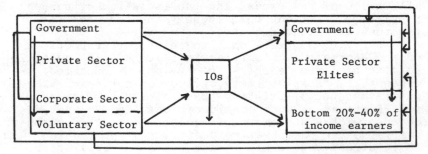

Figure 3.1  Development-related Resource Flows

where PVOs fit into the larger system of BHN resource
flows.  Figure 3.1 illustrates the possible direction of
all development-related resource flows among
governments, IOs, corporate entities, PVOs and various
target populations in the developing nations.  It should
be noted that the arrows represent flows of both
material and human, as well as monetary resources.  All
of the channels for resource flows to the developing
world are utilized to some degree in the current
aid-giving system.  However, the predominant paths
emphasized in the past have been those of direct
bilateral and multilateral assistance between
governments and IOs, as well as on private investment
flows from corporations and banks to governments or
economic elites in Third World nations.
     Figure 3.2, a simplified version of figure 3.1,
illustrates potential, noncorporate resource flows,
which could be expected to address the basic human needs
of the poorest segments of the Third World more directly.

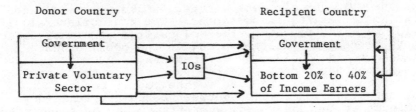

Figure 3.2   BHN Resource Flows

It must be stressed that private sector corporate flows
should not be seen as less important than other resource
flows retained in figure 3.2.  Indeed, macrolevel income
and employment producing strategies in the more dynamic
sectors of Third World economies should be expected to
continue.  Continued corporate involvement in the Third
World, coupled with a shift of offical assistance to
complement ongoing PVO efforts to promote BHN
strategies, might be expected to foster salutary
economic developments in both the urban and rural
economies.  Hence, the corporate paths are eliminated in
figure 3.2, only because they tend by themselves to
rarely, if ever, focus on what could be termed a BHN
strategy.  On the other hand, governmental, multilateral, and private voluntary assistance often do.
     Taking figure 3.2 as a simplified representation of
BHN resource flows, one can identify six distinct
resource flows that could be emphasized separately or in
combinations as elements of a larger BHN implementation

62

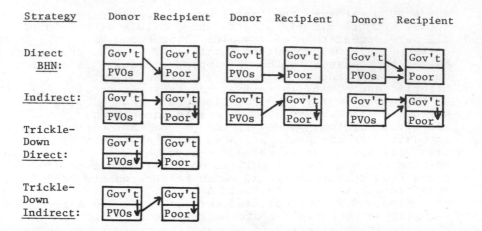

Figure 3.3  Alternative BHN Strategies

strategy.  Four of these strategies are bilateral and
two, multilateral in character.  The four bilateral aid
flow patterns can be further classified as either direct
governmental or direct PVO aid to the poor, or as
indirect aid provided by governments or PVOs to the
recipient government with the expectation that some
benefits will trickle down to the poor.  One can
distinguish even further between certain trickle-down
effects at the donor end, where funds may be funneled by
donor governments to PVOs, which may then, in turn,
either pass the resources on directly to the poor or
indirectly through the recipient government.  In short,
the four bilateral strategies may be termed direct,
indirect, trickle-down direct, and trickle-down indirect
strategies.  For illustrative purposes these strategies
are portrayed in the figure 3.3.  Clearly, there are
several potential combinations of such strategies that
could be pursued simultaneously between any two or more
donor and recipient countries.  In fact, it is rare to
find any one of these strategies in its pure form.
     As we have already pointed out, recipient
governments tend to prefer the indirect strategies
because they maximize recipient country control over
resources, thus diminishing potential penetration by
outside agents.  However, from the BHN standpoint, the
more directly such resources can be targeted toward the
poor the better.  Recycling of such resources through
host governments can reduce the  positive impact on the
poorest segments of the recipient country's population.
PVOs have shown the greatest enthusiasm for such direct
approaches, with donor governments showing some
inclination to move in the same direction.  In doing so,
donor governments have realized that it may be more

politically feasible to funnel official resources through PVOs than to undertake direct official programs in a recipient country which the latter may find unpalatable owing to the intervention issues that typically arise under such circumstances. Hence, as has been previously observed, one of the more promising strategies for realizing BHN objectives, while simultaneously mollifying recipient fears, is the trickle-down direct strategy. In short, while direct strategies may foster resistance between donor and recipient governments, and while indirect strategies are seen as increasingly unsuitable for BHN purposes by donor governments interested in shifting to such a development focus, the trickle-down direct strategy may provide a mutually acceptable path for both donors and recipients to pursue more extensive BHN objectives. This assumes, of course, that PVOs will be both willing and able to serve as intermediary vehicles for the transmittal of BHN programs, a point which we will examine more closely shortly.

The fourth bilateral strategy, which we have referred to as the trickle-down indirect strategy, is not a very promising alternative for BHN purposes. Although some developmental resources currently move in a trickle-down indirect fashion, the volume is limited if for no other reason than that most PVOs prefer to work autonomously rather than as providers of carte blanche assistance to host states. Indeed, it makes more sense for donor governments to provide development resources directly to a recipient government than to recycle them first through PVOs. In fact, one can assume that the recycling of development dollars by donor governments, PVOs, IOs and recipient governments, leads to higher administrative costs, as well as greater potential for waste and bureaucratic leakage. By contrast, one of the great advantages of direct bilateral aid strategies is that they get resources where they need to go with a minimum of waste and diversion.

Let us turn now to an examination of multilateral BHN strategies. As noted earlier, the signal advantage of multilateral aid is that it is not seen by recipient governments as having the political character that bilateral assistance does. Hence, to the extent that multilateral aid can be directed toward BHN objectives, political sensitivities can be minimized. There are two basic multilateral BHN funding strategies; one direct, the other indirect. Of course, it must be recognized that most multilateral funds originate with donor governments. In this sense, multilateral aid is essentially indirect aid. However, to the extent that multilateral funding is channelled directly to the world's poorest people, one is dealing with a direct BHN strategy. The more typical pattern of multilateral funding until recently, however, has been to channel

resources indirectly through recipient governments with
the expectation that the benefits would trickle down to
the poor.  The problem with such a practice is that
resources distributed in such a manner almost invariably
do not benefit the bottom 20 to 40 percent of a
recipient country's population.  Moreover, such
assistance is recycled twice; once through a multilateral bureaucracy and once through a national one.
Inevitably, resources are diminished owing to
administrative costs, even where a genuine BHN strategy
is pursued by both the recipient government and the
funding organization.  From a BHN perspective, then, it
is preferable to have both multilateral and bilateral
funds distributed directly to target populations.

It is not within the scope of this study to
demonstrate conclusively which of the six variations on
BHN aid flows discussed above is in fact the most
efficient.  Such a conclusion cannot be drawn given the
insuffiency of the data.  Indeed, a more elaborate
tracking of funds from governments, PVOs, international
agencies, and recipient governments would have to be
undertaken over a lengthy period of time to understand
the relative efficiencies of BHN aid strategies.
Nevertheless, given both the lower overhead costs PVOs
enjoy compared to governments and IOs, and the
propensity of PVOs to target their resources more
directly on the poor, one can conclude that expanded use
of PVOs as BHN assistance delivery vehicles would be
both feasible and advantageous.


INSTITUTIONAL DESIDERATA AND POLITICAL CONCERNS

Expanded use of PVOs as BHN development assistance
vehicles, faces a number of potential political
obstacles from a variety of sources.  These include
donor and recipient governments, the decentralized and
rather uncoordinated global aid-giving system, and PVOs
themselves.  These constraints must be fully assessed
before potential strategies for resolving them can be
entertained.

Donor governments may be reluctant to provide
resources to PVOs for BHN programs for a variety of
reasons.  In the first place, they may lack a serious
commitment to BHN goals, preferring to see aid directed
with more of a political or strategic focus.  Under such
circumstances the role of PVOs would not be seen by
donor governments as a particularly useful avenue of
assistance delivery.  Indeed many PVOs would be
reluctant to establish a closer partnership with donors
having essentially non-BHN motives or objectives.
Greater PVO/donor government cooperation presupposes a
genuine commitment by the governments to BHN development
objectives.

Even where governments are committed to BHN
objectives, they might prefer to pursue a direct BHN
program of their own without expanding the role of PVOs
in the process. Most DAC countries have at one time or
another over the past decade enunciated BHN development
objectives.[36] However, it is clear that substantial
amounts of such assistance have continued to address
traditional, non-BHN development concerns. Although
some effort has been made to ensure a more direct focus
on the needs of the poorest, high volumes of assistance
have yet to unambiguously reach them. Nor have all DAC
governments substantially increased BHN support through
PVOs. In some cases aid administrators in donor
countries have investments in their own official BHN
projects and would not care to see such funds diverted
to PVOs even where it might be demonstrated that the
latter could more efficiently address the needs of the
genuinely poor. Moreover, official development
assistance tends to focus on large-scale projects and
PVOs on much smaller ones. Hence, there is not always a
fit between what donor country aid officials and PVO
administrators see as priority programs. Finally, to
the extent that donor governments insist on tied aid or
partially tied aid, they will not see PVOs as an
attractive vehicle for such assistance. Indeed, PVOs
are usually not interested in participating in ventures
involving tied aid.

Potential obstacles to expanded PVO/government
linkages are not limited to the donor governments.
Recipient governments may also have reservations. To
the extent that expanded PVO/donor government ties are
effected, and to the extent that PVOs might begin to
expand beyond the traditional role they have played in
recipient countries, the latter may begin to have
reservations about the nature of PVO involvement. As
long, however, as the private, nonpolitical image and
identity of the PVO can be maintained, recipient
government concerns along these lines can be allayed.
Indeed, as we shall see shortly, PVOs are equally
concerned about the maintenance of their independent
identity. The key ingredient to any governments
resistance to or support of expanded PVO programs is the
degree of its commitment to BHN objectives. Where such
a commitment exists among recipient countries, less
reluctance should be expected to an expanded role for
PVOs. Still, a need would exist to coordinate recipient
government programs with those funded and administered
by external agents, including PVOs. Administrative
problems might be anticipated at this level even where a
recipient government has a clear BHN commitment.

Notwithstanding receptivity among both donor and
recipient countries to widened PVO participation in
development assistance, PVOs, themselves, must desire to
assume an expanded role before one can be realized. As

we have previously noted, economic pressures may be
moving PVOs toward greater receptivity to government
funding.  Owing to the limited availability of
charitable resources, many PVOs have come to the
realization that their existing resources will not
permit them to fund a growing number of potential
projects without additional income.  Still, PVO
officials have a number of concerns about the
consequences of accepting greater governmental funding.
A major concern is that the identity of the PVO might be
lost or altered.  At what point does a PVO cease to be
an independent entity relying on government support only
as a source of supplemental funds, and become instead a
mere dependent appendage of the government?  What
happens to the character of lean and efficient PVOs that
have been tempered by the rigors of seeking out sources
of revenue from the private sector when they begin to
rely on greater amounts of official aid?  If they become
too dependent, what would happen if governmental aid
were cut off?  Particularly among religious PVOs, the
question arises as to how missionary goals can be
squared with the secular aims of official assistance.
To what extent, they wonder, would they be required to
minimize evangelical activities in order to qualify for
government funds?[37]  These queries may overdramatize
the situation, but they reflect some of the fears that
PVO officials express about increasing reliance on
governmental sources of revenue.

Despite the hesitancy evidenced by many PVOs on the
subject of closer ties to governments, there are
mutually salutary ways in which PVOs and governments can
do business.  For instance, one problem many PVOs face
is the funding of recurrent costs of even rather modest,
small-scale BHN projects.  PVOs can rarely commit all of
the resources that may be required to complete a
multiyear project.  As a result, they often face the
unhappy task of abandoning promising but fragile
programs.  In such instances, government resources could
be of great help  by funding recurrent costs over a
longer period of time and improving the chances for
project survival.  Expanded use of the ocean freight
subsidies offered by AID is another area where there is
little reason for PVOs to be concerned about political
implications or loss of program control.  In these, and
other ways, modestly expanded cooperation between
governments and PVOs is already occurring and can be
expected to continue.

In addition to concerns issuing from particular
PVOs, it must also be recognized that inter-PVO
obstacles exist with respect to expanded PVO ties with
governments in pursuit of BHN development objectives.
Indeed, the decentralized structure of the international
aid-giving system militates against extensive
coordination and cooperation among aid-giving entities.

Just as a certain level of competition exists between
states regarding aid, so is there among PVOs a degree of
competitiveness for resources and programs. An
effective BHN strategy presupposes, however, that a
degree of coordination is established to avoid
unnecessary waste and duplication. Given the potential
obstacles to a more high-profile PVO participation in a
BHN strategy of development, how can sufficient
coordination be achieved to promote the successful
implementation of BHN programs?

The answer to this important question is in part
political and in part insitutional/legal in character.
Obviously, where the political will of recipient and
donor nations exists to meet BHN objectives, a way can
be found to efficiently coordinate and implement
programs designed to achieve such objectives. Part of
the problem is that the BHN approach has been caught up
in the global debates over the relative merits of the
NIEO and BHN regime-building approaches. But it is a
mistake to treat political will as though it were a
global phenomenon alone, at least if one expects to make
practical progress in the real world. Instead,
political will should be seen as a divisible, particular
phenomenon, capable of addressing particular problems in
particular countries. Nothing would fail so quickly (if
it could ever be established in the first place) as a
global BHN regime. If anything has been learned from
the history of development assistance, it is that
grandiose designs and programs imposed from the top do
not answer the basic needs of those at the bottom.
Certainly, then, BHN strategies of development should be
treated as malleable to local circumstances, and open to
variable implementation approaches.

Nevertheless, there are certain international or
regional arrangements that would promote the more
efficient development of particular BHN strategies.
Under the current system, a developing country that
desires to supplement its own BHN objectives, might seek
assistance from particular governments, PVOs and IOs.
Typically, it will bargain with each one to get whatever
assistance it can. Similarly, each government, IO and
PVO typically seeks to cut a deal in line with its own
priorities and capabilities. Although some
collaboration may exist in an effort to produce a
rational aid package, more often than not there is
little or none. In order to promote efficient,
long-term, and systematic BHN packages, however, there
is a strong need for consultation and coordination among
aid-giving entities.

A more rational BHN approach would call for a
country-by-country assessment of BHN objectives, and a
coordinated delivery of supplemental external assistance
through some central oversight mechanism. Instead of a
situation where each PVO has a separate agreement with

each host government, PVOs could work together to
develop an integrated, systematic package of BHN
programs.  This could be accomplished without destroying
the administrative autonomy of PVOs over their specific
programs.  In addition, such package proposals should be
integrated with the programs and projects of governments
and IOs.  The whole process could be overseen by a BHN
assessment and implementation team composed of
representatives from the host government, donor
governments, PVOs, and IOs--with the exact composition
of the team varying with the specific needs of the host
country.  In this way, a common BHN agreement,
specifying the particular roles, obligations, and rights
of each party, could be established.  Alternatively,
separate agreements could be reached between the host
government and aid-giving parties, in keeping with
current practice, but under broader oversight which
could reduce both the possibility of redundancy among
programs and the potential for programs working at
cross-purposes.  Bargains of this nature would clearly
be more appropriate than a global regime approach, and
would allow the actors to more directly confront the
needs of the desperately poor.  Such bargains would not
end the existence of developing country sensitivity to
external intervention, but they could ease the intensity
of those fears, and permit increased participation by
PVOs as vehicles for BHN assistance at the same time.


CONCLUSION

     If the saga of development efforts has demonstrated
anything, it is that there are no easy answers to global
poverty.  In this sense, the BHN approach should be seen
as a potentially viable alternative to past policies
that have demonstrably failed to meet the basic needs of
the world's poorest people.  But it should hardly be
viewed as a panacea to global poverty just yet.  Indeed,
the most important ingredient to the success of the BHN
approach will be the genuine commitment of governments
to BHN objectives.  As of now there is no global
consensus that the BHN strategy should be effected, let
alone agreement on how it could be implemented.  But the
absence of a global consensus does not mean, as we have
seen, that BHN strategies cannot be established on a
national or regional level.
     As for the role of PVOs in BHN development
strategies, the argument can be made that there is
considerable room for imaginative experimentation and
expanded participation.  This is not to suggest that
PVOs constitute the only or even the most significant
avenue for BHN assistance delivery.  Indeed, as was
observed earlier, PVOs currently account for only a
rather modest proportion of international aid flows.

They could not be expected to shoulder the administration of the estimated $15 to 20 billion a year that would be required to eliminate absolute poverty. On the other hand, they do constitute an especially suitable vehicle for transmission of BHN assistance, and they could be used in a more expanded and systematic way.

Whether PVOs are more actively incorporated into international BHN development strategies depends to a very large extent on the desire of donor and recipient governments, as well as IOs. PVOs exist in a state-dominated system and cannot force their will upon it. Moreover, they tend to have difficulty in organizing themselves in the name of pursuing a common PVO policy. Although several institutional efforts at inter-PVO coordination and consultation presently exist, many PVOs are reluctant to promote more extensive efforts. Forums such as the International Council of Voluntary Agencies (ICVA), the American Council of Voluntary Agencies in Foreign Service (ACVAFS), and Private Agencies in International Development (PAID), represent modest efforts at PVO coordination. Still, PVOs can not be expected to take the lead in effecting a more systematic and comprehensive BHN development approach. Although PVOs are unlikely to remain passive agents in the effort to promote broader BHN objectives, the lead implementation role is the more appropriate responsiblity of states and IOs. In the mean time, PVOs will continue, much as they have done in the past, to act as the conscience of the developed world, to educate people about the needs of the poor, and to take concrete steps to promote the welfare of the most desperately poor. But when it comes down to the question of how BHN objectives will be met, and to what degree resources will be committed to meet them, governments will make the critical choices. If they are serious about eradicating poverty and meeting basic human needs, they will do well to consider relying on PVOs as a means of delivering BHN assistance. As for the political obstacles that stand in the way of a more forthright BHN strategy by governments, they are considerable but hardly insurmountable. Indeed, as questions of sanity and humanity begin to converge, governments may find ways to overcome their political differences with regard to how basic needs should be met. And, as this inquiry has suggested, PVOs may be in more than a peripheral position to promote such an outcome.


NOTES


1. For a more extensive treatment of the history of development assistance and the evaluation of basic

needs thinking see Paul Streeten, et. al. <u>First Things
First: Meeting Basic Needs in Developing Countries</u> (New
York: Oxford University Press, 1981), and <u>idem</u>, "From
Growth to Basic Needs," <u>Finance and Development</u> 16
(September 1979): 28-31.

2.  See, Aspen Institute for Humanistic Studies,
<u>The Planetary Bargain: Proposals for a New International
Economic Order to Meet Basic Needs</u>, Report of an
International Workshop convened in Aspen Colorado, 7
July to 1 August 1975; and International Labor
Organization, <u>Employment, Growth and Basic Needs: A
One-World Problem</u> (Geneva: ILO, 1976).  Robert McNamara
also emphasized the need for a basic needs approach in
his "Address to the Board of Governors," 4 October 1976,
Manila, Philippines (Washington, D.C.: World Bank,
1977), and in a similar address given in Washington, D.C.
the following year.

3.  The literature on foreign assistance has
focused almost entirely on the role of interstate aid.
With regard to recent studies on BHN assistance, in
particular, the potential role of PVOs has been largely
ignored.  In Streeten's <u>First Things First</u>--one of the
more comprehensive treatments of BHN strategies--PVOs
are overlooked as potential BHN delivery vehicles.  So
it goes with much of the contemporary BHN literature.

4.  See the <u>Brandt Commission Report</u>, 285 for the
reference to PVOs.

5.  See Elliott Schwartz, <u>Private and Voluntary
Organizations in Development In Foreign Aid</u>  Office of
Management and Budget (OMB), (November 1976), which is
also abstracted in AID's <u>Development Digest</u> 18 (October
1980): 68.

6.  Aspen Institute, <u>Planetary Bargain</u>, 17-18.

7.  Previous aid strategies, such as the employment
creation, rural development, and poverty orientation
approaches did not place the same degree of emphasis on
local participation, nor the same degree of attention to
intrahousehold effects of economic policies that the BHN
strategy does.

8.  For and in-depth study of the problems involved
see Gharam Ghai, Martin Godfrey, and Franklyn Lisk,
<u>Planning for Basic Needs in Kenya: Performance, Policies
and Prospects</u> (Geneva: ILO, 1979), especially at
138-142, where administrative problems regarding
decentralized participatory planning is discussed in the
context of Kenya.

9.  This is especially emphasized in Streeten,
<u>First Things First</u>, 66-67 and 157-158; and in the ILO
<u>Report</u> of 1976, 60-61. See also, John Sewell, <u>U.S.
Development Agenda, 1980</u> (New York: Praeger Publishers
for the Overseas Development Council, 1980), 99-100.

10.  See, for instance, John McHale and Magda
Cordell McHale, <u>Basic Human Needs: A Framework for
Action</u> (New Brunswick, N.J.: Transaction Books, 1978).

11. For a trenchant analysis of the positive long-term potential of BHN strategies in respect to growth, see Streeten First Things First, 96-108. On the problems of transition see, ibid., 58-98.

12. Ibid., 183.

13. See, for instance, Roger D. Hansen, Beyond the North-South Stalemate (New York: McGraw-Hill, for the Council on Foreign Relations, 1979); and Johan Galtung, The North-South Debate: Technology, Basic Human Needs and the New International Economic Order (New York: Institute for World Order, 1980).

14. See Galtung, 35-39.

15. Ibid., 39.

16. Aspen Institute, Planetary Bargain, 8-9.

17. ILO, Employment, Growth and Basic Needs, 42.

18. Hansen, 262-264.

19. In its 1964 Directory of U.S. Nonprofit Organizations, TAICH distinguishes between voluntary agencies, foundations, and missions. Voluntary agencies are defined as "non-profit organization(s) established by a group of private citizens for a stated philanthropic purpose and supported by voluntary contributions from individiuals concerned with the realization of its purposes," at p. i. More recently the term private voluntary agency, or volag, has been interpreted more expansively to include missions and in some cases foundations. While the extant literature on BHN strategies largely ignores PVOs, there is a small but growing literature on the nature and functions of PVOs. Two general treatments of PVOs are particularly informative; John G. Sommer, Beyond Charity: U.S. Voluntary Aid for a Changing World (Washington, D.C.: Overseas Development Council, 1977); and Landrum Bolling and Craig Smith, Private Foreign Aid: U.S. Philanthropy for Relief and Development (Boulder, CO: Westview Press, 1982). A number of PVO case studies are also available. They include; on the Red Cross, David Forsythe, Humanitarian Politics: The International Committee of the Red Cross (Baltimore, MD: Johns Hopkins University Press, 1977); on Oxfam; Mervyn Jones, In Famine's Shadow: A Private War on Hunger (Boston: Beacon Press, 1965), and on CARE; Eugene Linden, The Alms Race: The Impact of American Vountary Aid Abroad (New York: Random House, 1976). An excellent book from the PVO practitioners standpoint is Elizabeth O'Kelley, Aid and Self-Help: A General Guide to Overseas Aid (London: C. Knight, 1973).

20. An examination of the annual reports of various PVOs demonstrates that overhead costs are generally quite low. CRS, for instance, sports an overhead of merely 1 to 2 percent, as do several much smaller PVOs. More typically, PVOs run overheads in the range of 8 to 15 percent with only a few reaching the 25 percent mark.

21. Budget figures can be found in the annually published reports and audits of PVOs.

22. Some PVOs started with a religious emphasis or with substantial participation by one or more religious groups, but subsequently evolved into a nondenominational focus. Such groups often go out of their way to project a more secular, or at least nonsectarian image.

23. This, of course, should not be taken to mean that secularly oriented PVOs have no concern for the mental or psychological well-being of the poor.

24. See Wynta Boynes, ed., U.S. Non-Profit Organizations in Development Assistance Abroad, 1978 Directory, published by TAICH in New York. The Directory lists over 400 organizations, but many did not report budgets as such, listing only the number of personnel engaged in foreign service.

25. Only those organizations that reported budgets were incorporated into the content analysis. In the case of many missionary organizations, 25 to 30 percent of their budgetary allocations were deducted to offset the 'nondevelopmental' features of missionary activity.

26. Tony Betts, "Development Aid from Voluntary Agencies to the Least Developed Countries," Africa Today 25, 4, (October-December 1978): 59-60, for a discussion on the prospects for bilateral funding of PVOs. See also, ibid., 49-59 for an excellent discussion of the development of inter-PVO consultation groups and PVO relations with international agencies.

27. The OECD's Development Cooperation Efforts and Policies of the Development Assistance Committee Reviews, contain records of corporate and governmental aid flows to LDCs on a country-by-country basis, but they do not report information for PVOs. Similarly, TAICH, does not report PVO assistance to LDCs on a country-by-country basis either. The decentralized and largley uncoordinated activities of PVOs makes centralized collection of PVO budgetary information a herculean task. Nevertheless, it is a task that should clearly be done on a regular basis. Unfortunately, PVOs and governments lack the incentive, managerial instincts, and money to do so.

28. See Schwartz, passim.

29. For thoughtful observations on this point, see Judith Tendler, Turning Voluntary Organizations into Development Agencies: Questions for Evaluation, Evaluation Discussion Paper No. 12, (Washington, D.C.: AID, 1982), 67-70.

30. See ibid, 84-92. See also, Ralph Kramer, Voluntary Agencies in the Welfare State (Berkeley, California: University of California Press, 1981).

31. Tendler, 20-47.

32. See, for instance, Sewell, 98-100.

33. Streeten, First Things First, 52.

34. Ibid., 6.

35.   In recent years PVOs have contracted with tne
World Bank for purposes of program development,
evaluation, and assessment.   They have also
subcontracted with the Bank for performance of
particular aspects of broader World Bank projects.   But
the prospects for broader PVO/Bank ventures are limited
for two reasons.   First, the Bank tends to be in the
macrodevelopment business while PVOs are more suited to
small-scale operations as a general rule.   Secondly,
countries must agree to allow PVOs to carry out specific
program tasks, and they often will prefer that their own
bureaucracies administer program funds, particularly
with regard to the more glamorous projects.   At the
national level, PVOs and governments have sought closer
institutional collaboration as well.   In the United
States, ACVAFS and AID have established numerous
informal lines of communication and cooperation.
Individually, PVOs may seek grants, contracts, or
cooperative agreements with AID.   For a more extensive
treatment see Bolling and Smith, 199-201.

36.   See, for instance, Steven Arnold, Implementing
Development Assistance: European Approaches to Basic
Needs (Boulder, CO: Westview Press, 1982).

37.   On this issue see, Elizabeth Schmidt, Jane
Blewett, and Peter Henriot, Religious Private Voluntary
Organizatons and the Question of Government Funding
(Maryknoll, New York: Orbis Books, 1981).   Indeed, this
work is currently the best available and most exhaustive
treatment on a whole range of issues regarding U.S.
government relations with U.S.-based PVOs.

# 4
# Development and the PVO: Incentives for Participation

*Arthur W. Blaser*

The literature on development is replete with references to the importance of participation, and to projects which failed because of their inability to reach a developing society's "grassroots".[1] The extensive literature on incentives for participation[2] has thus far been used to understand correlates of participation in labor unions and other domestic groups; but treatment of altruistic activity at the international level is usually reserved to a single footnote, while cross-cultural application of incentive theory is negligible. The application of incentive theory to participation will allow for more concrete conceptualization of the tasks which private voluntary organizations (PVOs) face. Not only will the relationships of PVOs be better understood, but so also will the utility of applying incentive theories to this type of organization.

The first section of this chapter examines the organizational environment of PVOs, that is, their relationship to people and governments. The second section outlines various organizational theories which purport to explain differences in participation. Various prescriptions for PVO autonomy, growth, and survival in a developing world are set forth in the concluding section.

THE ORGANIZATIONAL ENVIRONMENT OF PVOS

It is important at the outset to describe the organizational environment and range of actors with which PVOs interact to reach their goals. Figure 4.1 illustrates a selected variety of actors that PVOs interact with, including constituencies, governments, and indigenous PVOs (IPVOs). Only those actors and relationships relevant to this chapter are depicted. A full picture would indicate that all of the actors relate to one another and that other actors, such as host (Third World) governments also play important roles.

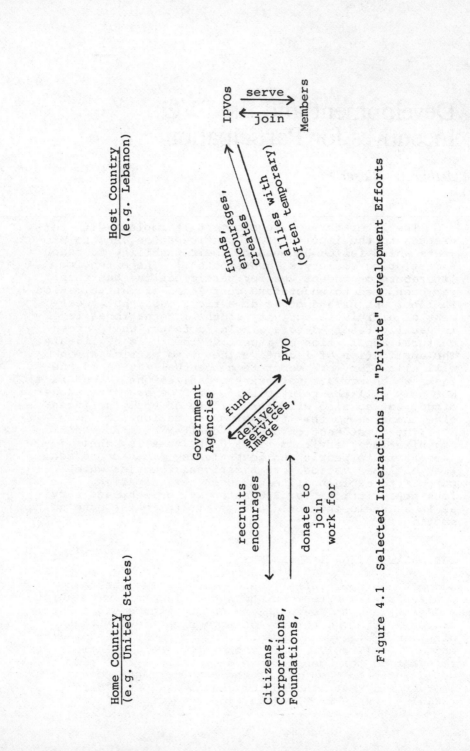

Figure 4.1  Selected Interactions in "Private" Development Efforts

Questions arising from this framework are summarized as follows:

1. Regarding home country participation in the PVO: What are the incentives that induce some individuals (or corporations or foundations) to send money to, join, or work in the field for the PVO? What disincentives explain the absence of some subgroups of society in PVO activity? (for instance, disproportionate involvement of a particular race, age, or sex.)
2. Regarding the PVO's relationship with governmental actors, such as the Agency for International Development (AID): What induces some PVOs to accept government ties? What are the disincentives that lead PVOs to reject or to limit government ties?
3. Regarding the relations of a host country PVO to the home country PVO: What can home country PVOs offer and how salient are such incentives for its IPVO? Why do many indigenous organizations avoid contact with western PVOs?
4. Regarding host country individuals and the indigenous PVO: What functions does the organization serve for members? What are some disincentives to organization membership?

ORGANIZATIONAL THEORIES

## Explaining the Problem and Solution of Collective Action

Much of the literature on collective action has dealt with the relatively easy cases of managing public goods, such as road maintenance and provision of utilities. Public goods are distinguished by non-exclusivity and jointness of supply. Unless there is coercion, or at least effective entrepreneurship, some individuals, the "free riders", will not contribute to the effort. Others will make only minimal contributions. The problem is multiplied manyfold when it is someone else's road that is being repaired. In such cases, there is disagreement over whether repair is needed (and if so how much). This process is complicated even further when cultural and linguistic barriers exist between those who need to act together. So it is with PVOs which rely on both private and public resources in their domestic environment to meet both private and public needs in a foreign environment. Cooperation to achieve such private and public ends can be very difficult to attain. Yet individuals, corporations, and governments do cooperate through PVO development activity. Social scientists' theories of recent decades offer a partial answer why. The theories also help us understand why some people do not participate.

Many social scientists have grappled with questions of group membership. There has been some progress: more information has been uncovered to explain why people join a greater variety of groups. Three stages in the process of theoretical development have been Truman's group theory, the political theories of James Q. Wilson, Amitai Etzioni, and others, and the economic theories of Mancur Olson. A fourth, but incomplete stage would apply these theories cross-nationally and to altruistic groups.[3] Attention to PVOs is part of this fourth stage. Table 4.1 offers a comparison between what I have classified as group theories, political theories, and economic theories. I will draw propositions from these theories and then discuss the implications of these propositions for PVOs.

## Group Theories, the PVO, and Development

David Truman's seminal work, The Governmental Process argues that political analysts should focus on group interests that struggle to influence the governmental process, rather than on government structures.[4] He suggests greater attention to the diverse interests of potential and existing groups as a basis for understanding politics. Although Truman focuses primarily on groups in the United States, he and others have claimed applicability of group theories to Western European countries.[5] Possible application to the rest of the world is not discussed.

Two aspects of Truman's group theory may offer insights to those who would understand, explain, or improve PVO development activity: its conception of group origins, and its prescription that groups are a basis of stability (and prerequisite for further social development). Vital to both aspects is Truman's pluralist view of politics as competition between multiple, overlapping groups which represent the diverse interests of members.

Looking at the origins of interest group activity may help us to understand when and where it would be propitious for PVOs to expand their membership, create new chapters or undertake new projects. To the extent that groups with similar origins may be likely candidates for coalition building, classification of PVOs and their indigenous counterparts by origin may isolate clusters with similar purposes and conceptions of development.

TABLE 4.1
Theories of Organization

| Type of Theory | Exemplar(s) | Scope of Theory | Type of Incentives | Organization and System Characteristics |
|---|---|---|---|---|
| 1. Group Theory | Truman, 1951 | Groups represent shared interests and are key actors in politics. | Purposive | Society consists of manifest or latent competing interests; latent interests will be activated when infringed upon greatly; groups overlap, precluding dominance, promoting stability. |
| 2. Political Theories | Wilson, 1973 | Voluntary, membership organizations, including political parties. | Purposive Solidary Material | Some organizations represent members' attitudes; in others, material gain is valued foremost; in others community is the primary value. |
| | Etzioni, 1961 | All governmental and nongovernmental organizations, including involuntary ones, e.g., prisons. | " (both + and −) | Above, plus use of coercion considered. |
| 3. Economic Theories | Olson, 1971 | All collective action, governmental or nongovernmental. | Material | Individuals usually make rational choices in joining associations. They generally advance self-interest, which means that organizations providing collective goods (national defense, global development, human rights) are difficult to maintain without coercion. |

Robert Salisbury offers a concise summary of two
conceptions of group origins set forth by Truman, labelled the proliferation hypothesis and the homeostatic
mechanism hypothesis.[6]  The former hypothesis is reflected
in two propositions, the second a corollary of the
first:

> P1:  Formation of organization is a consequence
>      of social differentiation, new technology,
>      and better communication.
> P2:  Societies with greater social differentia-
>      tion, newer technology, and better communica-
>      tion will have more interest groups, ceteris
>      paribus.

In fact, there does appear to be increasing concern with development over time.  This, coupled with
the fact that there is more PVO involvement in those
societies with the most differentiated social structures, lends prima facie support to the proliferation
hypothesis.  Paradoxically, in order for many links
between development agents to form, a modicum of development is necessary.

However, it is certainly inaccurate to say that
development is a necessary prerequisite to group activity.  Indeed, group action for development purposes
(e.g., traditional credit associations) is at the heart
of many Third World cultures.  Consistent with Truman,
a key reason for membership in such associations
(though seldom conceived as a matter for individual
choice) is purposive.  For example, people in traditional Third World contexts join burial associations
for the purpose of burial.  In addition, however, there
are salient solidary incentives (membership valued for
the opportunities to interact with others) that may
also be motivating factors.

There is a gap between the traditional organizations of the Third World and western PVOs, and it is
here that the validity and limits of the proliferation
hypothesis become apparent.  Ali Mazrui has illustrated
this point with reference to African culture, suggesting that:

> Many hastily assume that a history of collectivism
> in a traditional setting is a relevant preparation
> for organized collective efforts in a modern set-
> ting.  Unfortunately, much of the evidence points
> the other way.  Collective effort based on custom
> and tradition and kinship ties leaves Africa un-
> prepared for the kind of organized collectivism
> that needs to be based on command rather than
> custom, on efficiency rather than empathy, on
> rationality rather than ritual.[7]

Other analysts would reverse the responsibility, argu-
ing that it is western PVOs and modernity that are un-
suited to the balanced nature of traditional societies.
     Desirable or not, (and there have been some useful
indictments of PVO activities[8]) development, cultural
change, and increased mobility are likely to facilitate
a "critical mass" of collective action. For Truman,
the change would clearly be desirable, as indicated in
a third proposition:

> P3:   Creation of organizations representing pre-
>       viously latent groups leads to social order
>       and peaceful change.

Truman's prescription of a role for interest
groups in ensuring stability assumes that common interests exist and will be acted upon, and that the emergence of latent groups is not structurally constrained.
Truman's analysis concluded with the suggestion that:

> Whether the group-process eventuates in disaster
> will depend in the future as the past basically
> upon the effects of overlapping membership, par-
> ticularly the vitality of membership in those
> potential groups based upon interests held widely
> throughout the society.  These memberships are
> the means both of stability and of peaceful
> change.[9]

With respect to PVOs, this suggests activation of a wide
range of latent groups.  This might entail organizational efforts for women in development, communications,
rural development, and small enterprise management.
     In addition to the arguments that organizations
result from development, and that they provide a basis
for peaceful change, Truman proposes the homeostatic
mechanism hypothesis:

> When a single association is formed, it serves
> to stabilize the relations among the participants
> in the institutionalized groups involved.  At the
> time, however, in the performance of its functions
> it may cause disturbances in the equilibrium of
> other groups or accentuate cleavages among them.
> These are likely to evoke associations in turn
> to correct the secondary disturbances.  The forma-
> tion of associations, therefore, tends to occur
> in waves.[10]

This suggests:

> P4:   Proliferation of organizations occurs in
>       distinct stages.

Here the formation of new organizations breeds counterorganization, followed by stalemate. PVOs face two
forms of counterorganization: occasional isolationist
appeals suggesting that aid is counterproductive and
more common appeals that local needs are greater than
global needs. The homeostatic mechanism hypothesis can
easily be reconciled with the proliferation hypothesis,
with new differentiation creating new causes for concern, e.g., famine due to climate change, leading to
formation of PVOs concerned with climate control and
famine relief, then of business and farm groups that
seek to protect their material interests from uncertainty. Eventually a limit is reached to the number of useful organizations on both sides.

The wave image appears to bear some resemblance to
actual patterns of organization formation. One can
identify many PVOs which originated or expanded during
or following such crises as World War I, World War II,
(e.g., CARE) or drought in the Sahel (e.g., Africare).

Much of the current proliferation of voluntary organizations reflects an emphasis on individual or group
needs and solidarity, more suitable to organizations advancing exclusive interests than to PVOs. Future proliferation may, however, include greater attention to
such universal interests as development. Political culture has a major effect on how or where groups prolif-
erate--thus two societies at the same level of development will not necessarily have the same number of associations.

Group theory provides a simple answer to the question of why individuals and groups associating with
PVOs: people who share a PVO's purpose will join. This
is only a partial answer, since many individuals sharing
PVOs' purposes choose not to join. A complete answer
requires attention to additional incentives.

Political Theories

While group theory is a theory of politics, political theories as used here examine politics in groups
rather than groups in politics. The essence of this
approach is expressed by Wilson, who is considered an
exemplar of this group:

> the behavior of persons occupying organizational
> roles...is principally, though not uniquely deter-
> mined by the requirements of organizational main-
> tenance and enhancement and that this maintenance,
> in turn, chiefly involves supplying tangible and
> intangible incentives to individuals in order that
> they will become, or remain, members and will per-
> form certain tasks.[11]

Applying his thesis to political parties, labor unions, business associations, and civil rights associations, Wilson suggests a variety of incentives which may or may not coincide with members' self-interest. His framework has been applied and extended in other studies such as Jeffrey Berry's, which deals with public interest groups.[12] Considerable attention will also be devoted to a "political" typology of organizations, developed by sociologist Amitai Etzioni.

Wilson and Etzioni have developed frameworks which account for a wider range of motivations, and suggest that there is not necessarily a one-to-one correspondence between shared interests and organization membership. With respect to the PVOs this means that many people sharing an organization's purpose (development) may not join, while some PVO members may be as interested in affiliation with other members, or fringe benefits of membership, as in development.

The frameworks are summarized in Table 4.2. Etzioni claims applicability to all forms of organizations, governmental and nongovernmental. He suggests three kinds of power available to leaders, which may or may not be compatible with the three kinds of member involvement.

PVOs would be candidates for what Etzioni labels "typical normative organizations," i.e., they often have leaders whose power rests more on persuasion and manipulation of symbolic rewards than on remuneration or coercion, and followers whose involvement is based more on a high intensity motivation than on an alienative or a calculative one. Etzioni's treatment suggests the following propositions.[13]

P5: Organizational effectiveness is a function of the congruence of power applied by the organization and involvement of lower participants.

P6: In normative organizations, lower participants are most likely to be highly integrated in organization activities, and to accept elite control over organization activities.

For these propositions to be useful, organizational leaders would have to have some latitude over whose involvement is sought, and over the means by which power is applied. Incongruity can arise within the world of PVO activity. For instance, leaders may rely on remunerative power to reward members whose primary motivation is moral rather than acquisitive. One might also find calculative members (with paid positions, and hoping for higher posts) in organizations where leaders expect normative power to suffice.

TABLE 4.2
Political Theories of Organization

| Wilson's Incentive Type/ Etzioni's Compliance Structure Component | Definition | Implications |
|---|---|---|
| 1. Material (Wilson) | Tangible Rewards: money or things and services readily priced in monetary terms. | Business associations, political machines rely on these; little attention paid to substantive goals, stated purposes. |
| 2. Specific Solidary (Wilson) | Intangible, arising out of the act of associating; Can be withheld from others. Value comes from exclusion (e.g., offices.) | Often as bitter a source of conflict as material incentives; by nature impossible to provide all members with special status. |
| 3. Collective Solidary (Wilson) | Created by associating; Intangible and inclusive; Include fun, conviviality of being together. | Vital to avoid "political" conflict in such associations, though support of humanitarian cause may increase solidary incentives. |
| 4. Purposive (Wilson) | Intangible; derive from sense of satisfaction of having contributed to the attainment of a worthwhile cause. | Often become single-person efforts; Generally found in combination with solidary incentives; where purposive are prime, there will be a willingness to antagonize. |

5. Coercive Power (Etzioni)

Rests on physical sanctions or threats.

Works best where organization members' involvement is alienative, and intensely negative.

6. Remunerative Power (Etzioni)

Based on control over material resources and rewards, e.g., salaries and wages.

Works best where organization members' involvement is calculative, leading to utilitarian compliance

7. Normative Power (Etzioni)

Rests on allocation, manipulation of symbolic rewards and deprivations through employment of leaders, manipulation of mass media, allocation of esteem, prestige, symbols, and ritual.

Works best where members' involvement is morally based and intense. Leads to normative compliance. Vital in voluntary associations.

Incongruities arise, then, where basic incentives
and disincentives vary between an organization and its
members and between one organization and another which
may have an opportunity to interact.  Group theory suggests that a PVO should succeed when a sufficient number
of people share the group's purposes, and there has been
sufficient development to make latent groups manifest.
Political theories indicate that there may be failures
if different kinds of incentives are not taken into account.  They also indicate that the PVO organizational
network may be primarily purposive in nature, but not
exclusively so.

Full exploration of all potential incentives that
operate within and between groups would fill a volume.
In this chapter, it will be suffient to examine several more important examples.  The first three examples
apply to individuals or corporations which join or fund
a PVO.  They suggest other incentives which accompany
but do not replace, the salient incentive of a humane
cause.  The PVO will weight nonpurposive incentives in
its relations with corporations; there is generally a
significant material incentive, but a solidary disincentive to close ties.

1.  Most donors to PVOs are fully supportive of
    the groups's general purpose, but the pur-
    posive incentive may be accompanied by a
    disincentive, e.g., the agnostic who does
    not share the religious purpose of World
    Vision International, but donates because
    of an attraction to the development purpose.
2.  Many people who do not donate to or join a
    PVO may share the group's purposes intensely,
    but not join because of material and solidary
    disincentives.  For instance, Black Americans
    are underrepresented in PVOs.  This does not
    necessarily reflect disagreement with the
    purpose of global development; it may re-
    flect a greater proportional cost of donat-
    ing (in time and money), or a lesser feeling
    of belonging.
3.  To attract individuals organizations may in-
    duce people to belong to a program unrepre-
    sentative of true purposes.  Thus Americans
    join to give CARE packages, which have been
    discontinued, or to adopt foreign babies and
    foster children (still used as prominent ad-
    vertising by organizations which now conduct
    more ambitious projects aimed at structural
    change).[14]

The fourth and fifth examples apply to the association of PVOs with such governmental institutions as AID.

4.  Although there is agreement on the vague
    purposes of "development", orientations toward
    development may differ.  The material incentive
    for the PVO is again considerable, but govern-
    mental ties may bring with them solidary dis-
    incentives of a political and bureaucratic
    nature which most PVOs eschew.  PVOs often
    weigh the desired degree of AID funding (mate-
    rial incentive), versus the resistance to
    association with the government (solidary
    disincentive) and occasional compromises in
    definition of the development purpose.[15]

5.  Concern over the PVO-AID relationship has led
    to reforms.  The reforms suggest that even if
    there is agreement on the development purpose,
    increasing collective action requires stream-
    lining of administrative procedures and a
    large measure of autonomy for PVO projects.[16]

The sixth example applies to the difficulties of
PVO-IPVO association.  The IPVO often has purposes in
addition to development.  To supplement local ties with
transitional ones may be viewed positively, but will
occasionally be viewed as dangerous or inappropriate.

6.  The PVO-IPVO tie is sometimes frustrated by
    their different organizational structures,
    thus reducing a sense of involvement (solidary
    disincentive).  The PVO and IPVO may share
    the same general developmental purpose, but
    may differ over what it means and how it is to
    be carried out.  Pertinent in this regard are
    the comments of the Union of International
    Associations about INGOs:

    In some non-Western cultures there may be
    difficulty in locating organizational forms
    natural to that culture which could relate
    to a given INGO.  There may be resentment
    of any imposition of a new Western style or-
    ganization, and a lack of any socioanthro-
    pological skill to match very differnet styles
    of organization, or to adapt an INGO appro-
    priate to them...[17]

Some IPVOs, in contrast to some PVOs, would share
the sentiment of Julius Nyerere, that:

    Any act which increases the power of the
    people to determine their own affairs is an
    act of development, even if the act does not
    provide more bread or better health.[18]

The last two examples apply an indigenous population's association with the IPVO. The interests and values of the individual may differ from those of the society.

7. The process by which an individual joins an IPVO may differ greatly from that of PVOs. Some church, credit, and social groups functioning as PVOs foster a strong sense of belonging unobtainable where joining is a matter of calculated choice.

8. While most PVO members expect material losses, the opposite is true of IPVO members. For many of them, the IPVO provides capital, (e.g., tractors) difficult to obtain individually.

Analysis of PVO networks suggests a possible extension of Etzioni's theory. PVOs and AID are in a power relationship, as are PVOs and IPVOs. Affiliation may be very loose where such autonomous groups have common purposes; it may also be more restrictive. For instance, in the PVO/IPVO relationship, one might hope that IPVOs would share similar moral and solidary incentives with PVOs. In actual practice, independent IPVOs may fall in or out of favor with various PVOs over a period of time. This is because their involvement is in fact calculative and understandably linked to the question of which PVOs offer greater services. Wilson suggests that "Individuals will often contribute to large organizations without receiving any specific material benefit from it; organizations rarely will."[19] Thus,

P7: Utilitarian compliance and material incentives have greater applicability to coalitions of organizations (AID-PVO or PVO-IPVO) than to single, affiliated organizations.

Wilson draws attention to three kinds of incentives, in Table 4.2: material incentives, purposive incentives, and solidary incentives. While one might argue that existence of all three types result from characteristics inherent in human nature, it is evident that incentives vary greatly across societies and over time.

Wilson's distinction between solidary and purposive associations suggest that in the former conflict results from matters of "status, especially the distribution of recognition and the admission of new members."[20] However, patterns of conflict and harmony within purposive organizations, including PVOs, suggest that provision of solidary incentives is also vital to their success. While group theorists would suggest that development (and humanitarian relief) issues bring

members of the PVOs together, studies of a wide range
of organizations indicate that most members are introduced to group activities by friends. New members may
attend in part because they share the group's objectives, but they may also see group meetings (or identity with the group if it does not have meetings) as
useful for meeting people.

The tendency of single-minded attention to group
tasks to alienate members suggests:

> P8: Provision of general solidary incentives is
> important to the success of any voluntary
> organization.

Solidary incentives might even overcome material draw-
backs to coalition formation. Religious groups, trade
unions, and others are likely to affiliate with an organization like CARE for such solidary incentives as
the status of being linked to a universally recognized
humanitarian organization. Good or bad relations between organization personnel may also play a role.
This is not to deny the risk of too much attention to
solidary incentives--where group tasks are neglected in
reinforcing the aura of good feeling. In short, voluntary agencies must strike a balance between purposive
and solidary incentives.

Brief note should be made of cross-national PVO
links. There are societies in which the solidary incentive to link with other PVOs is a largely negative
one, namely to associate with any foreign group.
Because the PVO is an outside group, it will be viewed
with initial distrust by many people. Because of this
distrust, individuals who associate with the PVO may
have to forego material advantages in their own society.
For them to participate in a transnational development
coalition, would require that the purposive incentives,
(e.g., the long-range development of their society)
would outweigh solidary and material disincentives.

## Economic Theories

Group theorists focus on an identify of group purpose and members' interests; political theorists include a variety of incentives. The strength of economic theorists' efforts is their attention to incentives, generally material ones, which will be exchanged
for members' time. Thus, individuals rationally calcu-
late the decision to join; organizations are formed by
entrepreneurs who provide services to the group (e.g.,
development lobbying), and charge members the amount of
expense incurred plus a profit.

Classified here as "economic theories" are those
of Mancur Olson and the many others such as Salisbury,
Taylor, Barry, and Moe who have built upon his work. [21]
Of interest for understanding PVO activity are such
topics as: the collective goods/private goods distinction; the "free rider" problem in group activity to
gain collective goods, and the resulting "suboptimal"
provision of goods; the role of nonmaterial incentives;
and the role of entrepreneurs.

Collective goods or public goods, which include
national defense, clean air, clean water, human rights
and development, differ from private goods, including
automobiles, air conditioners, beans, and guns. The
major difference is that: "Those who do not purchase
or pay for any of the public or collective goods cannot be excluded or kept from sharing in the consumption
of the goods, as they can where noncollective goods are
concerned."[22]

Economic theorists' discussions of the free rider
problem and suboptimality of supply do have some applicability to PVOs. Olson suggests that individuals have
negligible impact on provision of collective goods. A
calculating individual, realizing that Oxfam's development efforts would not be significantly affected by his
or her participation, might decide not to contribute.
Where an individual fails to contribute (taking a free
ride at the expense of those who do), the supply of the
goods in question is suboptimal. Thus:

> P9: Organizations which seek to provide collec-
> tive goods will be subject to free riders;
> thus these goods will be suboptimally provided.

However,

> Voluntary Organizations which provide col-
> lective goods can induce contributions
> through promotion of selective incentives.

To demonstrate the propensity of humans to take free
rides Olson uses the example of the provision of law
and order:

> Almost any government is economically beneficial
> to its citizens, in that the law and order it pro-
> vides is a prerequisite of all civilized economic
> activity. But despite the force of patriotism,
> the appeal of the national ideology, the bond of
> a common culture, and the indispensability of the
> system of law and order, no major state in modern
> history has been able to support itself through
> voluntary dues or contributions. [23]

If people must be coerced in order to contribute to their own safety, there would appear to be little reason for them to contribute because of the warm feeling they experience knowing that perhaps one more Pakistani benefits from a development project.

Organizations wanting to encourage contributions from free riders may coerce them (as governments do through taxes and unions through strong-arm tactics), or may offer private goods as selective incentives. (Thus the American Automobile Association which lobbies for the collective "good" of more highways, offers such private goods as tour books, film processing offers, VISA credit cards, and insurance to its members.)

Few PVOs employ coercion, although a corporation which supports a PVO may create a strong "norm" toward contribution for a worthwhile cause. Many PVOs do, however, provide selective incentives, such as regular publications, conferences with prominent speakers, bumper-stickers, film-rentals, T-shirts and membership cards. Free riders can be, although often they are not, excluded from enjoying these incentives.

Even the less demanding forms of PVO involvement, such as the simple donations, require investment of time and postage with little prospect of immediate gratification. Without selective incentives such as newsletters or "adopted" children approaches, which tend to boost spirits, members might share the doubts of nonmembers about whether their efforts really do any good.

For U.S. citizens, the greatest selective incentive is provided in collaboration with the federal and state governments by the tax deduction. This is another reason, independent of support for PVO purposes, why those in higher tax brackets are more likely to participate. They could ride free, but the material disincentives are not prohibitive. Nonmaterial incentives help explain why groups like OXFAM and CARE exist, and why IPVOs affiliate with PVOs. Some economic theorists have introduced consideration of utilitarian optimism—where an individual would contribute to provide improvement in either his own condition, or in someone else's condition.[24]

In practice, some organization members are likely to be attracted to purposive incentives, consistent with group theorists' claims. There is hard data to support this claim for a range of organizations.[25] Indeed, one would suspect that purposive incentives would be even more powerful in PVOs.

Furthermore, in experimental settings it has been observed that, "the effects of free riding were much weaker than would be predicted by most economic theory."[26]

There are major differences between a laboratory experiment and the real world of PVOs. These would usually
make free riding less likely in the PVO world where
moral consequences of nonparticipation are apparent.
This, however, does not justify total rejection of the
economic theorists' contributions. Most successful
PVOs offer packages of incentives so that altruists'
(and corporations') material losses are minimized.
Combinations of minimal material disincentive, with
significant purposive and solidary incentives are likely to prove attractive.

Economic theorists suggest an important role for
entrepreneurs who would put such packages together.
Discussions of entrepreneurial activities indicate why
groups not directly concerned with development, including veterans, labor groups, and teachers may take part
in PVO activities or contribute money to them. Frolich,
Oppenheimer, and Young suggest propositions about entrepreneurial behavior, two of which may have relevance to
transnational PVO activity:

P11: Political entrepreneurs will diversify with
respect to both the supply of collective
goods and their sources of revenue as a
function of the presence of organizational
complementarities in their operations.[27]
P12: The more a political leader depends upon
donations, the more wary he will be of collective goods that are durable or have high
initial costs of supply.[28]

P11 suggests that once certain capabilities have been
acquired by an entrepreneur (e.g. coercion), he will
have incentives to provide other collective goods (e.g.,
law and order).

The examples used in the present discussion, and
the variety of incentives which individuals are suggested to have, are at variance with the analysis of
Frohlich, et. al. It is nevertheless the case that religious organizations, labor groups, and businesses,
owing to shrewd leadership, have led PVO activity.
Their association with the development issue is made
easy by the presence of some members who are purposive-
ly motivated, whether rationally or irrationally. They
also possess meeting places, tools for publicity, and
expertise: three of the biggest barriers to new development activity. It would follow that a PVO which
"shops" for affiliates might seek out established
churches, women's groups, or ethnic organizations whose
leaders want to expand the group's activities.

P12 illustrates the value of economic theorists'
assumptions once one broadens such terms as "costs" to
ensure applicability to PVOs.  It is true and significant that PVOs dependent on donations are reluctant to
take on new development issues for which initial costs
would be high.

The relation of durability to PVO activity can be
analyzed in two ways.  First, the collective good of
development is by nature nondurable.  If PVOs succeed,
they will end the justification for their existence or,
more likely, redefine "development".  The more PVOs
seek to foster self-sufficient projects, the greater
will be their withdrawal from participation after a period of years.  To the extent that a group's leaders
are motivated for purposive or general solidary reasons,
they might be willing to preside over their organization's phase-out.  Second, in reality, even with fundamental restructuring, hunger and poverty are almost
sure to continue, and new development issues will evolve
with new technology.  Political entrepreneurs have in
development an issue which appeals to millions of people, and which affects those in every occupation, reli-
gion, and region.  Individuals wanting leadership positions in church, labor, journalistic, or women's organizations may therefore find that development, when combined with the group's other purposes, offers a means of
attracting contributions.

The economic theorists' focus does therefore have
some applicability to PVO activity.  The intermittent
absence of large numbers of entrepreneurs when falter-
ing organizations need renovation, reflects "unprofitable" conditions in a broad sense.  So too the slow
growth in Western-style PVOs in the African, Asian, and
Latin American context.  The presence of entrepreneurs
who do not make material profit suggests that solidary
and purposive incentives predominate over material ones.
Even Lissner's discussion of the "politics" behind voluntary development agencies' altruism suggests that
the motives of group leaders are pure, perhaps even
too much so.[29]


RECAPITULATION AND PRESCRIPTIONS

The twelve propositions set forth in the preceding
section should offer some guidance and reassurance to
many PVOs and to many social scientists who claim wide
applicability for their theories of organization.  The
propositions appear to "fit" PVOs to differing degrees,
and to be confirmed in differing degrees by practice.
This section briefly considers challenges to the theories discussed in the previous section and suggests implications for theorists and PVOs.

One challenge faces the theorists themselves, who often argue that only one approach, usually their own, is useful. Wilson, for example labels Frohlich, Oppenheimer and Young's study as "almost devoid of empirical content."[30] Olson responds to group theorists with the claim that "the customary view that groups of individuals with common interests tend to further their common interests appears to have little if any merit."[31] Once the dust is cleared away there appears to be a basis for creation of more comprehensive social theory. Indeed, the more recent economic theoretical works combine insights of a variety of theorists to explain what each of their predecessors did and something additional. The disparate approaches have yet, however, to be integrated into a coherent framework applicable to organizations in a variety of societies.

A second challenge comes from Marxists and social theorists who challenge the approach of all incentive theorists: group, political, or economic. The alleged fallacy is that incentive theorists ask how individuals weigh competing incentives in deciding whether or not to contribute to or join a PVO or other organization, when they should ask how a society's economic base determines individuals' choices.[32] Rather than viewing Marxist theory and incentive theory as mutually exclusive, I would argue that even greater eclecticism is useful. While economic conditions may set the scale by which individuals weigh incentives, there is considerable lattitude for the PVO to attract and serve more individuals.

Even greater eclecticism and exploratory investigation is thus the first prescription for theorists of organization. Second, an exhaustive study applying the propositions such as those discussed here to a specific PVO would be useful both to theorists and to practitioners. It appears plausible that membership appeals to the media may be less fruitful than using networks of friends; it appears also that sympathy with a cause leads to membership more often when selected incentives are provided than when they are not. Attention to background characteristics, professed motives, and other group involvements of PVO supporters would also be relevant to psychologists, sociologists, and other scholars of organizational and movement activity.

A fundamental question for organizational theorists and practitioners is the applicability of rationality and utilitarianism in the context of PVO activities. This is generally assumed, and thought to be equally valid cross nationally. There are many adherents of creeds which profess higher goals than utility,

however.  Russell Means has suggested that the rationality of European civilization may be as short-lived as
the longevity which rationalists predicted for mysti-
cism.[33]  Theorists should seek a better understanding
of how these higher goals affect membership decisions
by potential PVO supporters.

The first of three prescriptions for the PVOs is
the suggestion that they come to grips with the dis-
crepancy between a frequent motive for support--the
desire to "do good" on an individual level, and the
structural changes necessary for successful development.
Oxfam, War on Want, and the Institute for Food and Development Policy are excellent examples (but exceptions
to the PVO rule) in their educational efforts.  To
really foster development, these groups suggest, West-
erners must bear significant financial disincentives
and many must enjoy an intense solidary we-feeling
with designated recipients.  This contrasts with the
notion that "we" are helping "them".

A second prescription has to do with common purposes.  PVO representatives are sometimes surprised by
the extent to which a struggle for justice in one
sphere does not transfer to another sphere.  This should
not be a great surprise, since the PVOs seldom define
their purpose as part of long-range strategy, with
implications for domestic policy, peace, and justice
issues.  Yet, PVOs should be more heavily involved in
common efforts to increase the salience and visibility
of these issues.  Indeed, to the extent that such common action leads to a higher awareness by the public
at large to these issues, and their bearing on development, all PVOs stand to gain.

The final prescription for PVO consideration is
the need for comparative analysis.  AID has become
more receptive to PVO autonomy, to strategies which
encourage IPVO participation, and to nonconventional
development strategies.  Further alternatives remain
along the lines of European models.  These countries'
governments have provided much greater material incentives for collective action with PVOs, without accom-
panying purposive or solidary disincentives.

These prescriptions only scratch the surface of
the assertions set forth in the previous section.
Additional work in this area may aid critical analysis
of PVO development efforts.  To the extent that they
value development, prospective researchers have a
purposive incentive to select PVO-related topics for
study.  There may also be a greater solidary incentive
to do so; witness the perceptive commentaries of
academics and activists who are beginning to represent
a true community of concern for development and for
human needs.  We can only hope that the reward structure of social science disciplines, of research

agencies and of the PVOs will provide sufficient material incentive. At stake is not only the development of knowledge, but potentially the development of human beings.

## NOTES

1. See especially John G. Sommer, Beyond Charity: U.S. Voluntary Aid for a Changing Third World (Washington, D.C.: Overseas Development Council, 1977). Romesh Diwan and Dennis Livingston, Alternative Development Strategies and Appropriate Technology: Science Policy for an Equitable World Order (New York: Pergamon, 1979).

2. See especially David Truman, The Governmental Process: Political Interests and Public Opinion (New York: Alfred A. Knopf, 1951); Amitai Etzioni, A Comparative Analysis of Complex Organizations: On Power, Involvement, and Their Correlates (New York: Free Press, 1961); and James Q. Wilson, Political Organizations (New York: Basic Books, 1973).

3. Little has been done however, to apply these theories in a genuinely cross-national way to altruistic organizations such as PVOs. An important step in the right direction has been: David Forsythe and Susan Welch, "Joining and Supporting Public Interest Groups: A Note on Some Empirical Findings," Western Political Quarterly (September 1983): 386-399, which studies U.S.-based human rights NGOs.

4. A useful review and critique of group theorists is G. Garson, Group Theories of Politics (Beverly Hills: Sage Publications, 1978).

5. See for instance Roy Macridis, "Interest Groups in Comparative Analysis, Journal of Politics 23 (February 1961): 25-26.

6. Robert Salisbury, "An Exchange Theory of Interest Groups," Midwest Journal of Political Science 13 (February 1969): 3-5. Key pages in Truman are 42-52.

7. "Political Engineering in Africa," International Social Science Journal 35 (1983): 285.

8. See especially Sommer, Beyond Charity, and Diwan and Livingston, Alternative Development Strategies, passim.

9. Truman, 535.

10. Ibid., 15.

11. Ibid., 13.

12. Jeffrey Berry, Lobbying for the People (Princeton, NJ: Princeton University Press, 1977).

13. Etzioni, 14, 112.

14. Sommer, 128-129.

15.   See especially Sommer, Beyond Charity;
Landrum Bolling with Craig Smith, Private Foreign Aid:
U.S. Philanthropy for Relief and Development (Boulder:
Westview Press, 1980); and David Hapgood, ed., The
Role of Popular Participation in Development, Report of
a Conference on the Implementation of Title IX of the
Foreign Assistance Act (Cambridge:   MIT Press, 1968).
16.   See for instance AID's preparation and over-
sight of policy papers reported by Edwin L. Hollander
in "Special Reprot:   Policy Profiles-AID Drafts Blue-
prints for US Economic Assistance," Horizons (July-
August 1983): 33-45.
17.   "Forum Background Sheet:  Problems Hindering
Actions of International Nongovernmental Organizations
(INGOs)," Transnational Associations (1980): 182.
18.   Quoted in Gunduz Y.H. Vassaf, "Community
Psychology in Search of a New Focus," International
Social Science Journal 35 (1983): 348.
19.   Wilson, 277.
20.   Wilson, 45.
21.   Six examples of the literature which are relevant to economic theories of organization follow:  Mancur Olson, The Logic of Collective Action:  Public Goods
and the Theory of Groups (Cambridge:  Harvard University
Press, 1971, is taken as the starting point by succeed-
ing economic theorists.  Olson suggests that rational
individuals will not contribute to provision of collective goods (such as human rights promotion) unless they
are coerced, or offered selective incentives.   Since
rational individuals are unlikely to contribute to
provision of collective goods through voluntary organizations, supplies of these goods will be suboptimal.
However, Salisbury, argues that Olson does not explain
why entrepreneurs start organizations.  He suggests,
following a discussion of material, solidary, and
expressive incentives, that entrepreneurs seek political
"profit".  Norman Frohlich, Joseph Oppenheimer, and Oran
Young, Political Leadership and Collective Goods (Princeton, N.J.: Princeton University Press, 1961), also
discuss provision of collective goods.  Their analysis
of political competition is designed to explain why
leadership arises.  See also Michael Taylor, Anarchy and
Cooperation (London:   John Wiley and Sons, 1976).
Taylor takes issue with Olson's assumptions about human
nature.  He uses game theory to discuss virtue and the
utility of altruistic strategies.  He argues that
humans will contribute to provision of collective
goods (such as development) without being coerced.  See
also Brian Barry, Sociologists, Economists, and Democracy (Chicago: University of Chicago Press, 1980), who
reviews economic and sociological theories of democracy

including Olson. Barry takes a favorable view of economic approaches (Olson and Downs), but suggests that they do not account for "sense of duty", the likely cause of contributions to Oxfam. Finally, Terry Moe, The Organization of Interests (Chicago: University of Chicago Press, 1980, finds a mixture of economic and purposive motivation in U.S. interest groups. Moe includes data based on a survey of printers, farmers, and others.

22. Olson, 15.
23. Olson, 13.
24. Taylor, Norman Frohlich, "Self-Interest or Altruism, What Difference?" Journal of Conflict Resolution, 18 (March 1974): 55-73.
25. Moe's analysis of such groups as the Farmers Union, Retail Federation and Hardware Association suggests that both selective incentives and group purposes attracted members.
26. G. Marwell and R. Ames, "Experiments on the Provision of Public Goods, I: Resources, Interests, Group Size, and the Free-Rider Problem," American Journal of Sociology 84 (May 1979): 13-35.
27. Frohlich, Oppenheimer, and Young, 54-55.
28. Ibid., 55-56.
29. Jorgen Lissner, The Politics of Altruism: A Study of the Political Behaviour of Voluntary Development Agencies (Geneva: Lutheran World Federation, 1977).
30. Wilson, 212.
31. Olson, 2.
32. See e.g., Wolf Heydebrand, "Organizational Contradictions in Public Bureaucracies: Toward a Marxian Theory of Organization," in Amitai Etzioni and Edward W. Lehmann, eds., A Sociological Reader on Complex Organizations 3d ed. (New York: Holt, Rinehart, and Winston, 1980).
33. Russell Means, "Fighting Words on the Future of the Earth," Mother Jones (December 1980): 23-28.

# 5
# The Domestic Environment of AID-Registered PVOs: Characteristics and Impact

*Hibbert R. Roberts*

Within the United States, Private Voluntary Organizations (PVOs), as instruments to promote development in lesser developed countries, have garnered increasing attention from public officials and scholars alike. Numbering among the reasons for this interest is that PVOs are claimed by their spokespersons and are seen by others, including public officials, to possess characteristics that uniquely qualify them to perform certain developmental tasks in less developed countries (LDCs) with greater effectiveness and efficiency than possible through the bureaucracies and programs of international organizations (IOs) and governments. For example, former Chairman of the American Council of Voluntary Agencies for Foreign Service (ACVAFS) and Executive Director of the American ORT Federation, Paul Bunick, in an appearance before the Senate Foreign Relations Committee submitted a written statement asserting that PVOs are more than "relief agencies, refugee organizations, or health and welfare organizations." They are, he argued: "...a strong force in development. They bring experience, knowledge of conditions and human resources at the community level. They are a symbol of hope at the 'people level' in most areas of the world." Moreover, the statement continued:

> Voluntary agencies are in an enviable position as regards human development activities since they live with people, they have simple structures, they serve the deep-felt needs of the people, and they act on what <u>the people themselves consider their priorities</u> (Emphasis in the original text).[1]

Recalling the 'New Directions' emphasis, i.e., providing direct assistance to the poorest people in LDCs rather than relying so heavily upon the questionable "trickle-down" effect of macrodevelopment projects, called for in the 1973 and 1975 foreign assistance funding legislation passed by Congress, Senator Hubert Humphrey wrote:

> ...we stipulated that private and voluntary
> agencies be increasingly encouraged to assist
> in this effort. We knew that whereas government-
> to-government programs were often effective in
> the capital assistance and large-scale training
> aspects of development, people-to-people initia-
> tives were often more successful in ensuring that
> the benefits of any kind of aid were shared by
> those most in need in the world's villages and
> slums.[2]

Indeed, according to John G. Sommer, the 1973 and 1975
development assistance legislation assumed that PVOs

> ...because of their historic tendency to work more
> closely with 'grass-roots' structures and because
> of their greater flexibility, have a potential
> for contributing substantially to the pioneering
> and experimentation required for the development
> of agricultural, health, educational, and related
> structures more appropriate to the needs of the
> poor majority.[3]

Echoing this belief in the "grass-roots" efficacy
of PVOs, Douglas J. Bennet, Jr. noted a few years later
in a prepared statement to the U.S. Senate about the
International Security and Development Cooperation
Act of 1980 that PVOs "...provide direct channels for
private, people-to-people efforts and are very active
in fostering self-help initiatives among the poor."
He further claimed: "One of the most significant
contributions by PVOs is building and strengthening
indigenous institutions."[4]

In sum, flexible, innovative, institution-building
development programs designed to meet the needs of the
"poor majority" and to induce its participation in local
decision-making processes are some of the major attri-
butes advocates claim for the overseas activities of
U.S. PVOs. That this people-to-people (bottom-up,
nonbureaucratic) rather than government-to-government
(top-down, bureaucratic) response to the current challenges of development is more efficacious and economical
is another trait often implied, if not openly avowed,
for PVOs by their proponents. But one must note that
not all PVOs would ascribe each of the foregoing characteristics to their own field activities in LDCs. Further
caution must be exercised, moreover, because much more
systematic evaluation of PVO activities overseas has
to occur before it will become possible to determine
with a fair degree of certainty the accuracy of the
claims made about the virtues of PVOs as agents of
development.

The validity of what Judith Tendler calls the
"articles of faith" of the PVOs is not directly at issue
here, however.[5] Rather, the purpose of this chapter is
to explore the possible affects of their domestic
environment upon the behavior of those PVOs registered
with the U.S. Agency for International Development (AID)
and therefore involved in some manner in development
assistance projects overseas. Underlying this focus is
the postulate that the "articles of faith," the behavior,
and the programs of PVOs are a function of the domestic
context within which PVOs must operate as well as their
interaction with the foreign environment in which most
of them conduct their developmental activities. No
pretense exists that this study will determine defini-
tively the amount and form of influence their home
setting exerts upon AID-registered PVOs or, consequently, its impact upon their projects overseas. The
heterogeneity of PVOs in terms of such factors as their
size, status, sources and amounts of funds, objectives,
and operational styles combine with the dearth of
readily available information about the formulation,
implementation, and results of the multiple and diverse
PVO projects in LDCs to permit only inferences and
suggestions. Yet, regardless of this inescapable
tentativeness, the following analysis does intend to
demonstrate that to ignore their domestic base is to
curtail one's understanding of PVOs as agents of
development.

In terms of their home environment, the more than
160 PVOs that have been registered with AID between the
years 1974 and 1981, despite many differences in size,
structure, wealth, and programs, are all by definition
nonprofit organizations. Consequently, the overwhelming majority of PVOs (exceptions will be mentioned later)
must ultimately compete sometimes among themselves and
always with approximately 300,000 other organizations
in order to obtain a share of the billions of dollars
(53.6 billions in 1981) donated yearly by U.S. citizens.[6]
Given this crowded, competitive environment, it is
obviously important for an individual PVO to find a way
to attract the attention and, most importantly, the
tax-deductible contributions of the American donor.
Simply put, barring other sources of revenue, e.g., AID
funds, a PVO's survival depends upon the success of
its fund-raising campaigns, and, in general, to establish the PVO as an organization whose programs and
objectives deserve financial support.

Aside from personnel and financial commitments,
a PVO's unending quest for income may entail additional
consequences. First, a PVO may be induced to tailor
its overseas program to maximize its fund-raising
potential among donors in the United States. To illustrate, the Meals for Millions Foundation (MFM) was

established for the purpose of transmitting to LDCs the knowledge and technology required to produce low-cost food supplements derived from locally available sources of vegetable protein. However, MFM's executive director, whether accurately or not, perceived that the U.S. public was less likely to support development projects whose results would take a relatively long time to unfold than the shipment of the U.S.-produced food supplement, "multipurpose food" (MPF) which could be used for the immediate objective of feeding starving people in various areas of the world. The executive director's perception proved accurate insofar as appeals for money to feed victims of man-made and natural disasters brought in enough donations to enable MFM to ship tons of MPF to food-deficit countries. Consequently, for more than two decades MFM concentrated much more heavily upon relief activities than upon its original objective of being an agent of development. Not so incidentally, this shift in emphasis probably did keep MFM alive within the combative arena of U.S. philanthropy. Yet, even though survival is a predictable objective of an organization and the relief of hunger a worthy task, the fact remains that MFM altered the major thrust of its program in response to a perceived need in rather than outside of the United States.[7]

Second, the potential for intense competition among PVOs also accompanies their need to get donations from the U.S. public. One reason for this assertion is that in any given year the amount of money available to PVOs engaged in overseas development is relatively small in comparison to the total contributions forthcoming from the U.S. public. Thus, over the ten year period of 1972-1981 only in 1974 did the donations for "a mix of organizations involved with foreign aid technical and educational assistance and foundation endowment" exceed 7 percent of the total dollars contributed. As a percentage of the GNP, moreover, total contributions for overseas activities have declined from 2.01 in 1972 to 1.83 in 1981.[8] It is also worth mentioning that in 1981 AID-registered PVOs reported receiving a total of $683,327,850 in private contributions[9] or less than 11 percent of $3.71 billions contributed to the "mix" of organizations and foundations defined above.[10] More startlingly, subtracting the combined totals of "private contributions" ($512,388,684) given to the ten largest recipients reduces the amount received by the remaining 134 PVOs to $170,939,166.[11] In other words, of the billions of dollars collected each year by U.S. nonprofit organizations, only a relatively paltry amount is potentially available to the overwhelming majority of AID-registered PVOs; a fact which leads to the inference that competition among these PVOs is almost inevitable.

While not all PVOs are likely to be equally engaged
in public fund raising, most of them will try to target,
capture, and hold a portion of the small U.S. philanthropy "market" that supports overseas assistance. A
few PVOs are fortunate enough to benefit from having
a clearly defined and responsive pool of potential
donors. In 1981, for example, six AID-registered Jewish
PVOs received $328,144,095, with the United Israel
Appeal's share being $253,851,000.[13] Also, church-
related PVOs (approximately eight) usually obtain a
part of their income from parent organizations and do
not have to depend solely upon an undifferentiated
pool of potential donors for financial support. Yet,
even if one were to assume that these fourteen or so
PVOs are free from the same degree of fund-raising pressure experienced by other PVOs, it should be remembered
that no PVO is ever going to feel it has sufficient
funds to accomplish all that ought to be done in the area
of development. Nor is it reasonable to think that
these PVOs are going to accept with equanimity encroach-
ments upon their "territory" by another PVO, regardless
of the worthiness of its objectives.

Lacking a fairly assured financial base such as
that enjoyed by Jewish and church-related PVOs, fund
raising has to be of unending, time-consuming concern
for the bulk of AID-registered PVOs. Because, among
other things, each PVO has to try to hit upon some
aspect of its programs or goals that will distinguish
it from all other PVOs who are also trying to obtain
donations from basically the same pool of potential
contributors, i.e., those relatively few individuals
who are willing to give to U.S. nonprofit organizations
with overseas projects. This is no easy task, since
AID-registered PVOs are all involved in some aspect of
development assistance designed ultimately to improve
the lives of people in LDCs. In other words, they
are all humanitarian organizations with objectives
worthy of support. Furthermore, typically it is difficult for a PVO to claim that its program is unique
either in terms of the people affected or the type of
assistance provided. A quick review of PVO program
statements indicates that, whether viewed along the
dimension of functional categories (health, education,
agriculture, commerce, labor, etc.), geographic distribution (Africa, Asia, Latin America, Middle East)
or particular groups (children, women, refugees, etc.),
assistance is forthcoming from several and frequently
many PVOs.[14] Thus, an individual wishing to donate
to a PVO that provides medical assistance would have
more than thirty organizations from which to choose.
The individual could then narrow his or her choice
by selecting a PVO according to the type of program or
geographic area being served. But, even then a

selection might have to be made from among two or more quite similar organizations.[15] No PVO by virtue of either its program or its worthwhile, humanitarian, nonprofit intentions can rest assured that no competition exists for the support of potential contributors.

Uncertain funding suggests, in turn, that PVOs may find it expedient to base appeals for money upon examples of successfully completed development projects, on promises of activities that will bring speedy, tangible relief to some pressing need, e.g., food shipments to famine stricken people, or plans to start/ continue a development activity whose impact will be positive, demonstrable, and relatively immediate. It is not argued that appeals of this nature are misleading or are not based upon an accurate portrayal of projects that do indeed address some development problem afflicting an LDC; certainly in the arena of development there is ample room for all kinds of projects aimed at the multiple needs existing in regions throughout the world. What is being argued is that fund raising creates its own dynamic which may impel PVOs, consciously or not, not just to shape their overseas programs to meet the perceived expectations of potential donors in the United States, as mentioned above, but also be hesitant about trying anything new. Once promises have been made or achievements in the field recorded, a donor-dependent PVO probably would find it extremely difficult to contemplate changing the focus or techniques of its efforts abroad. The very fact that a PVO exists means that it has had some success in tapping a segment of the philanthropy market, but any significant or rapid change might endanger this base of support. Moreover, if change in a PVO's program emphasis does occur, it will probably unfold gradually and will be as likely in response to domestic stimuli as to ones from abroad. Innovation, flexibility, and sensitivity to the needs of the world's poor majority, therefore, may not be characteristics possessed in abundance by every AID-registered PVO.

Ought one conclude from the foregoing that the philanthropic sector of the AID-registered PVOs' domestic environment induces only competition and costly fund-raising campaigns and serves solely to constrain their development assistance programs? Obviously, this is not the complete picture. First, regardless of the relatively restricted number of philanthropy dollars available for foreign aid, the fact remains that this money does supply many PVOs with the capability to conduct overseas operations. Second, competition for donations need not lead to enervating inter-PVO conflict. Indeed, ACVAFS, Coordination in Development (CODEL), and Private Agencies Collaborating Together (PACT) provide examples of organizations designed to promote cooperation and coordination among development agencies. Third, although the imperatives of survival for a non-profit organization may limit the validity of the "articles of faith" when applied to a particular PVO, the arena of U.S. philanthropy does afford room for a venturesome or new PVO to attempt novel ideas and approaches and, provided U.S. donors respond favor-ably, to test them in the field. Put another way, collectively, PVOs may exhibit greater fidelity to their proclaimed strengths than they do as separate entities because of the diversity of programs and organizations made possible through the financial sup-port coming from the diffuse and relatively unregulated U.S. philanthropic sector.

In addition to the private, philanthropic sector, the federal government forms another portion of many U.S.-based PVOs' domestic environment. More precisely, 156 U.S. PVOs were registered with the U.S. government through AID as of December 31, 1981. Since over one-third of these registered PVOs, among other things, obtained more than 50 percent of their income from federal funds, it seems appropriate to devote atten-tion to an analysis of AID-PVO relations in an effort to explore their possible impact upon the overseas activities of PVOs.[16]

The first and crucial step for a PVO that decides to establish formal ties with the U.S. government is to gain the acceptance of AID, that is, to become a registered agency. From AID's current viewpoint, there are four categories of registered organizations. Cooperatives and credit unions which rely "almost exclusively" upon AID for their funding and at the "urging" of AID conduct activities to increase the participation of poor people in "their countries' development." Also largely AID-funded, AFL-CIO Insti-tutes aim to strengthen "free" labor unions and to involve workers in economic and social development in LDCs. Family planning organizations, the third category, rely "heavily" upon AID to support their population control activities overseas. Nonprofit consulting firms provide "management and planning assistance" to PVOs in the United States and other countries and have been fund-ed by AID grants. Traditional voluntary organizations--PVOs--comprise the fifth category and are defined in the following discussion of AID's registration process.[17]

Successful registration requires that a PVO prove it meets certain criteria. The most important of these are as follows: (1) The PVO must be a "private non-governmental organization which is organized under U.S. law and maintains its principle place of business in the United States..."; (2) it must be a tax exempt, nonprofit, "voluntary organization, i.e., receives voluntary contributions of money, staff time or in-kind support from the general public."; (3) it must be, "or anticipates becoming, engaged in voluntary charitable or development assistance operations abroad..."; (4) it must be financially sound and follow standard accounting practices; (5) it must have an unpaid Board of Directors whose members, rather than paid staff, "constitute a majority in any decision."; and (6) it must use its funds and resources according to "stated purposes" and "without unreasonable cost for salaries, promotion, publicity, fund raising and administration..." (Costs are unreasonable if they exceed twenty percent of the "total cash and in-kind contributions" received by the organization. This limitation can be appealed.)[18]

Upon demonstrating that it meets AID's registration criteria and receiving a certificate of registration, a PVO becomes eligible to request support for its projects. AID assistance comes in five forms: (1) Freight subsidies and reimbursements for the shipping of supplies; (2) participation in U.S. government excess property programs; (3) PL 480 food for distribution abroad; (4) contracts; and (5) grants. Through 1981, seven types of grants were available to PVOs, i.e., matching (MG), institutional development (IDG), consortium (CG), operational program (OPG), institutional support (ISG), management service (MSG), cooperative agreements, and grants from U.S. government organizations other than the Bureau for Food for Peace and Voluntary Assistance.[19] The following table gives a rough idea of the significance of U.S. government assistance to PVOs.

TABLE 5.1
PVO Income and AID Support

| Year | Total Income of Registered Reporting PVOs | Total U.S. Government Assistance | U.S. Government Assistance: % of Total Income of PVOs | No. of PVOs |
|------|------|------|------|------|
| 1974 | 949,174,717 | 260,804,099 | 27 | 88 |
| 1975 | 950,774,176 | 353,588,008 | 37 | 87 |
| 1979 | 1,155,685,943 | 447,562,080 | 39 | 112 |
| 1980 | 1,550,514,226 | 618,159,220 | 40 | 124 |
| 1981 | 1,819,608,852 | 742,342,233 | 41 | 144 |

Source: U.S. Agency for International Development, Reports 1974, 1975, 1979, 1980, 1981. (See footnote 16)

As can be seen, the amount of income PVOs derive
from the U.S. government is not insubstantial and has
been growing steadily, albeit modestly, during the
last three years reported by AID. The 1973 "New Directions" legislation's call for AID to give greater
support to PVOs probably accounts for much of this
growth as well as the 10 percent increase in funding
that occurred between 1974 and 1975. Regardless of
the reasons for the rise in AID assistance, however,
it is evident that the U.S. government represents an
attractive source of income for PVOs wishing to aug-
ment the support won in the arena of U.S. philanthropy.

While more money for development projects is
probably the major benefit PVOs anticipate deriving
out of a formal association with the foreign aid arm
of the U.S. government, AID quite naturally also expects
its "partnership" with PVOs to be advantageous. From
AID's perspective, PVOs contribute to the developmental
assistance goals of the U.S. government in four important ways. First, the relations PVOs have with private
institutions in LDCs provide them with "a means for
effectively engaging the rural and urban poor in their
nation's development." Second, PVOs can serve as
instruments to educate the public about the needs of
LDCs and to get funds from the private sector of the
U.S. Third, PVOs engaged in overseas activities
illustrate the "basic American values of pluralism,
voluntary action and concern for others." Fourth,
PVOs can strengthen AID's efforts, "particularly with
respect to matters such as community level involvement."[20]

This mutually beneficial partnership between AID
and PVOs is not, however, free of problems. Both sides
recognize that one, if not the most, basic and intract-
able issue is how to preserve the touted flexibility,
independence, and people-to-people approach of PVOs
that receive grants, transportation subventions, PL
480 food, and contracts from a bureaucratic government
agency that must serve the national interest of the
U.S. as defined by legislation, directives, and regulations. AID's most recent policy paper dealing with
PVOs clearly demonstrates its sensitivity to this issue.
Thus, it is recognized that "...public and private
objectives and programmatic interests frequently do not
coincide. AID is accountable to Congress and the U.S.
public; PVOs must account to their contributors." The
paper further notes:

> AID, by its very nature as a government
> development agency, operates very differently
> from private and voluntary development agencies.
> AID is an instrument of our total foreign policy.
> As a result, in determining where it will

concentrate its resources for development, it must factor in a wide range of considerations.

The policy statement goes on to explain:

...while acknowledging and valuing those areas where AID and PVO interests do overlap and where AID and PVOs can and do work together, it is important to underline that the motivations, interests and responsibilities of these development agencies are not and should not be identical.

AID then defines its partnership with PVOs along "two major dimensions." Namely, "AID deals with PVOs both as intermediaries in conducting AID's programs and as independent entities in their own right."[21]

Aside from attempting to demonstrate an awareness and acceptance of distinctions between AID and PVOs, the AID policy paper explicitly sets forth the following policy objective: "to discourage dependence on U.S. Government financing of the international development programs of PVOs." Furthermore, to reach this objective and to comply with a legislative mandate, AID will require PVOs, as of 1 January 1985, to "obtain at least 20 percent of its total annual financial resources for its international programs from non-USG sources, with preference given for private funding, in order to qualify for matching grants, operational program grants and institution-building support." PVOs not meeting this requirement will be eligible only for "intermediary" assistance to "implement AID programs."[22] One can argue whether a PVO receiving 80 percent of its funds from the U.S. government is or can be independent, but the 20 percent nongovernment funds requirement does illustrate AID's awareness of the danger that registered PVOs may loose their identities and become mere extensions of U.S. government policy.

AID-registered PVOs, predictably, share their partner's concern about the issue of independence. Common sense and historical experience suggest that this mutually held concern is valid so long as a PVO chooses to maintain formal links with the U.S. government. Depending upon the foreign context of a U.S. government/ PVO project, for example, it is certainly conceivable that a local populace will not have the knowledge or interest to draw a distinction between a jointly funded project and one that is solely financed by U.S. government or PVO funds. In some cases this blurring would be of little consequence, but in others it might make the success of a PVO project problematical because of the existence of anti-U.S. government sentiments within the target groups. Moreover, aside from this problem of perception, one should also remember that the past

record of U.S.-PVO relations is replete with examples of
PVOs becoming the direct instruments of U.S. foreign
policy. U.S. PVO activities in Vietnam during the
1960s are a case in point. In other cases, PVOs alter
their projects to fit the policies of the U.S. government, e.g., CRS in India in 1976.[23] In fact, one can
surmise from this historical record that the only way
a PVO can with certainty avoid direct U.S. government
influence is to break its ties with AID and rely upon
the unpredictable and competitive, but more diffuse and
less intrusive, U.S. philanthropic arena to finance
its programs. The growing number of AID-registered
PVOs combined with the significance government assistance assumes in many of their budgets suggests that
few PVOs are or will be inclined to take this drastic
step.

Short of rupturing their formal links with the U.S.
government, it appears that PVOs rely upon an inter-
active process with AID to maximize their freedom from
constrictive and complex administrative regulations
and procedures. The focal point of the bargaining
that occurs is the Advisory Committee on Voluntary
Foreign Aid (ACVFA); a fifteen-member organization
which acts as a forum for AID and PVOs to "air matters
in a neutral setting" and as a source of "counsel on
the policies which govern programs involving voluntary
organizations."[24] In brief, although originally founded
in 1946 for the primary purpose of registering PVOs
with AID, ACVFA now aggregates, filters, and forwards
PVO concerns and recommendations to AID and provides
a conduit for the latter's response. A report of
ACVFA's activities in 1979 and 1980 affords interesting
insights into problems disturbing AID-PVO relations,
the process of addressing them, and the costs that
accompany a PVO's involvement in the governmental
sector of its domestic base.

The ACVFA accounts of its September, 1979 Tarrytown and June, 1980 Washington, D.C. meetings are the
most instructive.[25] The more than one hundred representatives of AID, PVOs, and other organizations who
attended the Tarrytown session identified seven problem
areas that required the attention of PVOs and AID.
Problems in the area of "perception and communication"
encompassed the need for AID and PVOs to acquire a
better understanding and accommodation of differences
and to clarify their policies and procedures. "Philosophical differences" gave rise to the question of
whether it might not be appropriate to separate PVO
funds from those "allocated according to geopolitical
constraints." The third and fourth problem areas
dealt with "structure," i.e., the "organization" of
AID and PVOs. With respect to AID, questions (suggestions) dealt with the desirability of making financial

support for PVOs "an explicit line item" in foreign
assistance appropriations; ensuring "core support" for
PVOs that would be "less constrained;" reducing the
"multiplicity" of AID offices and, hence, "confusion
and delays" confronting PVOs; establishing an organization within or outside of AID that would bear "sole
responsibility" for PVO-U.S. government relations; and
reducing the "ambiguity" in the relations between AID,
PVOs, and PVO affiliates overseas. PVO structural
issues concerned the desirability of: "categorization"
to "assist" AID develop a "better means of supporting"
diverse PVOs, establishing "consortia" of "new and
small" PVOs to reduce administrative burdens, and reducing auditing requirements while retaining "proper
accountability." A further question posed in this
problem area was: "What are the optimum levels of
government funding for PVOs that will enable them to do
what they want to do while still retaining their independent and private nature?"

The fifth, "functional," problem area raised points
about how to "streamline" the procedures entailed in
AID's approving and overseeing grants in order to reduce
adminstrative costs and delays experienced by PVOs and
to enable them to continue making "flexible" responses
in the field. Another issue questioned how PVOs could
"strengthen their capacity to perform effectively overseas" so they could acquire "greater independence" from
AID in the formulation, implementation, and evaluation
of their overseas projects. "Development Education"
and "Congressional Policy and Attitudes," the sixth and
seventh areas, included queries about what could be done
to get Congress to "relax" restrictions on AID, PVOs,
and ACVFA and to "adopt less restrictive" legislation
which would permit more "freedom of action" in the
AID-PVO partnership.

The Washington meeting, which had 230 participants,
echoes with greater specificity the problem areas defined at Tarrytown. Consequently, only a few of the
more pointed of the thirty-five recommendations made
at this meeting need to be highlighted in order to provide a fairly complete view of the issues involved in
the AID-PVO relationship. Regarding PVO "autonomy"
one recommendation was: "that PVOs communicate with
AID about differences in objectives. PVOs have their
own objectives which are not identical to those of
the organizations which fund them. This reality needs
to be kept in mind by AID." In terms of "monitoring/
reporting," ACVFA noted criticisms of AID-contracted
evaluators for "superimposing their evaluations on PVO
evaluations." It was also noted that: "Surprise visits
arranged by AID, with no or very limited consultation
with PVOs, are considered disruptive." Legislative
restrictions, project management, evaluation/account-

ability, audits of PVOs and their subgrantees, and financial management were further topics that brought forth recommendations for ACVFA's consideration.

As can be seen from the foregoing account of the ACVFA Tarrytown and Washington meetings, PVO concerns about arrangements with AID range from preserving and extending their autonomy in the face of AID's structural and procedural complexities and its evaluation and accountability processes as applied to PVO field pro- jects. One can opine that the costs for maintaining and nurturing their partnership must be heavy for both AID and the PVOs. AID, which must operate within the broad framework of U.S. foreign policy considerations and the web of regulations, statutes, and operational codes spun by Congress, the Office of Management and Budget (OMB), the Department of State, itself, and others, must also work with a group of diverse organ- izations that wants federal assistance but is impatient with the restrictions and complications which accompany it. The PVOs, on the other hand, find themselves involved in "red-tape" and an organizational labyrinth, both of which consume personnel time and institutional funds, and a relationship which threatens their autonomy.

Now, AID's PVO policy paper demonstrates that it is not insensitive to the problems PVOs face in their for- mal relations with the U.S. government, and ACVFA no doubt assumes correctly that "...AID wants its relation- ship with the PVOs to be as much like a partnership as possible, consistent with the realization that AID is the grantor and that PVOs wish to preserve their in- dependence."[26] The unavoidable reality remains, how- ever, that AID is the senior partner, it is the grantor, it does control the allocation of funds. This is not a unique nor a necessarily unreasonable state-of-affairs. What does make it rather interesting is that both partners seem to share to some degree the illusion that a PVO is "independent" when the location, duration, type, objectives, monitoring, and evaluation of its project must receive AID's approval before federal funds will be forthcoming. Combine this power with the actual assistance provided by the U.S. government via AID and surely it is reasonable to speculate about the latitude of action an AID-registered PVO retains. Some PVOs certainly can and do resist the diminution of their autonomy that seems to inhere in their AID ties. Ironically, their battle is not against an implacable foe. Rather, AID resembles the flame that attracts and may consume a moth that finds its light irresistable. AID's "New Directions" concern with microdevelopment, bottom-up development projects and its resources may prove to be an overwhelmingly attractive combination for some PVOs. To the extent that it does, PVOs will become appendages of U.S. foreign policy and, concomitantly, will lose any claim to adhering to their "articles of faith."

This now completed study of the interaction of AID-registered PVOs with two major sectors of their domestic environment suggests that the overseas projects of U.S. nonprofit agents of development may be the products of more than the identifiable, objective needs of the poor majority living in LDCs.  Indeed, it seems justifiable to argue that the U.S. PVOs' quest for funds makes them susceptible to a variety of domestic pressures that can influence the form and content of their overseas projects.  The philanthropic sector does help to sustain PVOs, but the amount of donations any single PVO can usually expect to attract is relatively limited and competition for contributions is sharp.  Hence, a PVO must make its appeals for money as attractive as possible to its potential donors. This means, in turn, that the PVO will attempt to formulate overseas projects that contributors will find attractive.  As for the governmental sector, the PVO is confronted with the necessity of shaping its developmental projects to fit the current criteria of AID. In neither instance does it follow that the projects formulated to satisfy those who may fund the PVOs are necessarily antithetical or irrelevant to the developmental assistance needs of recipients.  Both do suggest that the U.S. PVOs' domestic environment constrains their capacity to respond to the developmental requirements of LDCs and casts doubts upon their capacity to fulfill their "articles of faith."

NOTES

1.  U.S. Congress, Senate, Committee on Foreign Relations, Foreign Assistance Legislation:  Fiscal Year 1972, Hearings, 92d Cong., 1st sess., June, 1971, 410-11.

2.  Hubert H. Humphrey, "Foreward" in John G. Sommer, Beyond Charity:  U.S. Voluntary AID for a Changing Third World (Washington, D.C.: Overseas Development Council, 1977), vii-viii.

3.  John G. Sommer, U.S. Voluntary AID to the Third World: What Is Its Future? Development Paper 20 (Washington, D.C.: Overseas Development Council, 1975), 25.

4.  U.S. Congress, Senate, Committee on Foreign Relations, International Security and Development Cooperation Act of 1980, S. Rept. 96-732, 96th Cong., 2d sess., 1979, 106.

5. Judith Tendler, Turning Private Voluntary Organizations Into Development Agencies: Questions for Evaluation, Program Evaluation Discussion Paper No. 12 (Washington, D.C: AID, April, 1982), 2.

6. American Association of Fund Raising Counsel, Inc. (AAFRC), Giving USA: 1982 Annual Report, 6.

7. For a more complete analysis of the Meals for Millions Foundation, see; Hibbert R. Roberts, "Meals for Millions Foundation: Limits and Potential for International Aid," International Journal of Comparative Sociology 21, 3-4, (Sept.-Dec. 1980): 182-195.

8. AAFRC, 7 and 36.

9. U.S. International Development Cooperation Agency, AID, Bureau for Food for Peace and Voluntary Assistance, "Voluntary Foreign Aid Programs," (1981), 21.

10. AAFRC, 36.

11. "Voluntary Foreign Aid Programs," 1981, 21-27. Please note that of the 156 PVOs listed, 144 submitted data reports.

12. In 1981, for example, twelve PVOs received 95 percent or more of their total funds for overseas development from AID. Ibid., 34-35.

13. Ibid., 21-27.

14. Ibid., 5-20.

15. For example, in the area of dentistry, two PVOs, American Dentists for Foreign Service and Dental Health International, provide assistance--the former in Korea and Africa and the latter in Africa. Ibid., 6 and 9.

16. 1981 Report, 3. Unless otherwise indicated, please note that data about AID/PVO relations was obtained from the following sources. For 1974: AID, Bureau for Population and Humanitarian Assistance, Office of Private and Voluntary Cooperation, "Voluntary Foreign Aid Programs,' 1974, as presented in Sommer, U.S. Voluntary Aid to the Third World 60-65 (hereafter 1974 Report). For 1975; AID, "Voluntary Foreign Aid Programs," as presented in John Sommer, Beyond Charity U.S. Voluntary Aid for a Changing World (Washington, D.C.: Overseas Development Council, 1977), Table 4 (hereafter 1975 Report). For 1976-78; no data available. For 1979; AID, "Voluntary Foreign Aid Programs," 1979 (hereafter 1979 Report). For 1980; AID, "Voluntary Foreign Aid Programs," 1980 (hereafter 1980 Report). For 1981; AID, "Voluntary Foreign Aid Programs," 1981 (hereafter 1981 Report).

17. AID, Bureau for Program and Policy Coordination, "A.I.D. Partnership in International Development with Private and Voluntary Organizations," AID Policy Paper, (September, 1982): 5.

18. AID, "Conditions of Registration and Documentation Requirements," (November 30, 1982): 3-6.

19. 1981 Report, 32.

20. AID Policy Paper, (September, 1982): 1-2.

114

21. Ibid., 2. AID defines PVO intermediaries as being cooperatives and credit unions, AFL-CIO institutes, and family planning organizations. Ibid., 5-6.

22. Ibid., 3-4.

23. For a more complete analysis of these and additional examples of the U.S. government curtailing the independence of AID-registered and funded PVOs, see; Sommer, Beyond Charity, 97-101.

24. AID, "Report of the Advisory Committee on Voluntary Foreign Aid," (January, 1981), 4 (hereafter ACVFA Report).

25. ACVFA Report, Appendix IA, pp. I1-I5 and Appendix ID, I9-I14.

26. ACVFA Report, Appendix III, III-2.

# 6
# U.S. and Canadian PVOs As Transnational Development Institutions

*Brian H. Smith*

INTRODUCTION

Since the mid-1960s private voluntary organizations (PVOs) have significantly expanded their overseas aid activities in the Third World. Some of the older U.S. agencies--CARE, Catholic Relief Services (CRS), Church World Service (CWS), Lutheran World Relief (LWR)-- originated primarily as relief organizations during and immediately after World War II and focused most of their attention on war-torn countries in Europe. Over the past twenty years these and newer overseas aid-granting PVOs (totalling over seventeen hundred by 1981) that are home-based in other Organization for Economic Cooperation and Development (OECD) countries have diversified their activities and geographical focus to include development assistance to Asia, the Middle East, Africa, and Latin America in health, education, technical training and improvement, marketing and producer cooperatives, small credit financing and community development.

In 1968 the total overseas aid of these private agencies (the bulk of which was administered by the one hundred or so largest PVOs) was $510.2 million. By 1974 this had more than doubled to $1.22 billion and by 1980 doubled again to $2.4 billion. Throughout the 1970s their contribution hovered around 10 percent of the total annual bilateral and multilateral foreign aid sent overseas by OECD governments. When the value of contributed services is accounted for, the ratio of governmental assistance to voluntary agency grants is closer to 6:1.[1]

Governments in the North Atlantic countries have in fact steadily increased their own contributions to PVOs carrying out overseas relief and development assistance. Originally, when the older U.S. PVOs began in the 1940s governmental aid took the form of food, but now includes (and in Europe and Canada is predominantly) cash contributions for development projects. In 1973 OECD government grants to their respective PVOs

engaged in overseas activities totalled $315.4 million
but by 1977 had more than doubled to $734.5 million and
accounted for 33 percent of the total revenues of the
PVOs.[2]

In the United States public assistance to PVOs
for overseas work totalled only $80 million in 1964,
but by 1973 had reached $207.9 million, and by 1979
amounted to $627.6 million. In 1981, 125 of the 156
U.S. PVOs registered with United States Agency for
International Development (AID) received public
subsidies amounting to $742.3 million and this public
aid accounted for 42.4 percent of their total revenues
of $1.75 billion.[3]

## New Challenges for PVOs

All of these factors indicate the growing popularity PVOs enjoy in North Atlantic governments and
societies at large for being effective conduits of
foreign aid. The extant literature on PVOs has
chronicled the reasons for such expanding PVO
appeal--they are cost-effective, they bypass government bureaucracies and deal directly with poor
people, they support small private indigenous institutions in Third World societies and thus promote
local self-reliance.

Questions are also being raised as to whether
PVOs can now play an important catalytic role in wider
development issues by: (1) showing larger aid-granting
institutions how to be innovative in meeting basic
human needs; (2) empowering grass-roots groups abroad
to challenge and change within their own environments
the economic and political structures underlying
poverty and exploitation; and (3) influencing public
opinion as well as policy makers at home to make
changes in corporate and governmental policies
affecting global distribution of resources.

I am currently in the midst of a three-year
research project on PVOs as development institutions
that looks at aspects of all these questions. It
involves an examination of primary and secondary
documentary materials, structured interviews in home
offices of overseas aid-giving PVOs in eight North
Atlantic countries, and field visits to Colombia and
Chile to analyze the political and economic impact of
the indigenous private institutions and projects they
support. In this chapter I shall report on data
collected from the first stage of this research--
namely, structured interviews with forty representatives in twenty-two U.S. and Canadian-based PVOs
and eight representatives in governmental agencies
such as AID and the Canadian International Development
Agency (CIDA) that provide public aid to international
PVOs based in the United States and Canada.[4] I shall

subdivide the findings according to the following four
areas covered in these interviews:

1. <u>Goal Coherence</u>:  the degree to which there is
   consensus within the U.S and Canadian PVO
   community as to priorities in development-
   related activities abroad and at home.
2. <u>Political Character and Consequences</u>:  to
   what extent these PVOs are free of political
   limitations and costs while acting as conduits of aid from home governments and aiming
   at structural changes in developing countries.
2. <u>Proof of Effectiveness</u>:  the methods used by
   PVOs to evaluate the impact of the overseas
   institutions and projects they support on
   wider dynamics of development in these
   societies.
4. <u>Governance</u>:  decision-making and accountability mechanisms within PVOs affecting their
   relationships to donors as well as Third
   World partner groups.

In a concluding section I will indicate what implications the findings in these areas have for the three
larger questions about PVOs as agenda-setting agents in
development, as promoters of empowerment among the poor
in the Third World, and as educators and advocates at
home for global structural changes.


GOAL COHERENCE

In the official language of <u>all</u> fifteen of the
U.S. PVOs I interviewed there is a great emphasis on
promoting long-term development, as opposed to the
alleviation of immediate suffering.  All stress in
their literature (as well as during interviews with me)
the need to attack the structural causes of poverty by
promoting a greater awareness abroad and at home as to
its deeper causes, by enhancing skills and access of
the poor to resources, and by enabling the poor to
build local organizations to take collective action to
better their own socioeconomic situation--all of which
are parts of a basic human needs (BHN) or alternative
development strategy (ADS).
Nevertheless, despite the emergence of a common
language about goals among all types of U.S. PVOs in
recent years--language that resembles elements of
both the BHN and ADS approaches--I found that there is
quite a diversity in emphasis among PVOs in opera-
tionalizing what this rhetoric means in practice.
There are at least three quite different methods of
implementing the common set of symbols: (1) continuing
reliance on traditional assistential mechanisms

(especially food); (2) transfer of technical resources
and skills to the poor; and (3) building or strengthening private institutions and networks in the Third
World responsive to multiple needs of the poor as they
define them.


## Traditional Disaster-Aid Agencies

While the older U.S. organizations (those that
began as disaster aid agencies back in the 1940s) in
their official publications give emphasis to development as opposed to assistential work, they continue to
rely predominantly on material aid rather than cash
grants to support their overseas operations. CRS, CARE
USA, and Seventh-Day Adventist World Service (SAWS) all
still distribute a great deal of food (especially PL
480, Title II, Food for Peace from the U.S. government)
and other material aid (clothing and medicine) in
developing countries. Although the total amount spent
by CRS in 1981-82, for example, was $334.3 million,
material contributions (mainly food), freight reimbursements by governments to transport them, and staff
salaries accounted for all but about $30 million
(which then could be used as cash grants for development projects globally). CARE USA in 1981-82 had
$264.9 million in resources, but only $35.7 million in
cash went for development projects and the rest was in
the form of food and medical supplies, ocean freight
reimbursements to ship them, and cash for other overhead costs. Of the $16.2 million 1981-82 budget of
SAWS, only $2.5 million was in the form of monetary
contributions for overseas projects (see Table 6.1,
column 1).

All of these PVOs in their publications refer to
much of the material aid they send overseas as development assistance, since a good deal of it is not disaster or refugee aid but rather food donations used in
nutrition projects for mothers and children under
five, school-age children and elderly persons, and
food-for-work projects (in construction, irrigation,
and sanitation) administered by local governments.
They also try, as one CRS spokesperson told me, to use
food aid in such nonemergency circumstances to stimulate new community organizations around feeding centers
and food-for-work projects.[5]

Representatives interviewed in these three organizations (two in CRS, three in CARE USA, and one in
SAWS) responded to a list of six organization goals I
presented to them: (1) immediate alleviation of suffering; (2) increasing income and/or employment; (3)
improving skills and problem-solving capacities; (4)
building new community-run institutions and networks;

TABLE 6.1
Resources and Percentages Received From the U.S. Government by the 14 Largest U.S. Transnational PVOs (1981-1982)

Total Resources: $1,189.9 million
Resources from Government: $603.8 million (50.7%)

Column 1

Predominantly Relief

| PVO | Resources | % Government |
|---|---|---|
| CARE USA | $264.9 mil | 77.8% |
| SAWS | 16.2 mil | 73.4 |
| International Rescue Committee | 27.6 mil | 71.7 |
| CRS | 334.3 mil | 68.8 |
| HIAS | 11.8 mil | 52.9 |
| World Relief Corporation | 5.7 mil | 68.2 |
| World Vision Relief Organization | 13.7 mil | 36.7 |
| MAP International | 27.9 mil | 1.2 |
| Direct Relief International | 5.7 mil | .04 |
| Christian Children's Fund | 42.1 mil | 0.0 |
| | | |
| TOTALS | $749.9 mil | 64.5% |

63% of total PVO resources
80% of total government aid

TABLE 6.1
(continued)

Column 2

Predominantly Technical

| PVO | Resources | % Government |
|---|---|---|
| Association for Voluntary Sterilization | $11.5 mil | 95.2% |
| Community Development Foundation | 1.5 mil | 92.0 |
| International Education Development | .8 mil | 85.9 |
| Pathfinder Fund | 5.7 mil | 83.7 |
| VITA | 2.1 mil | 76.1 |
| Planned Parenthood Federation of America | 24.1 mil | 70.9 |
| National Association of Partners of the Alliance | 1.7 mil | 68.7 |
| Technoserve | 2.1 mil | 58.3 |
| AITEC | 1.0 mil | 55.7 |
| Institute for International Dev. | 1.1 mil | 44.4 |
| Institute of International Educ. | 60.2 mil | 27.4 |
| International Exec. Service Corps | 15.6 mil | 27.3 |
| Meals for Millions | 1.5 mil | 25.3 |
| Pan American Development Foundation | 5.0 mil | 21.4 |
| People-to-People Health Foundation | 12.9 mil | 20.2 |
| American ORT Federation | 8.8 mil | 16.7 |
| Credit Union National Association | 13.9 mil | 10.8 |
| National Rural Electric Cooperative Association | 20.5 mil | 8.5 |
| Heifer Project International | 3.2 mil | 6.0 |
| Mennonite Central Committee | 19.2 mil | 1.7 |
| TOTALS | $209.4 mil | 33.5% |

17.6% of total PVO resources
11.6% of total government aid

TABLE 6.1
(continued)

## Column 3

Multiservice Institution and Network Building

| PVO | Resources | % Government |
|-----|-----------|--------------|
| PACT | $ 3.8 mil | 97.8% |
| Asia Foundation | 7.7 mil | 86.5 |
| CODEL | 2.0 mil | 59.6 |
| Church World Service | 60.7 mil | 43.4 |
| Lutheran World Relief | 10.9 mil | 29.4 |
| Save the Children Federation | 18.4 mil | 20.6 |
| Domestic and Foreign Society of the Protestant Episcopal Church | 38.7 mil | 18.1 |
| National Board of YMCAs | 22.9 mil | 12.9 |
| American Friends Service Committee | 16.6 mil | 3.6 |
| Foster Parents Plan USA | 10.1 mil | 1.1 |
| Ford Foundation | 20.5 mil | 0.0 |
| Rockefeller Foundation | 13.1 mil | 0.0 |
| OXFAM America | 4.0 mil | 0.0 |
| UUSC | 1.2 mil | 0.0 |
| | | |
| TOTALS | $230.6 mil | 21.7% |

19.4% of total PVO resources
8.3% of total government aid

Source: Bureau for Food For Peace and Voluntary Assistance, AID, Voluntary Foreign Aid Programs (Washington, D.C.: AID, 1982).

(5) enhancing recipient bargaining power vis-à-vis local merchants, credit institutions, government agencies, etc.; and (6) empowerment of the poor to challenge and change dominant political and economic structures. All chose the first as the one most important for their organization in selecting projects to support abroad.

Hence, although the words have changed in the older and larger U.S. PVOs regarding mission definition, they still concentrate their energies in areas where they have a proven and admirable track record—immediate relief from hunger and sickness. During interviews I learned that many on the Board of Directors of both CRS and CARE USA are still primarily concerned with the delivery of goods and services to the poor and to victims of natural disasters and do not want their respective organizations to lose this traditional focus which has gained them countless admirers and supporters.[6]

The 10 to 12 percent of the budget of CRS and CARE USA (as well as SAWS) that is in the form of cash rather than material assistance is devoted to very technical projects—improved methods of agricultural production, water development, natural resources conservation, construction of schools, low-income housing, or health facilities. Hence, all six respondents from these three agencies ranked in priority as organizational goals, just after the immediate alleviation of suffering, increasing income and/or employment, and improving skills and problem-solving capacities of the poor.

While CRS, CARE USA and SAWS are three of the larger relief-oriented PVOs registered with AID, there are several others that continue to emphasize predominantly assistential aid. These include MAP International, the International Rescue Committee, World Relief Corporation, Hebrew Immigrant Aid Society (HIAS), Direct Relief Corporation, Christian Children's Fund, and World Vision Relief Organization. The combined resources of these PVOs, together with CRS, CARE USA, and SAWS, was $749.9 million in 1981-82, or 63 percent of the total resources of the forty-four largest U.S. PVOs (see Table 6.1, column 1).

## Technical-Assistance PVOs

The technical emphasis (characteristic of a minor part of the activities of traditional relief agencies) was the predominant emphasis in two other U.S. PVOs in my survey—ACCION International/AITEC, and the Pan American Development Foundation (PADF). Both of these organizations were founded in the 1960s and see the

causes of poverty in developing countries to be a lack
of access to critical resources such as credit and
appropriate technology.  They support microenterprises
with management training and loan guarantees, including
revolving credit funds for small business persons.
Representatives of both of these institutions during
my interviews ranked as priority goals for their
respective organizations items 2 and 3 on my list--
namely, increasing income and/or employment opportunities  for the poor, and improving their skills and
problem-solving capacities.

AITEC and PADF are representative of a whole
series of U.S. PVOs, several founded during the 1960s
when the U.S. government began to provide considerable
resources for private organizations engaging in the
construction of the technical infrastructure necessary
for development in the Third World.  Such organizations
include the Community Development Foundation (administered by Save the Children Federation), the Credit
Union National Association, the Association for Voluntary Sterilization, the Planned Parenthood Federation
of America, People-to-People Health Foundation,
American ORT Foundation, National Rural Electric Cooperative Association, Heifer Project International, the
Institute for International Development, the Institute
of International Education, International Education
Development, International Executive Service Corps, the
National Association of the Partners of the Alliance,
the Pathfinder Fund, Technoserve, and Volunteers in
Technical Assistance (VITA).

Some of these PVOs--such as the Credit Union
National Association, the International Executive
Service Corps, and the Institute for International
Development--also draw upon the expertise of the U.S.
business community, and provide technical advice and
training by active or retired U.S. private executives
for small businesses and credit institutions in
developing countries.

Although the combined resources in 1981-82 of these
eighteen PVOs (including AITEC and PADF) amounted to
only $188.7 million--a little over one-half of that of
CRS ($334.3 million), and three fourths of that of CARE
USA ($264.9 million) for the same year--many provide
essential technical services and resources for small
groups of entrepreneurs in developing countries.
Moreover, their combined contribution of $188.7 million
to technically oriented projects in the Third World in
1981-82 was three times that made to comparable projects by CRS ($30 million) and CARE USA ($35.7 million)
together, whose predominant emphasis overseas is still
assistential rather than technically oriented aid.

Moreover, there are some older relief agencies
that have shifted most of their emphasis away from

assistential activities to technical training and
improvement of production of basic commodities and
services. These include Meals for Millions/Freedom
From Hunger Foundation and the Mennonite Central
Committee, whose combined resources in 1981-82 totalled
$20.7 million. Together with the other eighteen
technically oriented PVOs, in 1981-82 the total
resources amounted to $209.4 million, or 17.6 percent
of the total aid of the forty-four largest U.S. PVOs
(see Table 6.1, column 3).

## Institution and Network Builders

The other ten U.S. PVOs I interviewed all emphasized in their mission definition the creation and
enhancement of indigenous private institutions in
developing countries that address priorities as they
define them. Some of the older relief agencies, such
as CWS and LWR, are de-emphasizing food and other
material aid and placing more efforts on supporting
with cash local private groups in developing coun-
tires--church-affiliated as well as some secular
community organizations--who are identifying problems
and addressing them with collective action.[7] Save the
Children Federation and Foster Parents Plan USA no
longer give support for individual children abroad, but
rather contribute money to grass-roots organizations
that are carrying out multidimensional and integrated
strategies to improve the educational, health, nutritional and sanitational facilities in communities
where children live, especially in rural areas.[8] The
Rockefeller and Ford Foundations also stress institution building--Rockefeller traditionally stressing
university facilities and research institutions, and
Ford more recently rural community organizations and
human rights action and research groups.[9] Oxfam
America and the Unitarian Universalist Service Committee (UUSC) both give support to new local or regional
private development institutions.[10] Coordination in
Development (CODEL) and Private Agencies Collaborating
Together (PACT)--both of which are federations of
several PVOs--give priority to strengthening local
community organizations that give low-income groups
an opportunity to take charge of their own destiny and
to have greater voice in critical decisions affecting
their lives.[11]
Many of these indigenous Third World institutions
(most of whom are PVOs themselves) administer or
contribute to grass-roots projects that are production
or technically oriented--agricultural and marketing
cooperatives, prefabricated housing construction,
training of paramedical personnel, etc. The emphasis

in the minds of U.S. PVOs, however, is not so much on
the transfer of technology to individual projects but
on supporting the emergence and expansion of indigenous
institutions that can initiate and carry out a whole
range of activities identified as priorities by their
recipient groups. These U.S. PVOs see their major
innovative thrust as promoting PVO counterparts in the
Third World that dispel isolation and hopelessness
among the poor and mobilize them for collective action.
Moreover, many of the projects carried out by these
local counterpart institutions abroad are in the area
of consciousness raising, such as women's solidarity
groups, literacy training, and adult education.

Some of the U.S. PVOs--such as CWS and UUSC--
also support network building and information exchange
among the various indigenous institutions they support
abroad. This often takes the form of sponsoring meetings of such groups from several countries in a region
to share information and strategies on community organization building.

Four other U.S. PVOs, which were not interviewed,
also belong to this third category of "institution
and network builders." They include the American
Friends Service Committee, the Asia Foundation, the
Domestic and Foreign Society of the Protestant Epis-
copal Church, and the National Board of YMCAs. Their
combined resources in 1981-82 amounted to $85.9 million.
Together with the other ten institution and network
builders the total resources amounted to $230.6 million
in 1982-82, or 19.4 percent of the total resources of
the forty-four largest U.S. PVOs (see Table 6.1,
column 3).

All ten of the U.S. PVOs I interviewed in this
category ranked very high as their organizational goals
items 4 and 5 on my list--namely building new community-
run institutions and networks, and enhancing recipient
bargaining power vis-a-vis local merchants, credit
institutions, government agencies, etc. Several of the
twenty-one representatives interviewed from these ten
U.S. PVOs commented on how these two goals fit togeth-
er--namely, the creation of private participatory
structures among the poor would lead to an enhancement
of their bargaining position with other important
social and economic groups or institutions that can
assist them.

Of the thirty-one persons I interviewed in all
fifteen U.S. PVOs, however, only three listed the
last item--empowerment of the poor to challenge and
change the dominant political and economic structures
in their environment--as the most important objective
of their organization. Moreover, all three were from
the same PVO--PACT.

It is not very surprising that respondents from

the first two clusters of PVOs--the three that are
assistential (CRS, CARE USA, SAWS), and the two that
are technically oriented (AITEC and PADF)--would not
rank empowerment high on their list of priorities given
their narrower focus. Of the eight persons prioritizing
objectives from these five PVOs, five ranked empowerment last, one listed it fifth, and two explicitly
rejected it as having any importance as an organizational objective.

What is interesting, however, is that persons in
the ten U.S. PVOs in category three--institution and
network building--ranked empowerment quite low as a
stated goal. Of the thirteen persons interviewed from
these organizations who prioritized the six goals,
two ranked it last, two placed it fifth, and two
explicitly rejected it as a goal. Only two ranked it
second, two placed it third, and three (all from PACT)
listed it first. Hence, only among five of these ten
PVOs did respondents rate "empowerment of the poor to
challenge the dominant political and economic structures in their environment" within the top three goals
of their organizations.

It would seem that such an objective might be
considered closely associated with the enhancement of
the bargaining power of the poor vis-a-vis local
economic and governmental institutions in their area.
U.S. PVOs on the whole, however, shun empowerment as
an explicit objective. Some respondents told me they
don't speak about this in their literature, but
believe that by strengthening local community organizations this will occur eventually as a spinoff.
Others simply rejected it as having no place in the
scope of activities of a foreign nonprofit organization operating in a developing country.

## Canadian PVOs

Canadian PVOs (who sent nearly $200 million over-
seas in 1981-82--or about one-seventh of the U.S.
total) tend to cluster very much in category 2 (technical aid) and 3 (institution and network building), with
much less emphasis on assistential work than their U.S.
counterparts. Of the $171.6 million sent abroad by
thirty-four of the largest Canadian PVOs in 1981-82,
only $42.4 million (24.7 percent) was predominantly
for relief-type aid (see Table 6.2, column 1)--as
opposed to 63 percent of U.S. PVO resources. Canadian
PVOs spent $33.3 million (or 19.4 percent of total PVO
resources) for technically oriented projects abroad
(see Table 6.2, column 2)--proportionately slightly
more than the total U.S. PVO aid in this category
(17.6 percent). In the area of institution and

TABLE 6.2
Resources and Percentages Received From the Canadian Government by the 34 Largest Canadian Transnational PVOs (1981-1982)

Total Resources: $171.6 million
Resources from Government: $59.8 million (34.8%)

Column 1

Predominantly Relief

| PVO | Resources | % Government |
|---|---|---|
| Canadian Red Cross | $12.0 mil | 61.6% |
| USC Canada | 5.0 mil | 23.9 |
| World Vision | 15.8 mil | 9.9 |
| International Child Care/Canada | 1.3 mil | 9.6 |
| Leprosy Relief (Canada) | 2.2 mil | 9.1 |
| Compassion of Canada | 2.1 mil | 7.3 |
| Christian Children's Fund of Canada | 4.0 mil | .5 |
| TOTALS | $42.4 mil | 22.4% |

24.7% of total PVO resources
15.9% of total government aid

TABLE 6.2
(continued)

## Column 2

### Predominantly Technical

| PVO | Resources | % Government |
|-----|-----------|--------------|
| Canadian Executive Service Overseas | $2.1 mil | 95.2% |
| Cooperative Development Foundation of Canada | 1.7 mil | 89.2 |
| Canadian Hunger Foundation | .6 mil | 78.9 |
| Mennonite Central Committee | 6.1 mil | 67.1 |
| Canadian Teachers' Federation | 1.4 mil | 48.5 |
| Foundation for International Training | 1.3 mil | 45.3 |
| Food for the Hungry/Canada | 1.6 mil | 44.4 |
| Canadian ORT | 1.9 mil | 35.9 |
| CARE Canada | 6.1 mil | 35.8 |
| Canadian UNICEF Committee | 7.6 mil | 35.5 |
| International Medical Assistance | 1.9 mil | 25.6 |
| OXFAM-Quebec | 1.0 mil | 15.3 |
| | | |
| TOTALS | $33.3 mil | 47.8% |

19.4% of total PVO resources
26.6% of total government aid

TABLE 6.2
(continued)

Column 3

Multiservice Institution and Network Building

| PVO | Resources | % Government |
|---|---|---|
| World University Service | $ 2.8 mil | 90.4% |
| Canadian Labour Congress | 1.1 mil | 81.5 |
| Interchurch Fund for International Development | 1.8 mil | 74.7 |
| Inter Pares | .6 mil | 57.4 |
| Canadian Lutheran World Relief | 3.0 mil | 54.3 |
| OXFAM Canada | .9 mil | 53.6 |
| Canadian Catholic Organization for Development and Peace | 14.7 mil | 46.5 |
| National Council of YMCA's of Canada | 2.4 mil | 43.3 |
| SUCO | 9.9 mil | 42.2 |
| CUSO | 24.1 mil | 37.4 |
| Anglican Church of Canada | 2.4 mil | 28.6 |
| CANSAVE Children | 2.8 mil | 28.1 |
| Overseas Book Centre | 5.2 mil | 17.3 |
| United Church of Canada | 5.7 mil | 13.1 |
| Foster Parents Plan of Canada | 18.5 mil | 12.4 |
| TOTALS | $95.9 mil | 35.9% |

55.9% of total PVO resources
57.5% of total government aid

Source: Canadian Council for International Cooperation (CCIC), Directory of Canadian Nongovernmental Organizations Engaged in International Development (Ottawa: CCIC, 1982).

network building, however, Canadian PVOs proportionately
far outstripped their U.S. counterparts. The thirty-
four largest Canadian PVOs dedicated 55.9 percent of
their resources to this objective (see Table 6.2 , column
3), as compared to only 19.4 percent by the forty-four
largest U.S. PVOs in 1981-82. Hence, in category 2
(technical aid) the proportions are close, but in
categories 1 (relief) and 3 (enhancement of institutions and networks) the Canadian and U.S. PVO proportions are practically mirror images of one another.
    Moreover, many of the Canadian PVOs in category 3
also link empowering the poor in developing countries
with supporting participatory institutions and networks
that enhance bargaining power. Of the nine persons
interviewed from seven different Canadian PVOs, six
ranked their organization's priorities and four of the
six listed bargaining enhancement, institution building
and political and economic empowerment as the top
three priorities of their respective institutions.
Spokespersons for Canadian Catholic Organization for
Development and Peace (CCODP), Canadian University
Service Overseas (CUSO), Service Universitaire
Canadien Outre-Mer (SUCO), and Oxfam Canada all
mentioned social justice or more equitable distribution
of resources as central to their notion of development,
and conversely that poverty was a structural problem
caused by a denial of power to low-income sectors by
those with wealth both in developing countries and in
the North Atlantic region.[12]
    According to Richard J. Harmston, former Executive
Director of the Canadian Council for International
Cooperation (CCIC), some of the largest Canadian PVOs--
such as CCODP and CUSO--unlike their counterparts in
the U.S., do not emphasize relief but rather a liber-
ationist or solidarity approach to development by
supporting those Third World institutions and networks dedicated to enhancing the political and economic
power of the poor.[13]

## Mission to Home Country: Influencing Public Opinion

    Another major difference between Canadian and
U.S. PVOs is how they define their missions to their
respective home populations. Canadian PVOs, much more
so than their U.S. counterparts, since 1968 have
considered a large part of their work to be educating
the Canadian public about the causes of underdevelopment abroad and encouraging Canadians to support
activities with peoples in the Third World, including
the establishment of networks of communication, inter-
cultural exhanges, and pressure on governments.
From 2 to 20 percent of the total budget of Canadian
PVOs supporting programs overseas is now allocated to

this education/advocacy function at home (CCODP, for
example, allocates 10 percent of its resources and
fifteen full-time staff to this activity).  Moreover,
the Canadian International Development Agency (CIDA)--
the foreign aid arm of the Canadian government--through
its Public Participation Program (initiated in 1971)
now allocates nearly $6 million annually for develop-
ment education by PVOs (as compared to $1 million by
AID).

Materials (including books, study guides, brochures, flyers, and film strips) are prepared by PVOs
and distributed throughout Canada via their own
regional offices or learning centers (partially funded
by the government), and to schools, churches, unions,
cooperatives, and community groups.  The content
includes basic information about living conditions in
developing countries with an attempt to show how these
conditions are affected by decisions made in Canada.
Sometimes these materials are explicitly political
in their analysis and orientation, and condemn specific
policies such as Canadian and U.S. government support
for some repressive Third World regimes, arms sales
to developing countries, and some overseas investment
and employment practices of multinational corporations.
Such materials often recommend specific action to
readers, such as letter-writing campaigns to governments and boycotts of targeted companies' products.[14]

Some Canadian government policy makers have criticized such activities for being political activism,
rather than education, saying that they reach only 10
to 15 percent of PVO constituents who are politically
aware and committed rather than the majority who need
a more nonthreatening and less demanding educational
approach.[15]  Others in the PVO community itself are
wary of such a political emphasis, since they believe
insufficient evaluation of its impact has been done
and that it does not promote fund raising.[16]

An evaluation of development education in 1981
conducted by the CCIC, however, while acknowledging
certain weaknesses in PVO educational programs (e.g.,
over-emphasis on school children and not enough
attention to businessmen and parliamentarians), stated
that there have also been solid results over the thirteen year history of these efforts in Canada.  The
report concluded that millions have been reached
directly or indirectly, that values such as equity,
cooperation, solidarity, and social justice have made
a breakthrough into public consciousness to varying
degrees, that the number of Canadian private organizations involved in international cooperation is on
the rise, that private donations and public subsidies
to international PVOs (most with development education
programs) have substantially increased, that "letters

132

to the editor" in newspapers concerning development
and world problems are growing, and that the media
are calling upon PVO development educators to obtain
information or analysis concerning international
events.[17]
    Only two of the fifteen U.S. PVOs in my survey
have given attention to this type of development education prevalent in many Canadian organizations--Oxfam
America, and the UUSC.  Oxfam prepares and distributes
brochures and films among its 3,000 affiliate groups
in the United States that include critiques of policies
of various governments and businesses (e.g., impact
audits of policies of the El Salvadoran and Guatemalan
governments), and advocate changes in U.S. policy
towards developing countries (e.g., no military aid
for Central America).[18]  The UUSC for the past several
years has been organizing bipartisan congressional
fact-finding trips to Central America to raise governmental and public consciousness as to the continued
repression being perpetrated by some governments in
the region receiving U.S. military and economic aid.
The UUSC distributes findings from these trips to its
8,000 member-contributors and publicizes them in the
media.[19]  Currently the UUSC is widening participants
on these trips to representatives from business, aca-
demia, the professions, and the media.
    No other U.S. PVO I interviewed engages in such
types of education/advocacy activities.  Several
respondents from the other thirteen U.S. PVOs told
me they provide general information about development
projects as part of their fund-raising materials and in
annual reports.  Some said the approach taken by
Canadian and some European PVOs was too controversial
and would not work in the United States.[20] Others claimed
a concrete picture of undernourished children is more
powerful than verbally explaining abstract structural
issues.[21]  One said that a letter from a child overseas whose community an American has helped is more
educational than all the books and articles on development.[22]
    A spokesman for CRS in charge of community edu-
cation and awareness told me:

    U.S. people respond better to appeals to the
    heart than to the head.  CRS has gotten a lot
    of negative feedback from individual donors
    when we have tried to make them aware of the
    deeper structural causes of injustice in Central
    America.  They have bought Reagan's argument
    that we have to stop Communism there.[23]

    These responses are typical of the majority of
U.S. PVOs--relief-oriented, technical supporters, as

well as institution and network builders. Development
education in terms of systemic analysis of deeper political and economic causes of poverty (some of which
are located at home) along with advocacy for specific
changes in current home government and business
policies has not thus far been a central part of U.S.
PVO objectives.[24]

Hence, among North American PVOs--U.S. and
Canadian--there is a great deal of variety in goals.
Although all use the rhetoric of a BHN or an ADS
approach, this means very different things in practice
among PVOs. Several of the larger and older PVOs
which are U.S.-based continue to work predominantly
with effects of poverty and rely heavily on traditional
means, such as food aid--although claiming to use it
in a new way--but now include as a minor part of their
activities some technical assistance. A whole new
generation of smaller PVOs tends to focus exclusively
on the strictly technical and resource multiplication
aspects of development. A third group (including
some older and some newer PVOs) emphasizes the building
of new private development institutions, community
organizations and networks carrying out a multiplicity
of self-chosen projects in both technical and
consciousness-raising areas. Finally, there are a
significant number of PVOs (predominantly in Canada)
who define development not only as institution and
network building, but as also including political and
economic empowerment of the poor. As a consequence
they support liberation movements abroad and challenge
some dominant governmental and business institutions
at home supportive of economic and political elites
in the Third World.


POLITICAL CHARACTER AND CONSEQUENCES

Despite the differences between U.S. and Canadian
PVOs over whether "empowerment of the poor to challenge
the dominant political and economic structures in
their environment" is an explicit goal of their agencies, I found a considerable consensus among all twenty-
two PVOs regarding the political implications of their
work. Respondents from only seven of the twenty-two
PVOs in my survey (six of whom are relief or technically oriented) said they believed that a strictly
apolitical stance was desirable and feasible--five
from the U.S. (CRS, CARE USA, Save the Children
Federation, AITEC and PADF), and one from Canada
(CARE Canada). Representatives in the other fifteen
PVOs (all institution and network builders)--nine from
the U.S. and six from Canada--said some political
impact of PVO activities overseas was inevitable.

The most common reason given by respondents in every one of the relief and technically oriented PVOs in my survey for opting for a strictly apolitical position was so that their organizations could operate in all types of regimes. They claimed that the alleviation of immediate suffering or the building of a technical base to improve the lot of the poor could, and should, go on regardless of the ideology of a particular government, and that their respective organizations work in all types of circumstances to achieve this.

George F. Kraus, the former Regional Program Officer for Latin America in CARE USA, stated this position as follows:

> I did not support Pinochet's philosophy in Chile, or that of the generals in La Paz, Bolivia, but CARE can do its work on technical grounds-- e.g., water projects--and work in any type of regime for the long-range good of the people.[25]

John P. Grant, Former Director for Latin America of Save the Children Federation (the only PVO in category three in my survey which opted for an apolitical stance), expressed his organization's position this way:

> We are apolitical according to our status. We are also trying to work in a variety of political environments. There are frequent political fluctuations in Latin America. We have to be apolitical so as to survive in rapidly changing contexts.[26]

Among all the other fifteen PVOs in my survey (who defined themselves primarily as institution and network promoters), an apolitical position was seen as practically impossible in their work overseas. Everyone of the twenty-five respondents from these fifteen organizations, however, distinguished between a political position, which they considered unavoidable given the nature of their work, and a partisan political position, which they felt was harmful and which they claimed to avoid assiduously.

All the U.S. and Canadian respondents in this group of PVOs indicated that building new, or strengthening existing, private institutions serving the poor had political implications with a "small p" since, when these institutions were effective, they would lead to a redistribution of power in society-- economic and political--in favor of their participants. One U.S. PVO spokesperson said that participation of people in decision making (a requirement his PVO

demands of its Third World receipient groups) is at
times political since it is based on an option for
democracy, and some governments are against this.[27]
Another U.S. representative acknowledged that PVOs have
a liberal bias in that they encourage participation
and collective action in addressing the causes of
poverty, and this, he said, is a political ideology.[28]
A Canadian stated that his PVO is political in the
sense that it attempts to "affect the distribution of
economic and political power in Latin America in favor
of the poor."[29]

All of these PVO spokespersons who acknowledged
the political implications of their work, however,
indicated that their organizations had a policy of not
giving aid to Third World groups closely tied to any
one political party or tendency. Such assistance,
many argued, would undermine their credibility among
the broad range of their recipients abroad, would
create serious problems with Third World governments,
and upset their donors at home.

Several indicated that at times the overseas
groups they supported had a political orientation but
not an explicit tie to, or control by, a political
party or movement. A spokesperson for PACT said that
"we support a development process even if associated
with a political tendency," provided that the
recipient organization is not part of a political
party or movement.[30] Another from CWS emphatically
ruled out any support for groups closely identified
with parties, but stated that "a progressive political
position can be maintained by working with groups
seeking structural change."[31] A representative of LWR
acknowledged that the "majority of indigenous agencies
we support in Latin America are in opposition to the
policies of those in power," but if they are part of
a political organization, movement or party they
receive no aid.[32] A person in CCODP said that this
organization absolutely rules out assistance to
specific parties, but that it does give aid to those
who are among the broad front of groups working for
progressive changes favoring the poor.[33]

While the arguments defending the positions of
both groups of PVOs--those seven opting for a clearly
apolitical stance, and those fifteen defending a
political, but nonparty-affiliated stance--are clear,
concrete realities may not always reflect such rhetorical positions. There is some evidence indicating
that strictly relief and technical activities cannot
easily be divorced from political implications, and
factors in some developing societies also prevent a
clear division between politically "progressive" and
"partisan" action--especially in the eyes of those with
the dominant economic and political power.

## The Feasibility of an Apolitical Position

Rev. Msgr. Roland Bordelon, CRS Director for South America, admitted that, while on the level of intention it is necessary and possible for a relief-oriented PVO to have an apolitical position, in the order of implementation it is very difficult. He stated that:

> As soon as you accept a dollar from a government--whether it be Sweden, Canada or the U.S.--there is a political tinge. As soon as you work under approval from a host government, e.g., Chile or Peru--there will always be a little political tinge.[34]

CRS participated from 1975 through 1978 in the Minimum Employment Program (PEM) of the Chilean government by contributing food packages destined for workers in partial payment for their labor in public works projects. This program, however, has been highly exploitative of workers in that it has not paid them the legal minimum wage and has also used such laborers in productive (not merely marginal) jobs, thus replacing many full-time public employees. Moreover, none of the PEM laborers receive social security or health care, nor are they guaranteed work on anything more permanent than a day-to-day basis. In the perspective of most Chileans, PEM has not been a service to the poor but one more manipulative instrument of the government against them.[35]

CRS participated in PEM for three years largely for political reasons. Groups within Chile brought pressure to bear on AID (CRS' single most important benefactor), convincing U.S. government officials that PEM was a step toward alleviating unemployment and hunger in Chile in 1975. AID, in turn, urged officials of CRS in New York to contribute some PL 480 food to PEM despite some internal reservations on the part of the CRS staff. The Chilean Catholic Church's local affiliate of CRS, Cáritas, acted as the local conduit of the food packages for PEM. Many Chileans in the working classes were scandalized by this very ambiguous and political action by local and international agencies of the Church, and saw it as furthering the Chilean junta's exploitative policies. CRS and Cáritas withdrew from PEM in 1978, not because of the moral or political implications of PEM, but because AID no longer considered Chile a priority area for its Food for Peace program and thus reduced its PL 480 programs in that country.[36]

Other large U.S. PVOs also have difficulty in staying free of politics. While representatives in CARE USA, for example, indicated to me that their

organization takes an apolitical stance, the reality
in some cases may be otherwise. Thomas Kines, National
Director of CARE Canada, in assessing the position of
his U.S. counterpart, felt there is at times a definite
political orientation in the decisions of CARE USA:

> The U.S. branch of CARE is most sensitive to
> what the U.S. government wants. When we meet in
> New York to discuss worldwide CARE projects, some-
> times when we seem to agree that CARE should not
> pursue some projects on technical grounds, the
> New York directors say, "Wait a minute. AID wants
> us in there. Get AID on the phone right now and
> let's talk to them about this."
> When this happens I get angry since CARE USA
> claims to be nonpolitical.[37]

In both of these specific instances the image and
choices of the two PVOs involved (CRS and CARE USA)
were influenced by a factor discussed in other chapters
of this book--namely, reliance on government subsidies.
In 1981-82, over two-thirds (68.8 percent) of CRS'
total resources came from the U.S. government, and
public subsidies or contracts constituted over three-
quarters (77.8 percent) of CARE USA's budget (see
Table 6.1, column 1). It is simply impossible for U.S.
PVOs under such conditions to avoid some identification
with the U.S. government in the eyes of recipients
overseas and inclusion of AID preferences in decision
making in home offices about their own global priorities. A problem arises, however, when, as other contributors to this volume have suggested, such identification in image or in fact with home government foreign
policies significantly undermines a PVO's credibility,
as well as ability to respond to Third World needs as
these are articulated by its partner and recipient
groups abroad.

In 1981-82 80 percent of U.S. government aid to
the largest forty-four PVOs went to nine organizations
who are predominantly relief-oriented (see Table 6.1,
column 1) because food aid and related subsidies constitute the great bulk of U.S. governmental assistance
to the nonprofit sector in foreign aid. However, many
of the smaller technical, institution and network
building PVOs are also heavily dependent on federal
aid in the form of cash subsidies and contracts (see
Table 1, columns 2 and 3). In fact, fourteen out of
the thirty-four PVOs in Table 6.1 listed in the
latter two categories depended on AID for 40 percent or
more of their income in 1981-82.

Among the twenty-four persons I interviewed from
all eleven U.S. PVOs in my survey that receive some
form of U.S. government aid, twenty indicated that

there were serious limits on their organizations'
overseas credibility or freedom of choice resulting
from such assistance.  Several mentioned that their
institutions had decided to forego the use of such
assistance in Central America in recent years so as
not to appear identified with U.S. foreign policy
objectives in that region and thus lose the confidence
of many in need they were trying to help in the area.
Twenty of the twenty-four indicated that their organizational freedom was impaired as a consequence of
government support.  The U.S. State Department had
forbidden them from using public subsidies in countries
it politically blacklisted in Latin America--not merely
Cuba but also post-revolutionary Nicaragua, and pre-
invasion Grenada.  AID also had an additional list of
country priorities (based on aggregate per capita
income data) where it wanted PVOs to use the bulk of
its funds, but this excluded many middle-income
countries of the Americas where PVOs are active among
the majority of the population that still remains very
poor--Mexico, Colombia, Venezuela, Brazil, Argentina,
and Chile.

Finally, thirteen of those twenty indicated that
at one time or another AID had pressured them to
support, or not support, specific projects, and several
believed this was due primarily to political objectives
of the U.S. State Department.  When such wishes of AID
clearly went beyond a PVO's own criteria for project
selection (acknowledged in the terms of the AID grant
itself)--for example, projects were technically weak,
or did not involve local recipients sufficiently in
design or operation--the  PVO could successfully fend
off such pressures.  At other times, however, there
was nothing a PVO could do but to comply--e.g., when
AID had earmarked its PL 480 food aid for certain
countries, or even specific areas of one country, due
to the political or military importance those areas
had for U.S. foreign policy interests.

Hence, it would appear that for a PVO that
receives significant U.S. governmental aid to claim it
has an apolitical character is not always accurate.
Both its image and choices are at times shaped by the
objectives of U.S. foreign policy.[38]


## The Costs of "Progressive but Nonpartisan" Politics

There is also evidence that the distinction made
by many PVOs between desirable progressive political
positions and undesirable, and avoidable, partisan
political identifications is  at times too facile.  The
context in many developing countries makes it very hard
to realize such verbal divisions in the concrete due to

politically polarized environments. Choices have to
be made, and in the eyes of elites in such divided
societies actions even indirectly affecting the distribution of resources will be looked upon as politically partisan.
Dr. Laurence Stifel, Vice-President and Secretary
of the Rockefeller Foundation and Director of its
former Education for Development Program, stated the
problem as follows:

> We do not aim to take a partisan political
> stand, but certain projects we support overseas
> are seen as such by some groups in host
> countries. Family planning programs are con-
> sidered to be cultural imperialism by some
> people. Our emphasis in improving the skills
> and production of small farmers is seen by
> large landholders as partisan politics. We also
> try to work with reformist groups in government--
> this can be perceived as biased by conservative
> political groups. In education, some intellec-
> tuals consider us too conservative and represen-
> tative of the interests of the established powers.
> We sometimes, therefore, get criticized by both
> sides of the political spectrum.[39]

This is quite understandable given the entrenched
interests in countries where there are wide divisions
between rich and poor and where any attempt to close
such a gap is termed partisan politics by those with
privilege. It sometimes, however, involves much more
than distorted perceptions, or partisanship being in
the "eye of the beholder". Serious consequences can
and do occur when actions are interpreted as being
partisan, and people have been known to lose their
lives in projects not intended to appear partisan by
foreign PVOs who supported them.
Oxfam UK in Oxford, England acknowledged in its
1981 annual report that many of the participants in
the self-help projects it has assisted in El Salvador
have been killed or missing:

> Eighteen months ago, Oxfam was involved in
> supporting nine projects in El Salvador. They
> were unremarkable in Oxfam terms--health and
> education programmes, agricultural development
> among peasant farmers, a legal aid surgery and
> self-help housing projects.
> Today, virtually all of them are in abeyance,
> or have been completely destroyed. Some have
> changed their form to survive and deal with the
> emergency.
> In April (1980) Oxfam's Central American

field staff reported that 17 Salvadoreans who
had worked on Oxfam-supported projects in El
Salvador had been killed by the Army or by
government-controlled paramilitary forces, and
that upwards of 300 people who had benefited in
one way or another from the projects were dead
or missing.

Up until the end of the year, our Central
American Field Directors had asked for restraint
in reporting the mounting toll of death and
disappearances.  They feared publicity might
endanger people still engaged in the projects.

They released the figures in April (1981)
believing that an international outcry might be
the only method of stopping the slaughter of
innocent victims.[40]

Despite the fact that many PVO representatives in
my survey--especially from Canada--felt very proud of
the fact that their organization was working to
empower the poor, and insisted that they took a
progressive but nonpartisan political stance in
selecting groups and projects to support overseas, only
one person in the forty I interviewed expressed a
similar concern as Oxfam UK in this cited report
regarding the consequences of PVO actions on the lives
of recipients in the Third World.  Laurence Simon,
Director of Policy Analysis in Oxfam America, indicated
that political impact on recipients must always be
taken into account when a PVO decides upon any significant public action abroad or at home:

Formation of a cooperative can often be an
overtly  political act.  We must anticipate the
consequences...We found in our impact audit of
Guatemala that the most direct targets for assas-
sination were persons active in rural development
projects funded by both AID and private nonprofit
organizations.  Funders must be more cognizant
of this.  Therefore, PVOs  are not nonpartisan
without qualifications.

We feel we must speak out in the U.S. when
U.S. economic or political policies negatively
affect the recipients of our aid overseas--
especially when our recipients overseas so
request us to speak out (e.g., on the impact of
U.S. military assistance).

Sometimes, however, we avoid a public stance
here for fear of hurting our recipients.  These
costs have to be weighed.[41]

This kind of weighing and sifting of the actual
political repercussions of an organization's actions

regardless of its intentions would appear to be absolutely essential, and undoubtedly does go on within
many U.S. and Canadian PVOs who work overseas.  It is
interesting, however, that only one of the forty whom
I interviewed in North American PVOs mentioned this
as an important problem in deciding the political character of their organizations.

I discovered no evidence during my interviews nor
in examination of documentary materials in PVO offices
to justify accusations made during early 1983 in
Reader's Digest, the Washington Times, and on the 60
Minutes CBS-TV program that PVOs support "Marxist-
Leninist" movements overseas or provide aid to armed
revolutionary groups.[42]  Some of the same groups
attacked in these communications media--such as CWS,
CRS, and Oxfam America--were also involved in my own
survey, and I find such attacks unfounded and
irresponsible.

However, I did sense a certain uncritical reflection among respondents in my survey who did not
acknowledge the politically partisan implications of
their organizations' actions, especially when these
even indirectly threaten those with economic privilege
in the Third World.  In the realm of power struggles
which these institution and network building PVOs
cannot avoid, neat verbal distinctions often do not
hold true.  People can pay with their lives in one
country for something that in another context would be
considered an acceptable course of action to solve a
problem.


Political Advocacy at Home

A final dimension of political character--and
where U.S. and Canadian PVOs again differ consider-
ably--is the issue of whether or not PVOs attempt to
influence the policies of their own home governments.
Of the fifteen U.S. PVOs in my survey, representatives
in nine said that their organizations do try to affect
or change the politics of the U.S. government.  However, persons in six of the nine PVOs all gave as
examples actions taken individually or collectively to
influence only those government policies directly
affecting their specific activities--e.g., AID grants
to PVOs, PL 480 food levels and regulations, waivers
for PVOs on AID country priorities, AID efforts to
oversee PVO activities, getting a share of the Caribbean Basin Initiative (CBI) money to be channelled
through PVOs.  Representatives in only three U.S.
PVOs--CWS, Oxfam America, and UUSC--indicated that
their agencies try to influence aspects of U.S. foreign
policy going beyond their own specific organizational

operations--e.g., the lifting of U.S. government
economic embargoes against Cuba and Vietnam (CWS), the
establishment of more equitable U.S. immigration
policies for Haitian refugees (CWS), and the curtail-
ment of U.S. military aid to El Salvador and Guatemala (Oxfam and UUSC). All three of these U.S. PVOs
admitted, however, that their advocacy efforts in both
Congress and the executive branch have not been effective as yet in changing U.S. government policies on
any of these issues.[43]

Representatives in six of the seven Canadian PVOs
I interviewed, however, not only acknowledged that
part of their political thrust was to impact on Canadian government policies but in every case the examples
given were broad issues not relating only to CIDA-
PVO relationships. These included trying to get the
Canadian government to renew official aid to Cuba
(CUSO), Vietnam, and Kampuchea (CCIC), pressuring CIDA
to provide assistance to Nicaragua after the 1979
revolution (CCODP), urging parliamentary restrictions
on Canadian trade with South Africa (CCODP), insis-
ting that the Ministry of External Affairs take a
more independent stance from U.S. foreign policy
towards Central America (Oxfam Canada) and Namibia
(CCIC), advocating that the Canadian government do
something about political prisoners in Guatemala
(SUCO), asking the Prime Minister that import duties
on certain goods from Tanzania aimed at saving a
handful of Canadian jobs at Exxon be lifted (Inter
Pares), and petitioning the government to place more
emphasis on basic needs and human rights in its
foreign aid programs (CCIC).[44]

While in several instances spokespersons from
these Canadian PVOs acknowledged that success had been
only marginal or not forthcoming, they also pointed
to some cases where the government changed its policies
after PVOs exerted direct pressure--the sending of
Canadian government grain to Nicaragua as well as
contributions to its literacy campaign; the lifting
of import duties on the Tanzanian goods; the expres-
sion of concern for Guatemalan political prisoners by
the Canadian ambassador.[45]

While there have been no adverse reactions as of
yet to such political advocacy positions taken by PVOs
in relation to Canadian government policy, some believe
that Canadian tax laws could in the future be used to
limit such activities. The Canadian Charities Act
prohibits tax-exempt organizations from engaging in
political activities, including lobbying to influence
government policies. The language is vague but broad,
and some feel that Revenue Canada could interpret the
lobbying clause more strictly and thus remove tax
exempt privileges for some PVOs that attempt to

influence Canadian foreign policy.  CCIC has spoken
out, in fact, on the need to make the wording of the
law more precise, but to date no change has occurred.[46]
Interestingly, this concern among Canadian PVOs
about their independence being threatened by political
advocacy is also now shared by many U.S. PVOs regarding
their own situation in the United States.  Although few
PVOs engaged in overseas activities try to influence
U.S. foreign policy to the same degree as their
Canadian counterparts, many domestic service oriented
U.S. PVOs do engage in concerted efforts to influence
government welfare policies.  In January 1983 the
Office of Management and Budget (OMB) in the Office
of the President issued a circular (A-122) adding new
restrictions on political advocacy.  It demanded that
all recipients of federal funds separate their
advocacy functions from their service programs or
lose government grants.  It also broadened the definition of political advocacy by tax-exempt nonprofit
organizations beyond that used by the Internal Revenue
Service to include practically every form of participation in the governmental decision-making process.[47]
OMB withdrew the circular in March 1983 in face of
strong united opposition by 250 domestic and foreign-
oriented PVOs, joined by several military contractors
and commercial organizations doing business with the
government whose use of federal funds would have been
curtailed as well by the directive.  Subsequently,
after much discussion with government contractors in
the business community and a relaxation of many of the
accounting burdens they were subject to before the
A-122 controversy orginated, in November 1983 OMB
issued a new set of proposed restrictions on lobbying
by all of the private sector.  Although some of the
limitations disagreeable to the nonprofits were
removed (strict separation of advocacy and program
functions, use of federal funds to offer advice to
Congress not explicitly requested in writing), other
activities involving federal funds continued to be
ruled out--e.g., several forms of information gathering
and constituency education regarding Congressional
actions.  Moreover, the recent proposals also seek to
establish OMB and each government agency as the arbiter
as to what constitutes legitimate advocacy activities
by tax-exempt groups even beyond the detailed definitions of lobbying in the U.S. tax code.[48]
Hence, the whole realm of what constitutes permissible politics by a PVO is currently ambiguous.
Intentions to avoid politics completely cannot be
actualized consistently by North American PVOs that
receive federal aid, and decisions made in home
offices can sometimes contribute to unforseen and
dire partisan political consequences for recipients

abroad. Moreover, while transnational Canadian PVOs
attempt to play a more active role in shaping some of
the foreign policy decisions of their government than
do U.S. PVOs, in both countries the PVOs are vulnerable
to actual or potential government efforts to narrow
the definition of permissible lobbying by tax-exempt
organizations.

## PROOF OF EFFECTIVENESS

Among the respondents in my survey--both in PVOs
and in government agencies subsidizing PVO activities
abroad (AID and CIDA)--it was acknowledged that to date
U.S. and Canadian PVOs have not developed adequate
evaluation techniques to assess the overall impact of
the programs they support abroad.  There were several
reasons given for this:

1. There is insufficient time and a lack of
   adequate resources to conduct thorough
   evaluations;
2. It is hard to evaluate small-scale projects
   with standard techniques designed for large
   problems--e.g., the log-matrix method used
   in AID;
3. It is difficult to assess many of the most
   important but intangible results of PVO
   efforts in development--e.g., the enhancement
   of attitudes of hope, self-esteem, and
   awareness among the poor;
4. Insistence on thorough evaluations undermines
   trust between donor PVOs and recipient groups
   and institutions in the Third World.

Several PVO representatives indicated that their
staffs were overcommitted with work, their resources
limited, and new project requests from Third World
groups constantly mounting.  They are able to get
financial audits and monitoring completed, but in-
depth evaluation of projects is much harder under such
circumstances.  Progress reports are required on a six-
month or annual basis by recipients, and staff persons
from the donor PVOs do make field visits at least once
a year to most projects and write up their own impres-
sions.  Occasionally an outside evaluator--from the
U.S., Canada, or the host country--will be brought in
to prepare an assessment, but this is not a regular
procedure.  Moreover, reports by recipients or PVOs
are frequently done in summary fashion and the information is uneven.  Some PVOs do not have separate
departments or offices for evaluation, while others
(CARE USA, SAWS, CUSO) have only recently created them.

Representatives from some PVOs--including CRS, CARE USA, PACT, Foster Parents Plan USA--acknowledged that they are able to generate impressive quantitative data from project reports--e.g., the number of people fed, children educated, wells dug, new loans offered, units of production increased, etc. However, they do not have methods of evaluating other and equally important issues less subject to statistical assessment, such as improvements in overall quality of life and world view of recipients, changes in power relations in the region, the possibilities for long-term continuity and replicability of projects--all of which are central to BHN or ADS approaches to development.

Moreover, in many PVOs there is no systematized internal learning process or feedback loop from past experiences to present and future decision making. Reports and memos are in files, but often there is no formal method of retrieving such information. Much remains unwritten in the personal consciousness of staff. "Institutional memory," according to one person, "has been staff continuity."[49] When staff changes occur, the memory is gone.

In addition, institution and network building by its very nature, according to several PVO spokespersons, requires trust. Insistence on thorough evaluations (especially when done by North Americans) can undermine this value. Dr. Richard Scobie, Executive Director of UUSC, remarked that, in general, UUSC has not made a systematic attempt to evaluate the impact of its network building in Central America and India since "emphasis is on building a trusting relationship" with Third World groups.[50] Rev. C. William Smith, Project Director for Central America, the Caribbean and Brazil in CCODP (the fourth largest Canadian PVO engaged in overseas aid), expressed a similar view:

> We rely on our network of contacts in a country
> at the beginning of the process in selecting
> projects to inform us of the political character
> of a new group--i.e., are they really for the
> poor? Once we have decided to fund, we ask for
> very little information during or after the
> project...We want to establish a partnership
> with these groups.[51]

Often in such circumstances self-evaluations are done by the recipient organizations of the projects they have carried out after completion. Frequently these do not follow any set pattern or methodology, or they answer only very general questions agreed upon by both recipients and donor organizations. Although these allow for much input by recipients and often serve as the basis for further funding, they do not provide in-depth and systematized analysis of the wider impact of projects on the local environment or the life-styles of the residents.

All of these reasons for a lack of standardized methods to judge the qualitative impact of PVO projects are cogent and understandable. Nevertheless, the unevenness of evaluations of PVO projects does not help to prove PVO claims that they are more effective than governmental agencies in certain areas of development assistance--e.g., innovation and replicability of techniques, extensive involvement of recipients in decision making, enhancement of the bargaining position of low-income sectors with other institutions in their environment. While such arguments are often used in fundraising efforts and requests for governmental support, there is insufficient evidence in current PVO evaluations to substantiate these claims solidly and consistently.

Dr. Judith Tendler's study in 1981 of seventy-five evaluations of PVO projects in AID files led her to the conclusion that such claims often cannot be proven with the methods used currently by PVO evaluators. Frequently these evaluations stressed (as mentioned by several PVO respondents in my own survey as well) quantifiable data while overlooking the qualitative issues. They also tend to be insular in their focus, since they rely predominantly for evidence on PVO staff or those directly involved in leadership positions in projects. There is little interviewing of nonleader beneficiaries, community members not participating in or benefiting from projects, other community organizations, or those working for government agencies in the same area. Nor is the experience of learning from development efforts by public sector organizations in the same services taken into account for comparative purposes. Tendler concludes that:

> ...Literature and knowledge is by and about PVO organizations, not about the world and the problems in which the project is taking place, or about the general class of problems being dealt with and the experience in dealing with them. Given the kinds of persons not interviewed, and the kinds of literature not cited, it is understandable that PVO evaluations do not give much of a feeling for the areas in which PVOs are innovative, the extent to which the decision-making processes they promote are participatory, and the extent to which their projects reach the poor.[52]

Some progress in PVO evaluation has been made in the past few years, in part due to pressure and subsidies by the U.S. and Canadian governments. AID since 1979 has funded a series of workshops on evaluation methods for PVOs (with forty or so PVOs participating) sponsored by the American Council of Voluntary Agencies for Foreign Service (ACVAFS). One outcome of these workshops has been the publication in 1983 of a book by ACVAFS aimed at helping PVOs significantly improve their project assessment techniques without mimicking evaluation methodologies of larger agencies not applicable for small-scale, grass-roots projects.[53]

In Canada CIDA now sometimes offers 10 percent extra cash for PVO projects to cover costs of evaluations. CIDA has also recently established an Office of Evaluation in its Special Programs Branch that will carry out itself, or contract, assessments of PVO projects subsidized with CIDA funds. Moreover, CCIC-- the umbrella agency of ninety Canadian PVOs--in recent years has been conducting three-day workshops for project officers of its member PVOs with outside professional evaluators.[54]

All of these are positive signs that U.S. and Canadian PVOs are now more interested in systematic evaluation of their overseas projects. Much improvement is needed, however, in this area. Moreover, it will require a sustained commitment of time and resources by PVOs to generate the kind of information needed to substantiate better their claims about solving generic development prob_ems in the areas of basic human needs more effectively than governments.


GOVERNANCE

## Decision Making

Decision making inside PVOs involves much input from the field. New projects are initiated not from home offices but from abroad, and almost universally start from private Third World institutions approaching a transnational PVO for support. Only two of the PVOs in my survey--CARE USA and PADF--said that they occasionally provide the impetus for a new project, and then it would be one of their field representatives, not the home office, who would suggest an idea to a Third World group.

Eight of the twenty-two PVOs have no field representatives stationed in Latin America--and three others have three or less to cover the whole region.[55] These PVOs rely heavily on field representatives from other PVOs (including contacts they already have in each country) to advise them on the merits of new proposals when they originate.

PVOs, however, after some input from their own

field representatives, those of other PVOs, or some
host-country groups, make final decisions about projects in their home offices in the U.S. or Canada--not
in the field nor in conjunction with Third World
representatives.  Usually headquarters' staffs have
authority to approve small projects ($5,000 to $25,000)
without going to the boards of directors.  The home-
office staffs also usually establish procedures for
project reports which field representatives and/or
recipient groups follow, but (as mentioned in the
previous section) these are in many instances flexible
and negotiable.

Hence, while projects normally start at the grass-
roots overseas and opinions are fed into headquarters
from abroad, no PVO in my survey has a decision-making
process which gives Third World groups a determinative
role as full partners in project selection.  The
discretion allowed to such overseas counterparts or
network members is in the reporting and evaluation
procedures, not in choices about allocation of
resources.

Third World PVOs are beginning to become uneasy
with what they consider a lack of real collaboration
with their North American counterparts who speak about
partnership but who continue to make the key decisions
about projects and funding allocations by themselves.
An appeal for more dialogue on what genuine partnership entails was made by Third World spokespersons at
a joint meeting of U.S. and Latin American PVOs
sponsored by the Advisory Council on Voluntary Foreign
Aid of AID in Jamaica in March 1983.[56]  The message of
several Latin American PVOs to their U.S. counterparts,
according to Paul Maguire of AID was that together
they must move beyond their past type of relationship
where North Atlantic PVOs are givers and Third World
PVOs are recipients.[57]

This feeling was also articulated by Tim Brodhead,
Director of Inter Pares and formerly Executive Director
of CCIC.  According to Brodhead, future collaboration
of North Atlantic and Third World PVOs will require
changes in how the former relate to the latter and
also how the former develop new roles at home:

I believe NGOs in the North Atlantic region are
in the twilight of their historical era.  They
began in the post-World War II era to bring money
and resources overseas, and they encountered
little resistance or critical challenge in foreign
countries.  Now, however, the Third World is
coming of age.  They have their own NGOs--and
these nonprofit organizations are especially well
developed in Latin America.  They want to be
treated as more equal partners, and also want to

know what North Atlantic NGOs are doing back home
to impact on attitudes, affect government and
business policies, and confront poverty and other
social problems. North Atlantic NGOs must be
ready to adapt to a new role abroad and at home if
they are to do something creative in the years
ahead.[58]

Thus, while overbearing paternalism does not seem
to characterize the relationships between North American and Third World PVOs in decision making, neither
does equal partnership. Such would require much more
sharing of authority than exists now, and a mutual
agenda-setting process by both groups regarding global
issues affecting development in the First and Third
Worlds.

## Accountability

All U.S. and Canadian PVOs are governed by boards
of directors who normally make final decisions about
larger projects and who are the ones ultimately responsible to the public in each country for the organizations' activities and use of funds overseas. Financial audits are carried out by reputable accounting
firms, and several of the larger PVOs carry out their
own internal audits as well. Those receiving public
funds must also provide the U.S. and Canadian governments with detailed financial accounting information
at regular intervals. Published annual reports include
budgetary information and audits are public documents.
Misuse of funds by recipient groups appears to be
quite rare. PVO representatives indicated during
interviews that termination or serious modifications
of projects because funds were being used other than
for what was agreed upon is seldom necessary.
Moreover, the efficiency of PVOs in using donor
money is impressive. Administrative and management
expenses are generally kept within the vicinity of 5 to
6 percent of total budgets, as compared to 20 to 30
percent spent on overhead by government-to-government
AID programs.[59]
In many instances, PVOs can also undertake similar
projects, albeit on a smaller scale, as bilateral or
multilateral public agencies and for much lower costs.
Some water development projects in Latin America, for
example, that have been sponsored by CARE Canada, have
been done at a cost of $6 per benefited household,
whereas the same projects would cost CIDA $60 per
family assisted and the Inter-American Development
Bank (IADB) $160.[60]
Hence, in the financial realm accountability and

efficiency both on the part of recipients abroad and
by PVO home offices to their donors seems to be good.
This is a major reason PVOs enjoy so much popularity
both with the U.S. and Canadian governments and the
general public in both countries.

In the area of information about projects, institutions, or networks supported overseas, however, the
methods of accountability to donors and the general
public in the U.S. and Canada are less strict. Annual
reports and periodic newsletters or brochures sent to
contributors normally include only brief summaries of
each major overseas activity of the PVO, usually on a
region-by-region basis. Lots of pictures are included
to make the projects more real to readers, but only
summary verbal sketches are given. It is not that
PVOs want to hide information from the public.
Rather they feel most donors are not interested in
reading long reports. More information can be obtained
by writing to headquarters if anyone so desires.

There are limitations, however, on just how much
information can and will be provided. PVOs will often
want to protect confidentiality for the integrity (or
the safety) of their overseas recipients. Most PVOs
treat documents they have in their files on overseas
programs as strictly privileged information, and do not
allow anyone outside staff and the board of directors
access to them. CCODP as a matter of policy, for
example, does not share any of the self-evaluation done
by recipients of its aid with outsiders (except CIDA
when it funds a project), and gives to no one names
of persons involved in the programs it supports.[61]

Such procedures, while instilling confidence among
recipients and creating a trustful relationship
between PVOs and Third World groups, are not conducive
to providing the home-country publics with a clear
idea of precisely what is being accomplished in overseas programs. Contributors, as well as the populace
at large, must rely heavily on the integrity of the
PVO that something is going on to improve the lot of
the poor overseas, and undoubtedly much is being done.

However, annual reports and other fund-raising
materials of some PVOs will often stress certain
catch words such as "aiding the grass-roots poor,"
"participatory," "self-help," or "innovative" to
characterize the projects they support. Such "articles
of faith," as Judith Tendler calls them, do not always
reflect what PVOs are actually doing. In her study of
seventy-five PVO evaluations, she concluded that,
despite the limitations of methodology used in many of
these evaluations (as described earlier), it is evident
upon reading them that a considerable number of PVO
projects do not live up to these descriptive adjectives
given to the public about their work. Tendler concludes

that PVOs do help needy people overseas, but many
projects do not reach the poor majority, or the bottom
40 percent at the grassroots.  A good number also support Third World programs or groups that do not
involve popular participation in decisions, and many
are not innovative at all since they rely on known
techniques of service delivery approaches.[62]  It is not
a question of project failure that is at stake.  Rather,
concludes Tendler, PVOs are providing important
services, but often not that qualitatively different
from those of governmental agencies:

> ...The work of PVOs may best be characterized as
> expanding or improving under existing techniques
> the delivery of public services.  In many cases,
> successful projects will involve a style that is
> top-down, though enlightened, and decentralized.
> Participation may or may not be involved.  In
> certain cases, moreover, PVOs may be successful
> more as precursors to government than as
> innovators.
>
> Finally, PVOs will in many cases be providing
> a service to local elites that was previously not
> available, thereby contributing to the economic
> development of a region.  They will not, in these
> cases, be reaching the poor directly.  They may
> be reaching the poor indirectly, however, through
> spread effects; or, the economic growth consequent
> upon their actions may worsen, rather than
> improve, the income distribution.  In these
> cases, PVOs will be practicing a community-level
> version of trickle-down or nontargeted approaches
> to development--just what PVOs and others have
> criticized the larger donors for.[63]

PVOs are reluctant, however, to present themselves
to the general public as being similar to governmental
agencies.  To raise funds they want to stress how
different they are, and yet the reality would seem to
be otherwise in many instances.  Some exaggerations,
therefore, characterize how PVOs present themselves in
their publications.

Another area of exaggeration occurs among some PVO
fund-raising media ads which place great emphasis on
starving or sick children an organization is helping.
The public can easily receive the impression that any
money contributed by a sponsor will go directly to
alleviate the immediate suffering of a specific child.
In fact, donors are sometimes assigned individual children with whom they can and do correspond.  However,
some PVOs who use child-sponsorship techniques to
personalize the donor-recipient relationship do not

ensure that a contributor's dollar gets to the child he
or she is sponsoring. It does go to the area the child
is living in, but is used for projects that will
improve the socioeconomic status of the whole community
and not just the children--e.g., health and educational
facilities, agricultural development, credit unions,
well-digging, home construction, etc.

While such an evolution in the orientation of
organizations such as Save the Children Federation and
Foster Parents Plan USA has moved them off the relief
track to the institution-building aspects of development, the impression given to the U.S. public at times
is still the former image. A careful reading of the
annual reports or newsletters of these two agencies
makes clear this newer structural emphasis. Television
and magazine ads often do not, however, convey this image.

A major reason for this is related to what was
mentioned in the section under goal coherence--i.e.,
the tendency among the U.S. public to respond better
to fund-raising techniques based on appeals to the
heart than the head. While this may very well be true,
it also does not help educate U.S. citizens about what
is needed to eradicate the deeper causes of poverty
abroad, nor does it inform them that these are actually
what many child sponsorship programs are now trying to
address. If some of the traditional disaster aid PVOs
now describing much of their present assistential work
as "development assistance" are to be criticized, then
others who have moved beyond this and yet want to
continue to have a relief image for some fund-raising
purposes are to be criticized as well. In both cases
accountability to the public is not completely accurate.

This problem of "reality distance" between what a
PVO is actually supporting overseas and where the
hearts and heads of its donors are is critical for
other types of nonprofits as well. For example, in the
case where a church-related organization is supporting
politically progressive but nonparty affiliated institutions and networks abroad, there can be a gap between
the mentality of its staff and the people in the pews
who contribute to these overseas activities through
their local church congregations. Sometimes what such
PVO staff personnel consider "progressive" is not what
the average churchgoer has in mind. Rather than give
detailed information to donors, or even try to influence
their political attitudes, an organization's staff will
go ahead with programs on the basis of their own
knowledge and moral convictions of what is needed to
improve the lot of the poor and oppressed in developing
countries.

The staff at CWS is better informed than the
average Protestant churchgoer as to what is going on
overseas, since they are in regular contact with Third

World church groups who know well the needs of their
own people.  Moreover, CWS does not tell one story to
its church affiliates at home and carry out another
with their money.  It is not, as suggested by one
critic on the CBS-TV 60 Minutes program in January
1983, an issue of deception or lying by Church
executives in the National Council of Churches (NCC)
to their people about some of the activities of
CWS.[64]

There is, however, a gap between the Church
agency's staff and the contributors.  One analyst of
the uproar caused by the 60 Minutes program, who
claims to know and admire some of the NCC staff,
believes the overall effect of the CBS report was a
distortion.  Fr. John Reedy, C.S.C., claims, however,
that the NCC has a problem in the distance that has
developed between its sponsoring churches' members and
the mentality of many of its professional staff who
shape the programs and projects of CWS, its overseas
aid-giving arm.  Reedy concludes:

> My impression is that a huge gulf separates
> the experience, the sensitivity, the judgments
> of many NCC staff members from the awareness and
> practical judgments of local clergymen  and the
> members of their congregations.
> The Council must do a better job of communi-
> cating to its constituency the experience and con-
> victions of those who formulate the programs.
> The staff needs to be more sensitive to the level
> of understanding of the church members in formu-
> lating the various programs.
> It is unhealthy--ultimately self-defeating--
> when a professional staff of any organization
> allows too much distance to develop between
> itself and its membership.
> In the long run, that kind of a gap can be
> more damaging than the treatment you might get
> from the 60 Minutes crew.[65]

Hence, while there does not seem to be a lack of
financial accountability nor of efficient use of
funds by U.S. and Canadian PVOs, information accountability to donors is sometimes limited and exaggerations
do occur in fund-raising techniques.  Moreover, the
absence of extensive disclosure of overseas activities
to the public by most PVOs can at times create perception gaps between what their donors think they do and
what their overseas recipients actually accomplish with
the contributions.  When such a gap is significant, a
PVO is vulnerable to attack by its critics or worse--
it can create disillusionment among its supporters.

CONCLUSIONS

Over the past twenty years the number, as well as the activities, of U.S. and Canadian PVOs supporting overseas programs in developing countries have grown significantly. Their cost-effectiveness in delivering services, their contacts with indigenous private local groups in the Third World, and their ability to engage in small-scale projects at the grass-roots level have all increased their popularity in the eyes of the general public and government legislatures interested in improving upon the somewhat disappointing results of large scale public foreign aid programs in meeting basic human needs of the poor overseas.

There is also a wide variety of approaches to the problems of poverty within the North American PVO community. This provides both multifaceted strategies to address these complex issues, and a choice for PVO donors--both private and governmental--who have a broad range of options to which they can contribute to aid the global poor through the nonprofit sector.

## Agenda-Setting Role Not Well Substantiated

While there is no doubt about the efficiency of PVOs in using resources, there is still uncertainty as to how innovative they are and how much they act as agenda-setting agents in basic human needs or alternate development strategies. Much more field research on these issues is necessary.

Evidence from my interviews and study of documents in the home offices of a cross-section of U.S. and Canadian PVOs indicates that innovation and replicable model building by PVOs may not be as extensive as is sometimes believed. A great part of U.S. PVO resources (almost two-thirds) is administered by a handful of large organizations whose primary focus is still on the delivery of food, clothing, and medicine to alleviate immediate suffering. While such relief aid is absolutely essential for many occasions, and PVOs can often get it there faster and more effectively than governmental agencies, it is not clear that it is contributing to the overcoming of deeper obstacles to long-term development as some agencies are now claiming. Some say they are stimulating around such activities (e.g., in food-for-work projects) the creation of new problem solving community organizations, but much more study is needed than has been done so far to prove this argument.[66]

In the realm of technical assistance PVOs are undoubtedly providing very important resources and skills in many locales where they are simply

nonexistent--e.g., primary health care services, and
credit and management training for small businesses and
cooperatives. Some of these are truly innovative--
e.g., the work that AITEC is doing in the realm of
credit and training for consortia of microenterprises
previously thought to be bad loan risks and impossible
to assist by banks and governments.[67] However, in many
instances--in health services, for example--technical
aid projects do not receive adequate evaluations to
pinpoint their truly innovative qualities.[68]

Nor is there sufficient wider contextual or follow-
up analysis done by PVOs to determine when and under
what conditions these projects act as catalytic forces
in a locale for more and better service delivery by
governmental agencies and/or profit-making organizations. PVOs may very well be surrogates for, or com-
plements to, these other larger institutions in a
region but not necessarily innovators of new and replicable techniques nor even precursors for them to do
more. While this is not bad, much clarification is
needed on precisely where the uniqueness and agenda-
setting contributions of PVOs are in creating better
methods for fulfilling basic human needs.

## Empowerment Hard to Verify

In terms of being empowerers of the poor to
construct their own organizations that can effectively
voice interests and redress the grievances they have
vis-à-vis dominant economic and political elites, the
rhetoric is at times great but adequate information is
sparse. This is due both to the lack of sufficient
evaluation resources and techniques, and also to the
mixed opinion in the PVO community about these as being
legitimate goals. U.S. PVOs will endorse the creation
of alternate networks of participation as desirable,
but seldom commit themselves publicly to empowerment
due to their fear of its political connotations--and
yet many claim they are hoping to achieve this by
supporting progressive, but nonpartisan, political
groups abroad. The Canadians are much more explicit
and consistent about their goals in institution
and network promotion, and many endorse in their statements and literature the goal of changing power relations as an essential ingredient of development.

However, in neither U.S. or Canadian
PVOs provide their donors or the general public with
much qualitative data on what effect indigenous
organizations are having on generic structural
problems of poverty or on power relations in a region.
Latin American groups rightfully resent being closely
studied by "gringos," as many U.S. social scientists

have done since the 1960s.  Neither can their success
always be chronicled either in Latin or North America
for fear of even more dire consequences than those they
are already suffering in repressive contexts.

While these are cogent reasons for U.S. and
Canadian PVOs to remain vague about some of their
institution and network building activities abroad,
they can leave themselves open to questioning by
friends and foes alike due to scant disclosures on
their accomplishments in this area.  It is not merely
the protection of confidentiality for overseas recipient groups which is important, but also maintaining
impeccable credibility at home about their claims.
When information or perception gaps emerge, donors can
wonder about what is actually being accomplished
abroad and, as media events (Reader's Digest article,
60 Minutes TV program) have indicated, those out to
undermine the good work of PVOs will try to exploit
such puzzlement for their own partisan political
purposes.

One theorist has argued that a core purpose of
the nonprofit sector is to operate in those areas
where the public (buyers of goods and services, and
contributors to charity) has no way to police producers by ordinary contractual devices--e.g., where
the possibility of cheating to increase profits is
great due to absence of effective marketing competition, or where the service is to be delivered to a
far-off place beyond the possibility for donors to
communicate directly with the beneficiaries of their
gifts.  The nonprofit organization, whose legal commitment is to devote its entire resources to the delivery
of promised services, becomes a more attractive intermediary between giver and recipient in such situations.[69]  This relationship of confidence is not being
undermined by PVO staff pilfering of donor funds, but
it could be affected if some of the rhetoric being
used about overseas programs is not backed up better
by solid evidence of results.  This pertains both to
those PVOs who provide limited public information on
the wider impact of their counterpart institutions'
activities abroad, and also to those who use exaggerations in fund raising.


Financing: Key to Independence Abroad and Advocacy
at Home

Ironically, the great popularity of PVOs inside
the U.S. and Canadian governments over the past
twenty years has led to a great windfall of new
resources from legislatures but has also created new
problems which will be hard to solve.  It has been

governmental, not private, aid that has enhanced the
growth of, and now sustains, the extensive activities of
the traditional relief agencies, that has been responsible for the creation or expansion of many technical assistance organizations, and which has provided
the stimulus for some older and some newer PVOs to
shift to institution and network building abroad.
Nonetheless, concomitant to increased public aid there
have been limits on autonomy.  While these are seldom
in the form of blatant political requests, subtle
pressures exist that negatively impact on the freedom
and flexibility of many PVOs.  A very dangerous effect
has been the almost unperceived attitudes of deference
for, and even anticipation of, government wishes that
has seeped into the mentality of some PVO executives
and staff, especially in the United States.70

While the Canadian situation is different in the
sense of fewer government restrictions on PVOs than
in the United States, overall dependence on governmental aid by Canadian PVOs is almost as great, and
in some controversial areas it is proportionately
larger--institution and network building for empowerment of the poor, and development education and
advocacy at home.  Such heavy dependence on government
for PVO activities which potentially could cause
political embarrassment for the government abroad and
at home is risky.

The continued role of PVOs as global educators
and public advocates regarding needed international
structural changes to address Third World poverty
adequately will be very much conditioned by their
sources of financing.  Significant dependence on
public aid will certainly place limits on how freely
and frankly U.S. PVOs can criticize and try to change
the economic and political policies of the U.S. government towards developing countries.  The current efforts
by the OMB to impose more controls on nonprofit groups
that try to influence governmental decision making is a
clear sign that even before most U.S. PVOs start to
play a significant role in the realms of development
education and advocacy for changes in foreign policy
the range of permissible action is being restricted.

Again, the Canadian situation is different in
these areas due to the greater willingness of the
government to sustain public criticism by its grantees
of its foreign policies than is the U.S. government.
Whether these commitments to education and advocacy
at home will continue as freely in the future in
Canada, and become a model for more U.S. PVOs to do
likewise, remains to be seen.

If North American PVOs--both U.S. and Canadian--
become more attuned to the voices of counterpart PVOs
in developing countries (especially Latin America) and

try to establish more collegial processes for decision
making with them about development priorities and
resource allocations, they likely will be asked by
their overseas partners to play a greater role at home
to make people aware of needed policy changes in
multinational corporations and governments. Such
education and advocacy roles need not be strident or
lacking in constructive criticism. They will, however,
require some risk taking and a willingness by PVOs to
lose some support in the private sector among those
primarily interested in treating the effects, not the
causes, of poverty abroad, and in the public sector
among government officials unwilling to subsidize
open criticisms of their own decisions.

At the end of my interview with J. Robert Busche,
Assistant Executive Director of LWR, he outlined his
vision for the future of PVOs in the North Atlantic
region that support socioeconomic projects in developing countries. He said that he hoped someday three
things would happen to give PVOs a more concerted
impact on economic and political structures underlying
global poverty:

1. Greater coordination of goals and strategies
   among transnational nonprofit organizations
   so as to eliminate the great dispersal of
   PVO energy that now exists.
2. Flowing from this closer cooperation among
   such PVOs, a concerted effort on their part
   to push their respective governments to
   change policies that perpetuate unjust international structures--e.g., imbalance of trade
   relations, lack of monitoring of international investments, escalating arms sales,
   etc.--and a refusal to act as conduits of
   governmental aid abroad until such changes
   were underway.
3. A joint refusal by North Atlantic PVOs to
   carry out any aid activities in developing
   countries unless the host governments in
   these societies guarantee certain minimum,
   but clearly defined, structural changes on
   behalf of the majority poor--e.g., equitable
   land reform.[71]

Whether Busche's dream is utopian or realistic
is debatable. Were it to be realized, even greater
contributions could be made by PVOs to enhancing
basic human needs and alternate development strategies
than they are doing at present.

NOTES

1.  Jorgen Lissner, The Politics of Altruism: A
Study of the Political Behavior of Voluntary Development
Agencies (Geneva: Lutheran World Federation, 1977), 37,
49-51.  Organization for Economic Cooperation and
Development, Development Assistance Committee (OECD-
DAC), Development Cooperation, 1981 Review (Paris:
OECD, 1981), 182.
2.  Lissner, Politics of Altruism, 41; OECD-DAC,
Development Cooperation, 1979 Review (Paris: OECD,
1979), 111.
3.  Elizabeth Schmidt, Jane Blewett, and Peter
Henriot, Religious Private Voluntary Organizations and
the Question of Government Funding: Final Report
(Maryknoll, NY: Orbis Books, Probe Series, 1980), 10;
Bureau for Food for Peace and Voluntary Assistance,
U.S. International Development Cooperation Agency,
Agency for International Development (AID), Voluntary
Foreign Aid Programs (Washington, D.C.: 1982), 21-27.
4.  My selection of PVOs was not made in random
fashion.  Rather I tried to include many different
types of organizations so as to do justice to the rich
variety that exists in the PVO community--large and
small, old and new, religiously affiliated and
secular, funded completely by private funds or supported by a combination of governmental and private
resources, exclusively development-oriented or
combining both relief and development activities.

The U.S. PVOs I selected were: ACCION Inter-
national/AITECH; CARE USA: Catholic Relief Services
(CRS); Church World Service (CWS); Coordination in
Development (CODEL); Ford Foundation; Foster Parents
Plan USA; Lutheran World Relief (LWR); Oxfam America;
Pan American Development Foundation (PADF); Private
Agencies Collaborating Together (PACT); Rockefeller
Foundation; Save the Children Federation; Seventh-
Day Adventist World Service (SAWS); Unitarian Univer-
salist Service Committee (UUSC).

The Canadian PVOs visited were: Canadian Catholic
Organization for Development and Peace (CCODP);
Canadian Council for International Cooperation (CCIC);
Canadian University Service Overseas (CUSO); CARE
Canada; Inter-Pares; Oxfam Canada; Service Universi-
taire Canadien Outre-Mer (SUCO).

I normally interviewed in each of these twenty-two
U.S. and Canadian PVOs the person most responsible for
the oversight of projects and programs the organization
supported in Latin America.  In some of the larger
PVOs I also conducted more than one interview with
persons having different responsibilities, and
different perspectives on the organization's overseas

activities. Multiple interviews were conducted in the
following ten PVOs: CARE USA and CARE Canada; CRS; CWS;
CODEL; CCODP; Foster Parents Plan USA; Oxfam America;
PACT; the Rockefeller Foundation.

Funding for this aspect of my research project
(which occurred between August 1982 and August 1983)
was provided by the Program on Nonprofit Organizations
at Yale University's Institute for Social and Policy
Studies, the U.S. Inter-American Foundation, and the
National Endowment for the Humanities.

5.   Interview with Dr. William Pruzensky, Regional
Director for Central America, CRS, New York City,
October 18, 1982.

6.   Interview with Rev. Msgr. Roland Bordelon,
Regional Director for South America, CRS, New York
City, October 12, 1982; Interview with George F. Kraus,
former Regional Program Officer for Latin America, CARE
USA, New York City, January 4, 1983.

7.   Interview, Rev. Oscar Bolioli, Director, and
Rev. Antonio Ramos, Assistant Director, Latin American
Office, CWS, New York City, January 6, 1983; Interview
with J. Robert Busche, Assistant Executive Director,
LWR, New York City, January 5, 1983.

8.   Interview with John P. Grant, Regional Director
for Latin America, Save the Children Federation,
Westport, CT., March 25, 1983; Interview with Kenneth
H. Phillips, National Executive Director, Foster
Parents Plan USA, Warwick, RI, June 10, 1983.

9.   Interview with Dr. Laurence D. Stifel, Vice
President and Secretary, and Dr. Mary M. Kritz, Assis-
tant Director for Population Sciences, Rockefeller
Foundation, New York City, January 14, 1983; Interview
with Jeffrey M. Puryear, Program Officer, Developing
Country Programs, The Ford Foundation, New York City,
January 14, 1983.

10.   Interview with Joseph Short, Executive Director
Oxfam America, Boston, April 1, 1983; Interview with
Dr. Richard S. Scobie, Executive Director, UUSC,
Boston, October 25, 1982.

11.   Interview with E. Brown, Coordinator
for Latin America and the Caribbean, CODEL, New York
City, January 7, 1983; Interview with James F. O'Brien,
Director of Project Fund, PACT, New York City,
December 30, 1982.

12.   Interview with: 1) Rev. C. William Smith,
Project Director for Central America, the Caribbean and
Brazil, CCODP, Montreal, December 15, 1982; 2) Jorge
Rodríguez, Coordinator for Americas Programs, CUSO,
Ottawa, January 21, 1983; 3) Enrique Ramirez,
Assistant Director, Latin American Division, SUCO,
Ottawa, February 21, 1983; and 4) Lawrence S. Cumming,
National Secretary, Oxfam Canada, Ottawa, June 2, 1983.

13.   Interview with Richard J. Harmston,

Executive Director, CCIC, Ottawa, January 21, 1983.

14. For a description and analysis of development education in Canada—based on interviews in 1981 with 140 persons working in ninety PVO's—see CCIC, Study of International Development Education in Canada: Final Report (Montreal: Cooperative d'animation et de consultation, May 1982).

15. Interview with Romeo Maione, Head of NGO Division, Special Programs Branch, CIDA, Hull, Ontario, February 22, 1983.

16. Interview with Thomas Kines, National Director, CARE Canada, Ottawa, May 31, 1983.

17. CCIC, Study of International Development Education in Canada, 69-71.

18. Interview with Joseph Short, Oxfam America.

19. Interview with Dr. Richard Scobie, UUSC.

20. Interview, Rev. Laurence, Olszewski, C.S.C., Coordinator of Diocesan Affairs, CRS, New York City, October 12, 1982.

21. Interview with George F. Kraus, CARE USA.

22. Interview with Kenneth H. Phillips, Foster Parents Plan USA.

23. Interview with Lynn Marshall, Development Director, CRS, New York City, October 12, 1982.

24. A proposal to substantially expand development education by U.S. PVOs was issued in late 1983 by a joint working group of the two national federations of PVOs that support overseas projects—the American Council of Voluntary Agencies (ACVA), and Private Agencies in International Development (PAID). The proposal recommends more efforts by U.S. PVOs to educate their constituencies and other attentive publics in the U.S. as to the structural impediments to genuine development, the links betwen local and global problems, and the existence of transnational inequities. The proposal, however, refrains from any political or economic analysis as to the causes of underdevelopment, does not give any specifics as to what transnational inequities entail, and does not encourage a critical advocacy position by PVOs vis-à-vis any overseas policies of the U.S. government or U.S. multinational corporations. Joint Working Group on Development Education, "A Framework for Development Education in the United States" (Washington, DC: PAID and ACVA, November 1983) (mimeographed).

25. Interview with George F. Kraus, CARE USA.

26. Interview with John Grant, Save the Children Federation.

27. Interview with Kenneth Phillips, Foster Parents Plan USA.

28. Interview with Carlos Castello, Regional Representative for Latin America, PACT, New York City, January 6, 1983.

162

29.  Interview with Rev. C. William Smith, CCODP.
30.  Interview with James F. O'Brien, PACT.
31.  Interview with Rev. Oscar Bolioni and with
Rev. Antonio Ramos, CWS.
32.  Interview with J. Robert Busche, LWR.
33.  Interview with Rene Guay, Director for South
America, CCODP, Montreal, February 21, 1983.
34.  Interview with Rev. Msgr. Roland Bordelon, CRS.
35.  Jose Adunate, S.J., and Jaime Ruiz-Tagle P.,
"El empleo mínimo:  ¿ayuda social o verguenza
nacional?," Mensaje (Santiago) 29 (June 1980): 257-63.
36.  Interview, Daniel Santo Pietro, former New York
staff member of CRS for Latin America, New York City,
August 13, 1981.
37.  Interview with Thomas Kines, CARE Canada.
38.  The situation is less problematic in Canada.
The Canadian government has fewer political, economic
and security interests in the Third World--and
particularly in Latin America--than the U.S. government.
It consequently allows more freedom of action to PVOs
that receive its assistance.  Although seventeen of the
thirty-four Canadian PVOs listed in Table 6.2 depend
for 40 percent or more of their resources on CIDA, the
Canadian PVO representatives in my survey expressed
much less concern about their credibility and freedom
due to such assistance.  In the Ministry of Economic
Affairs country blacklists for political reasons exist
but are shorter than in the United States.  (Cuba is the
only Latin American country listed.)  Country priorities
based on economic considerations, although applicable
for official bilateral governmental aid, do not yet
apply to CIDA funds channelled through PVOs.  Finally,
Canadian respondents felt that their recipient groups
abroad--especially in Latin America--had much less
problem taking Canadian governmental assistance
through them than indirect governmental aid through
U.S. PVOs because of the Canadian government's
relatively benign policies in the Third World.
39.  Interview with Dr. Laurence Stifel, Rockefeller Foundation.
40.  Oxfam UK, Oxfam: Review of the Year, 1980-81
(Oxford: Oxfam UK, 1981), 16.
41.  Interview with Laurence Simon, Director of
Policy Analysis, Oxfam America, Boston, March 8, 1983.
42.  Rael J. Isaac, "Do You Know Where Your Church
Offerings Go?," Reader's Digest (January 1983), 120-25;
CBS-TV Network, "The Gospel According to Whom?," 60
Minutes 25, 19 (January 23, 1983); Allan Brownfield,
"Behind the Effort to Cut Off Aid to El Salvador,"
Washington Times (February 24, 1983).
43.  Interview with Rev. William Wipfler, Director
of Office of Human Rights, National Council of
Churches, New York City, January 27, 1983; Interview

with Laurence Simon, Oxfam America; Interview with Dr.
Richard S. Scobie, UUSC.

44. Interview with: 1) Richard J. Harmston, CCIC;
2) Rev. C. William Smith and Rene Guay, CCODP; 3) Jorge
Rodriguez, CUSO; 4) Enrique Ramirez, SUCO; 5) Tim
Brodhead, Inter Pares; 6) Lawrence S. Cumming, Oxfam
Canada.

45. Ibid.

46. Interview with Robert Miller, Research Associate, Parliamentary Centre (Ottawa, Canada), Montreal,
June 1, 1983.

47. PAID, "Selected Legislative Issues for PVOs,"
PAID Third Annual Forum, Washington, D.C. (May 4-6,
1983), 5 (mimeographed).

48. Monday Developments (PAID Newsletter) 1, 21
(November 1983): 3; Felicity Barringer, "OMB Releases
Proposed Restrictions on Lobbying by Contractors,
Grantees," Washington Post, 3 November 1983.

49. Interview with Jeffrey M. Puryear, Ford Foundation.

50. Interview with Dr. Richard S. Scobie, UUSC.

51. Interview with Rev. C. William Smith, CCODP.

52. Judith Tender, Turning Private Voluntary
Organizations into Development Agencies: Questions
for Evaluation, Program Evaluation Discussion Paper No.
12,(Washington, D.C.: AID, 1982), 127, 131-32.

53. Daniel Santo Pietro, ed., Evaluation Source-
book for Private and Voluntary Organizations (New York:
ACVA, 1983).

54. Interview with Richard J. Harmston, CCIC;
Interview with Xeno Santiago, CIDA, Hull, Ont., Feb. 22,
1983.

55. Seven of the twenty-two PVOs have no overseas
field representatives at all--CCODP, Oxfam Canada,
Inter Pares, SUCO, Rockefeller Foundation, PACT and
CODEL. An eighth, Oxfam America, has none in Latin
America. Three other PVOs have three or less in Latin
America--CWS (3), LWR (1), and UUSC (1).

56. PAID, "Speical Report: ACVFA in Jamaica,"
Washington, D.C. (March 18, 1983), (mimeographed).

57. Interview with Paul Maguire, PVO Coordinator,
Latin American Bureau, AID, Washington, D.C., May 19,
1983.

58. Interview with Tim Brodhead, Inter Pares.

59. Bureau for Food for Peace and Voluntary Assistance, AID, Voluntary Foreign Aid Programs, 28;
Landrum R. Bolling, Private Foreign Aid: U.S. Philanthropy for Relief and Development (Boulder, CO: Westview Press, 1982), 190-91.

60. Interview with Romeo Maione, CIDA.

61. Interview with Rev. C. William Smith, CCODP.

62. Tendler, Turning PVOs into Development Agencies, iv.

63.   Ibid., vii.

64.   CBS-TV Network, "The Gospel According to Whom?"

65.   Fr. John Reedy, C.S.C., "Council vs. 'Sixty Minutes,'" The Witness (Dubuque), 17 July 1983, 4.

66.   One AID-sponsored study that focuses on the creation of self-sustaining, problem-solving organizations through food-for-work projects is Pirie M. Gall and James C. Eckroad, "Evaluation of the PL 480 Title II Program in the Dominican Republic: Final Report," International Science and Technology Institute, Inc., Washington, D.C., January 1983 (mimeographed). While acknowledging some innovation by U.S. PVOs, the study also points to many areas for improvement, and concludes that relief rather than community development still characterizes some of these projects.

67.   For a recent study of one such credit institution to supply loans to small business persons originally founded by AITEC in Northeast Brazil see Judith Tendler, Ventures in the Informal Sector, and How They Worked Out in Brazil, Evaluation Study No. 12, (Washington, D.C.: AID, March 1983).

68.   David F. Pyle, "Framework for Evaluation of Health Sector Activities by Private Voluntary Organizations Receiving Matching Grants," Bureau for Food for Peace and Voluntary Cooperation, AID, Washington, D.C., May 1982 (mimeographed).

69.   Henry Hausmann, "The Role of Nonprofit Enterprise," Yale Law Journal 89, 5 (April 1980): 835-901. This article was also reproduced as PONPO Working Paper No. 1 by the Program on Nonprofit Organizations, Institution for Social and Policy Studies, Yale University, 1980.

70.   Joseph Short, Executive Director of Oxfam America, articulated this judgment (also expressed previously in the text by the National Driector of CARE Canada) as follows:

Groups which have contracted with the U.S. government for a long time, or who receive a large percentage of their budget from the U.S. government, have a government mentality. They think as the government does. They don't have to be told what to do by government.

71.   Interview with J. Robert Busche, LWR.

# 7
# Voluntary Agencies and the Promotion of Enterprise

*Robert W. Hunt*

This chapter has two major purposes: first, to introduce some central issues in PVO activities that are of relevance to the promotion of small enterprise (SE) development, and second, to provide a summary of what we know about where and how voluntary sector projects best promote SE development work. The chapter is, in large part, a synthesis of a body of evaluation literature, much of it sponsored by the United States Agency for International Development (AID).[1]

The search for more conclusive information on PVOs and development requires both more differentiation of the PVO project activities and more evaluation of them. Most of the limited research on PVO impact has been conducted in response to specific in-house needs. Rarely have there been full scale investigations of the impact of PVO sectoral program activity. This is particularly true of PVO activities in the SE sector. Yet this is one area where voluntary groups have been involved in significant numbers.[2] It is also one where, since the concerns for equity and outreach to the poor often focus on employment promotion, PVOs are more likely to be involved in the future. For these reasons, this chapter will focus specifically on the SE sector and the PVO role in it.

## SE DEVELOPMENT: SOME INITIAL CONSIDERATIONS

The problems of poverty and joblessness have raised interest in the potential contribution of PVOs to development. More specifically, they have underscored the need for assisting small enterprises in developing nations. Enterprises classified as "small" have from one to as many as a hundred or so employees, though more often than not they have fewer than five, and usually only minimal resources in terms of fixed assets or working capital.[3] They are widely dispersed, with evidence now suggesting that they exist in larger numbers than previously believed in the most remote and poorest of communities.[4]  Because they are relatively easy to establish, and tend to rely on simple technologies, they provide more managerial and job opportunities--especially for the less skilled--than other forms of enterprise.  There are strong indications that in the poorer rural areas of Third World countries small enterprises are primary or secondary sources of income for half of the families.[5]  It follows that they have the additional effect of keeping populations dispersed, certainly more than programs which center on the promotion of development through large scale industrializaton. Their impact on the distribution of skills and opportunities may increase the possibility for stable and democratic change.[6]

Many SE programs have been developed over the past few decades.  Major funding agencies and developing nation governments themselves have been deeply involved in SE development in recent years.[7]  Efforts that once focused on the generation of "modern" industrial firms have tended to broaden and to encompass greater concern for much smaller firms with less chance for growth and for eventual integration with the larger commercial and industrial sector.[8]  Credit, extension services, and training continue to be the major forms of assistance, with the provision of basic infrastructure, which is typified by the construction of large numbers of industrial estates in the 1960s, declining as a source of support.

In spite of these efforts, development agencies have enjoyed only mixed success.  For one thing, the firms they attempt to assist are often fragile and dependent on one decidedly overworked individual.  The entrepreneurs themselves are commonly lacking both in knowledge of the marketplace and in financial reserves necessary for survival.  Such difficulties are multiplied with the founding, expanding, and adapting of businesses in a competitive setting.  This is particularly true where large institutions (banks, governments), bent on the promotion of capital intensive business, generate a variety of disincentives for small firms.

Public officials have been disappointed in the face of these difficulties.  But they have continued to believe that small enterprises are a crucial means for dealing with the daunting problem of unemployment. They have begun to raise hard questions about how to promote small business.  One consequence has been a striking increase in the advocacy of systematic evaluations of projects and of firm performance.  Both public and private sector organizations have become interested in the comparative evaluation of the impact of enterprise project.  The World Bank has completed a

major review under the auspices of its Development
Enterprise Department and many PVOs have begun to look
more systematically at the long term social effects of
their enterprise projects.  AID has recently undertaken
evaluations sponsored by the offices of Evaluation,
Multisectoral Development and Private and Voluntary
Cooperation.

An effort will be made in this chapter to build
upon these evaluations and relevant other literature to
summarize what we now know about success in the SE
development sector.[9]  Subsequently the role PVOs can
play in the promotion and development of small
enterprise will be considered more specifically.


## A SUMMARY OF RESEARCH ON SE DEVELOPMENT

Many early SE projects were infrastructural--
involving, for example, the development of power,
transportation, and communication facilities, as well
as industrial estates.  Some of this continues, but
most SE projects over the past decade, have been
focused on credit, extension services, and a variety of
training programs.  Credit programs have been common
and fairly well defined, but there is an increasing
tendency to draw on the various other inputs to
supplement lending activities or substitute for them.
Project variety is thereby multiplied.  Moreover, there
has been a growing tendency to introduce employment
promotion activities as components of rural development
and other projects.  This makes it still more difficult
to get a reading on the comparative significance of
particular project components.  In fact, it is hard to
know just what it is that the SE sector encompasses.
Partly as a consequence of this ambiguity, there have
been few efforts to evaluate SE projects.  However, the
prominence of the sector has increased as the range of
options available to donors in bringing change has
diminished.  As a consequence, many large donor
agencies, including AID, the World Bank, and the
International Labor Organization (ILO), have become
more active in supporting research and evaluation on
the SE sector.

Preliminary findings from these donor efforts, and
from the literature on enterprise projects, provide
information that is summarized in this chapter.  The
discussion is organized around the major project
inputs, (such as credit and training) despite the
overlap and ambiguity which this sometimes produces.
Subsequent to the consideration of each of these
inputs, a list of propositions will be provided.  These
highlight central themes and summarize relationships
most supported by the existing literature.

As a means for further clarifying the significance
of the various project inputs, their effects will be
contrasted with those of the most significant external
forces impinging on SE development.  These external
factors will be analyzed under the heading of
nonproject influences on enterprise activity.  We will
conclude that the most successful projects are those
aimed at improving a whole system of relationships, not
just activities at the level of the firm itself.

## Credit and Small Enterprise Development

Economic and Entrepreneurial Aspects of Credit.
Most small enterprises are financed by the income and
profits of owners and the savings of their families, or
by borrowing from those who serve as suppliers and
dealers.  These facts, coupled with evidence that
credit difficulties are often symptoms for managerial
or market related problems, raise doubts in the minds
of some as to the importance of credit in SE
development projects.[10]  Despite this, the need for
credit is invariably listed by small entrepreneurs at
or near the top of their list of problems.  Surveys
indicate that cash shortfalls and lack of access to
formal credit institutions are major reasons for the
fragility and failure of these businesses.[11]  Many
project designers and managers, in fact, regard credit
problems as the primary obstacle to the promotion and
the protection of small firms, to the ultimate
realization of their potential as promoters of
employment opportunities, and to more equitable
development.  Of the projects recently evaluated by
AID, those of the Institute for International
Development Incorporated (IIDI), of the UNO project in
Brazil, are among the most committed to this conclusion.
There is significant evidence that the flow of
credit does have substantial effect on both the number
of new firms, and their level of success and survival.
Some can be found in the report by Goldmark, Rosengard
and Money on the Upper Volta project of Partnership for
Productivity (PfP).  The authors suggest that this
project's impressive capacity to generate large numbers
of loans in a short time may have had a major impact on
enterprise development in the very poor eastern region
of the country.  Approximately half of the loan
recipients interviewed (about 20 percent of the total)
had substantially increased their sales volume,
clientele, and disposable income and had diversified
their product lines.[12]  Such reports are typical in
the literature on small enterprise, with credit
programs linked to the rapid increases in the numbers
of firms as well as in the sales and income of existing
firms.[13]

These results have been markedly increased by
organizational changes and management reforms,
including efforts to increase interaction among a
project's staff and the potential beneficiary community
and to improved efficiency in the processing of loan
applications.  An example of the significance of such
changes appears in the experience of the UNO project
for microenterprise development in Brazil.  This
project featured efforts to deal with the rather slow
dispersal of credit to informal sector entrepreneurs in
the northeastern state of Pernambuco.[14]  Program
operations were decentralized so that none of the
targeted beneficiaries was far removed from an UNO
office.  Program staff then had ample opportunity to
interact with clients and potential clients.  Coupled
with this was an agreement with the state bank
(BANDEPE) to speed up the processing of loans.  A
reorganization of the bank's operations reduced the
time needed to secure loan approvals by 90 percent.
These two steps were apparently responsible for the
substantial improvement in loans processed per staff
member, and the total number of loans granted by
UNO/Caruaru.  Many of the same improvements were later
made in the original center of project activity, the
city of Recife, with the result that the rate of loans
granted there has recently doubled.[15]  There are
other reports of decentralization of this sort working
to the same effect in PVO projects in Kenya.[16]
     A capacity to group clients into cooperatives or
business associations may provide additional
efficiencies in the development of credit programs.
Groups cut the costs of promotion and processing credit
applications, and allow for more aggressive follow-up
and collection efforts.  They also provide important
information to project officials on client needs.[17]
For instance, a recent evaluation of SE projects of the
Dominican Development Foundation (DDF) found
administrative costs of loans and extension services to
informal sector entrepreneurs in solidarity
associations to be less than half that for slightly
larger, still informal sector firms which were not
grouped.[18]  Moreover, in an evaluation of PfP's
commercial and enterprise development project in Upper
Volta, the record of two women's cooperative in
channelling resources to low income market women was
seen as particularly noteworthy.  These co-ops had
initiated group development activities in conjunction
with the credit process, and had secured high levels of
on-time payments by borrowers.  This program was seen
as a potential model both because of its social impact
and economic cost effectiveness.[19]  On the other
hand, a PVO such as IIDI has developed credit programs
based largely on a policy of accepting all borrowers
that come for assistance, provided they meet its

lending criteria. Despite the success of its programs (noted below), there have been concerns expressed over the difficulties IIDI has had in managing its diffuse and widely dispersed clientele. Efforts to keep track of clients, to provide advice and to secure scheduled payments, have generated more paper work. Loan application forms were made more complex and personal contact with loan applicants decreased. The result was that fewer loans got made while administrative costs remained high.[20]

When credit project goals emphasize the need to sustain enterprise profitability and entrepreneurial income, research suggests that extended loans to relatively larger enterprises, and loans for fixed investments, are most likely to contribute to those ends.[21] Some of the evaluation materials suggest that credit to microsector firms may only rarely produce self-sustaining enterprises.[22] Even those strongly favoring assistance for the microsector admit that the apparently positive impact of credit assistance to these firms can be misleading. O'Regan, Schmidt and Sebstad found an increase in gross incomes of about 30 per cent in the more than 150 microfirms aided by a credit program of the National Christian Council of Kenya. But they also saw a tendency for these increases to level off after a period of time and concluded that this occurred because of the need for owners to consume most of the profits to meet family needs. Without more reinvestment in the enteprise itself, the long-term impact of the loan would be minimized.[23] These conclusions may be premature, since firms used for family projects may well support other business endeavors. They may also support long-term human benefits which can have great significance; including not only better food and more education for family members, but the psychological gains which can come from the successful use and repayment of loans by those with little previous experience with the formal credit sector.[24]

This consideration of enduring impacts, coupled with the need to consider the benefits and costs of reaching the smallest firms, suggests a central question for credit programs. Can they be both effective in promoting economic change and business growth on the one hand, and create impacts which are equitable on the other? Indeed, do credit projects believed successful sometimes do as much harm as good, in a social as well as an economic sense?

## Credit: The Social and Personal Implications

The Social Dimensions of Credit. Concerns for the social effects of credit programs have been more

pronounced since the beginning of the "New Directions"
era in development assistance.  Early efforts to see
that credit went to the least advantaged focused on
attempts to categorize recipients on the basis of
family income and firm size.  Alternatively, they
tended to require that money went only to the
unemployed or to young people just starting out.  These
tactics continue to be used to facilitate an equitable
distribution of resources.[25]  Often they are not
successful.  It takes dedicated leaders and a better
management information system than most project
managers have available to enforce an equitable
distribution.  One effective approach has been to limit
loan size.  This tends to discourage the more
advantaged individuals, who have less incentive to seek
such small-scale assistance.[26]

Size limits may be less necessary, but still
helpful, where organizations of poor recipients exist.
"Solidarity groups" make it possible for the very poor
not only to get loans, and repay them, but to become
effective mediators between the most deprived and more
powerful interests in the community.[27]  One of the
reasons suggested for the improved performance of the
UNO project in reaching poor entrepreneurs in and
around the Brazilian city of Caruaru was the decision
by project officials to support the creation and
activities of a special administrative unit solely for
establishing associations and cooperatives for the
informal sector businessmen and women who were to be
served.  Forming these groups can be very difficult,
but there is increasing evidence that the time and
effort involved can reap economic as well as social
benefits.[28]

However, even projects which get money to the poor
can easily end up bolstering the power of local
elites.  In one study where an effort was made to trace
the use of loan funds, it was found that substantial
resources were going to raw material suppliers and
wholesalers to pay full price for goods on delivery.
No discounts were offered, and prices remained at the
inflated rate set by suppliers accustomed to providing
goods on credit.  For the customers, the arrangement
was apparently satisfactory in that it offered a means
to secure the good will of the supplier-patrons for
some future time when money might be in short
supply.[29]  Risk minimization strategies of this sort
are rational enough from the perspective of the
entrepreneur who must operate in a system of patrons
and clients.[30]  But they also hinder the ability of
small firms to enter and survive independently in a
larger marketplace.[31]

Answers are easier when the focus shifts from
firms and owners to jobs and the distribution of
benefits to workers.  According to the experience of

development agencies, the larger of the small firms are
likely to produce substantial numbers of new jobs,
especially in the manufacturing sector. A good example
of this is the IIDI effort in Honduras, which stressed
support for all businesses (manufacturing or not) which
seemed likely to survive and grow.[32] However,
critics of this approach point out that we really know
little about what job creation means; whether jobs
produced actually increase the amount or broaden the
distribution of income available in a region.[33] If
the existing new technologies turn out to be less labor
intensive than old ones, jobs may actually be lost.
There are also concerns about the quality of jobs in
the SE sector. Some see dangers in offering these jobs
as solutions for underemployment precisely because they
turn out to be lower paying ones than those in larger
scale enterprises, and because they often provide fewer
of the extra benefits. Those firms which do produce
the largest numbers of employment opportunities are
typically larger and more affluent.[34]

Some of these findings are challenged, however, by
those who favor strategies that promote the direct
employment capacities of beneficiary firms. They argue
that low quality jobs are better than none. Moreover,
where the jobs created do result in new employment, the
quality issue may be less significant. But it may be
insignificant in any event. A short-term,
intermittent, low-skill job may precisely fit the needs
of the partially employed, especially rural women who
need the flexibility such jobs provide in order to
continue to meet their traditional obligations. Such
jobs also can provide opportunities for men to earn
enough income to allow them to remain with their
families rather than seek work elsewhere. Such social
benefits can be substantial, even though difficult to
document.[35]

With the growing interest in the potential of
informal sector economic activities, the issue of
employment has emerged as a major project goal.
Innumerable microfirms exist in developing nations; and
they intrigue development professionals as potential
channels for reaching the urban and rural poor. On the
one hand, most appear unlikely to grow, even though
they may survive for extended periods of time. They
are also unlikely to generate many new jobs in the
usual sense. However, evaluations suggest that they
may reduce underemployment within owner families. This
is a factor which those assessing the PfP project in
Upper Volta regarded as partial compensation for the
relatively few jobs created by the assisted firms.[36]
Furthermore, microfirms may have significant employment
impacts beyond the family. They may provide more
economic linkages to local, smaller firms than larger
ones do, depending on the type of firm in question and

the amount of information on goods and services available in the local market.[37]

The differences reviewed here point to the potential trade-offs among jobs, equity, and rural development goals in the design of SE projects. Such dilemmas can be resolved only through consideration of systemic questions that are usually omitted in project formulation and evaluation. For instance, what are the general outcomes needed for a community, in terms of the quality of life for all citizens? There is little attention given in SE evaluation materials concerning this type of outcome. Yet, as these dilemmas become more evident, they will stimulate concern for such questions in the literature on SE development. They also will provide important terms of reference concerning the roles PVOs can play in promoting small enterprises and, through them, community welfare.

Nonproject Sources of Credit and Financial Assistance for the SE Sector. Several questions can be raised regarding nonproject inputs into the SE sector. How effective are inputs from development projects compared to policy changes in the dominant domestic institutions of a developing country (i.e., banks and governments) in stimulating SE development? Do these institutions and policies on some occasions dwarf the effects of project inputs? More positively, can they provide even greater boosts to SE development than enterprise projects? No doubt they sometimes can.[38]

For instance, small enterprises in developing countries benefit substantially from growth in consumer income. Contrary to the expectations of many economists, demand elasticities are quite favorable even for rural enterprises producing and selling simple products.[39] Consequently, government programs to aid agricultural development may provide a significant financial boost for rural enterprise, particularly where projects actually reach the poorest in the countryside. Though demand elasticities are favorable for small enterprise products generally, they are particularly so when income gains by the poorest enterprises are taken alone.[40]

Other sigificant government actions influencing the financial status of small enterprises--in this case negatively--include trade regulations. Exchange rates and tariffs often provide discriminatory advantages for more capital intensive businesses. The same has been said of tax laws, which in many instances provide concessionary rates for bigger enterprises.[41]

Alternatively, governments have sometimes been willing to require that banks raise their percentage of loans to the small business sector. Some governments have created loan guarantee programs to facilitate

these efforts. These programs have not often been
successful since it is difficult to guarantee
compliance. However, there are exceptions,
particularly when banks alone or in conjunction with
other agencies, provide concessionary assistance in the
context of a broader development program.[42]

Whether or not these policy factors are more
significant than projects in a given instance is
difficult to determine. Anyway, the most important
thing is to understand how SE project designers and
managers can adapt to these factors, or change them in
ways supportive of their own goals. We will deal more
with this issue later. For now we can say that few of
the projects evaluated have dealt systematically with
these questions. There are occasional references to
the need for project officials and beneficiaries to
have more influence over government economic
policy.[43] There have been some efforts by PfP to
build upon existing governmental institutions in Upper
Volta as a means of stimulating the rural SE sector
through the promotion of agricultural production and
income[44] But the fact is that little is known about
the financial significance of these domestic factors in
comparison to project financial assistance.

Conclusions on Credit. The following conclusions
can be drawn from the discussion on credit:

1.  The relative availability of credit for SE
    influences the rate of formation of new firms
    and the overall sustainability of small
    enterprise, at least in the short term.
2.  Impacts are more likely to be felt, and
    broadly distributed, where credit applications
    can be processed rapidly and loans well
    monitored. Efficiency of this sort is a
    function of:
    a.  the proximity of credit institutions to
        those served, since the decentralization
        of operations has been shown to relate to
        an increase in the number of loans made;
    b.  the extent to which beneficiaries and
        potential beneficiaries can be effectively
        grouped, as through cooperative credit
        associations, solidarity groups and the
        like, with this, in turn, being the
        product of the availability of a variety
        of incentives to participants;
    c.  The experience the credit agency or
        intermediary body has in a given region;
    d.  the knowledge of the SE sector acquired
        and available to the credit body, as
        through a census of SE;
    e.  staff management skills; and

  f. relationships to formal sector credit institutions.

3. The impacts of credit on firm profitability and the income of the entrepreneur and his/her family are more likely to endure when loans:

  a. are for longer rather than shorter terms;

  b. are for fixed rather than working capital;

  c. are provided to firms which are larger than microsector enterprises.

4. Credit, especially when provided to entrepreneurs who have not previously borrowed from public institutions, seems to be associated with the recipient's level of self-confidence and dispositions toward planning. Its impacts are most positive when loans are carefully tailored to the recipient's capacity to repay.

5. Where credit is not effective in improving the business performance of SE, and problems faced are other than basic structural obstacles (e.g., powerlessness), the main limits on the effectiveness of credit are most likely to be:

  a. the fact there is little demand for products produced.

  b. the fact that the management skills of the recipient entrepreneurs are minimal (though this in turn may be a product of personal disadvantages);

  c. the nonavailability of raw materials;

  d. regulations affecting procurement and operations generally.

6. Unless credit programs are specifically designed to account for social and economic differences within communities served, they will very likely reinforce inequality by promoting additional opportunities for the more privileged. Issues of equity, empowerment, and community development as integral concerns of credit projects can add to opportunities for both growth and equality among individuals and within communities served.

7. Where opportunities for introducing social controls and minimal, the most effective mechanisms for promoting equality of opportunity among potential borrowers are requirements which:

  a. limit credit to those with minimum income;

  b. require that assets of borrowers and their firms do not exceed given levels;

  c. strictly limit the amount available for any given loan. (The smaller the loan, the more likely that poorer individuals, and especially women, will benefit.)

8. Credit which is targeted to organized groups
   of the poor is more likely to have an
   equitable effect. (The process of finding
   and/or supporting the development of such
   organizations usually involves considerable
   "front end" costs for the organizing efforts
   and the project may therefore appear costly in
   the short run.)
9. Where the creation of jobs is of primary
   interest, the best results are likely where
   credit is provided:
   a. for longer terms;
   b. to new firms, especially as opposed to
      the expansion (often capital intensive) of
      existing ones;
   c. to firms larger than microenterprises,
      those generally called small or medium
      scale;
   d. to manufacturing enterprises more than
      those involved in service activities, and
      both of these more than those involved in
      retail trade.

## SE Development Through Extension and Training

Many studies of small enterprise have highlighted
the importance of managerial skills in the survival and
success of such firms.[45] As a consequence, the
provision of training opportunities and various
advisory services have been components of most small
enterprise projects, particularly in recent years.[46]
Some feel that these inputs are more important than
credit, particularly for firms that have survived the
early "start-up" crises.[47] A recent evaluation of a
microenterprise project of the DDF tends at least to
support a strong priority for management training and
advisory services. In this case, the most significant
explanation for expansion in sales, fixed assets, and
employees receiving credit was not the amount of
credit, but the degree to which the entrepreneurs were
using management skills taught as part of the
assistance program.[48]
Where there is criticism of extension and training
services it is of failures to match sufficiently the
opportunities provided with beneficiary needs. Some
failures are seen in psychological terms, such as where
there is a lack of appreciation of the applied
behavioral science research on the relationship of
personality and enterprise development. This is
striking since in many parts of the world this work and
supportive evaluations have strongly influenced project
design and development.[49] More commonly, concerns
with failures in program and beneficiary compatibility

occur where sophisticated business courses are aimed at
owner-operators of the smallest businesses, which are
unlikely to grow in any case.  Critics increasingly
argue that simpler training efforts may not only
suffice but be superior.  Some call for limiting
training and advisory services to such subjects as
separating personal and business accounts, starting an
account at a bank, and maintaining and repairing
tools.[50]  Teaching such simple processes, and some
rudiments of record keeping has been shown to relate to
improved business operations among small rural firms in
several nations.[51]  Alternatively, programs that
require the completion of formal training courses for
the approval of loans are seen as likely to fail.
Trainees in these cases are likely to offer only
perfunctory responses to the course material.  Moreover, any changes in the way such individuals operate
their businesses are unlikely to extend beyond the
period of supervision associated with the loan.[52]

A counterargument is suggested by the experience
of the DDF.  A recent evaluation of training efforts
with informal sector firms suggests that even when
there is some reversion to former ways, microenterprise
owners know and display more effective management
practices than they did before training was
provided.[53]  But, there are other examples to be
found of training and extension efforts, particularly
for the smallest of businesses, which provide advice on
things unconnected to the entrepreneur's needs.[54]
Such incompatibilities in the UNO project in Brazil led
Tendler to question the expenditure of nearly a third
of available resources on training.[55]

These results make the reported successes of the
Opportunities Industrialization Centers International
(OICI) in three African nations seem somewhat
anomalous.  Yet, two recent evaluations of OICI's
entrepreneurship training courses have indicated that
fairly standard business training programs were
extremely well received by trainees.[56]  They also
appeared, to the evaluators and many public officials
in the countries, to be affecting business performance
in a positive way.  Still, these data may fit with the
other conclusions on training.  For one thing, OICI is
primarily a training body, and has built its reputation
in the United States with vocational programs aimed at
assisting the least skilled.  It may be that recipient
nations and trainees working with OICI know that they
will receive only training and not financial
assistance.  Moreover, and probably more important,
most of the trainees in the OICI projects are operating
firms larger than the informal sector enterprises which
Tendler and others evaluated.  The record on the
response to training by entrepreneurs from firms of
this size is much more positive.[57]

Training for extension agents and business faculty should also vary with the level of firms they are to serve. Studies of microfirms suggest that those agents and teachers with fewer business skills but more skills in problem solving do superior work and are better received. Those who are technically well trained are likely to be bored with the work and ineffective.[58] Alternatively, where larger firms are serviced, these individuals need to have a broad command of management material and business knowledge, plus a sense of the particular dynamics of small firms and the problems they face at various stages of development.[59] Where there are supportive services for extension of agents and trainers, their work is also facilitated. For example OICI develops a number of advisory bodies at each of its training sites to provide regular analyses of market conditions and instructional materials for its faculty and field officers.[60]

The capacity to deliver training and extension services to small entrepreneurs is also made easier by the availability of mutual support groups, or "solidarity" associations of beneficiaries. These can include trade and manufacturing associations. Where such associations are effective (recall the case of the women's group in Upper Volta; or the case of the cooperatives formed in stage two of the UNO project), they can reduce the costs of promoting development programs and of dispensing services. They may also become involved in training and extension activities on their own behalf in order to gain legitimacy and support among other potential group members.[61]

Nonproject Supports: Equivalents and Substitutes for Training and Extension Services. There is a growing recognition that the owner-managers of small enterprises in many cases have the ability and resources to carry on operations and even to do better when left alone. There is also evidence that certain social conditions and psychological dispositions predict to successful business careers. Such nonproject factors provide much of the tangible and intangible support that is needed for success.[62] Support is also provided by business experience itself; those who have had an opportunity to "learn by doing" are more likely to succeed. In fact, prior business activity is one of the best single predictors of success with small enterprises, while most studies find that levels of formal education are unrelated to success.[63] A few training programs have recognized the importance of previous business experience as the strongest single reason for development agencies to provide credit, training, and extension services.[64] This does not mean that other assistance is unnecessary. It means that there may be a more

effective relationship between development agencies and
extension agents on the one hand, and the SE on the
other, if there is recognition of how to utilize
nonproject elements such as apprenticeship systems.  To
this end, there is an inclination to view informal
training efforts as something on which projects can
build.  Support for traditional apprenticeship systems,
or the encouragement of them, may well be a relatively
inexpensive and effective way of supporting types of
training activity commonly seen associated with success
in business.[65]

Beyond the contribution of training through
apprenticeship programs, business leaders have
considered at least two other means for assisting in
the development of small enterprise.  These include
efforts to establish links between large and small
enterprises so that the latter have assured markets for
their products, while the former can secure regular,
relatively low cost supplies of intermediate goods.
Banks have been supporters of these types of programs,
as have trade and manufacturing associations.  The
latter have in many cases also worked to create a
number of consultancy services for small firms.  Often
they have not been very effective because of the
difficulties of providing appropriate advice to a
diverse body of enterprises.[66]

Governments are, of course, involved in the
development of extension services for small
entrepreneurs.  Public regulatory policies have
important, if indirect, implications for the training
and advisory needs of small enterprises. Changes in
public policy may assist small business more than many
training or extension activities.  For instance,
licensing procedures required for business operations
in most developing nations, minimum wages policy, and
employee benefit regulations can pose major problems
for small enterprises.  Small entrepreneurs either need
a reduction in regulations or access to extension
agents with brokering skills to handle these problems.
In any event, government regulation is a critical
determinant of the types of extension and training
services needed by small businessmen and women.  These
political and bureaucratic influences, along with
broader social factors, need to be accounted for in
project decision making, just as are domestic and
international financial influences.

Conclusions on Extension and Training.  The
following conclusions can be drawn from this review of
the evaluation literature on extension and training in
SE development.

1.  Years of formal education does not relate to
    entrepreneurial dispositions or to business

success, at least in a direct way.

2. Business training courses are likely to
   contribute to the improvement of
   entrepreneurial skills and business
   development where: the trainees' firms are
   relatively large; training is integrated with
   other program inputs; and trainees are
   personally motivated for business success.

3. Basically the same relationships are true for
   management advisory services. They contribute
   most to the stability and growth of tiny and
   small firms when efforts are made to provide
   advice and information tailored to immediate
   business needs.

4. The most successful training and extension
   service institutions have staffs with skills
   relevant to the types and sizes of enterprises
   served, sources of regular information on the
   needs of beneficiaries and enterprises, and a
   capacity to judge the relevance of training
   and advice provided.

5. Training and extension services for the poor
   are most effective when the beneficiaries are
   organized into mutual support groups. Such
   groups can reduce costs for reaching scattered
   small enterprises, and can facilitate the
   exchange of advisory and training services
   among them.

## Institution Building and SE Development

In the previous section we reviewed the
implications of credit, extension, and training on SE
development. We turn now to a discussion of
institution building which is a common concern of PVOs
and which has strong implications for the relevance of
SE development in meeting the needs of the poor. This
is mainly true because a broadly focused concern for
institutional development can assist planners and
managers to avoid the discrete and static emphasis
common in most SE projects.

There are costs to the approaches to SE project
design and evaluation approaches that emphasize
specific inputs, such as credit or extension services.
They can generate serious dilemmas, which can threaten
basic project goals. We have already discussed some of
the dilemmas posed in the credit and technical
assistance projects. For instance, do we promote
employment even if it means supporting the most
privileged individuals? Similarly, when do the social
costs become too great to tolerate? Are the gains made
in working with the very poor entrepreneur sufficient
to offset the relatively low level of jobs their firms

will provide?  What are the trade-offs between credit
and training?  How are these affected by the nature and
stage of the firm's development?  At a more general
level, can we reduce the vulnerability of a project
directed at the poor by associating government
officials and agencies with it to provide financial and
political support?  Could this also cause a reduction
in the project's independent base for action?  Can we
have beneficiary participation and efficient projects?
Is it even likely that we can increase returns on
investment if organizational support is provided to
very small enterprises, given recent findings on the
relative economic efficiency of these firms.[67]  Are
there times when it would be preferable to work to
change public regulatory policy rather than to provide
project type benefits?

Attempts to deal with such concerns have been
largely responsible for the emphasis on multisectoral
or integrated development projects over the past
decade.  Such projects encompass a much wider range of
concerns, and more beneficiaries within a larger
geographic area.  In contemporary SE projects,
extension services are more clearly allied with credit
programs, and perhaps coordinated with activities of
private sector banking institutions.  Integrated
projects may take on institution-building components
such as greater attention to the development of a board
of directors, and to the creation of support networks
which may extend to international actors.  This all may
lead to "check lists" whereby various targeted
individuals and institutions are monitored to ascertain
whether the expected effects and relationships are
produced. How many women are being assisted?  Are
invaluable ecological resources being damaged?  What is
the effect of the project on the price of intermediate
goods?

Critics admit that integrated approaches to
project design and evaluation represent an improvement
over past efforts.  But such approaches still are
viewed as too dependent on a tradition of analysis
which minimizes system-level concerns.[68]  Some
critics think SE development should be based on the
institutionalization of roles and relationships which
facilitate and support productive activities by the
poor--and the rest of society.  Design and evaluation
based on an institutional approach would emphasize the
interaction of a large number of individuals and
organizations.  It would measure success in terms of
the ability to establish sustainable linkages between
individuals, enterprises, the market, the political
system, and communities.  The institutionalization of
SE projects involves nothing less than the development
of a way for projects to coexist with, and contribute
to, a system of enforceable norms that support

sustainable change.  After further specifying what
institutionalization means in the context of SE
evaluation, we will use the concept in two ways.
First,  we will introduce a final group of activities
found in the literature to be associated with SE
development.  Then we will draw on the concept of
institutionalization to focus an analysis of the role
of PVOs in enterprise development.

The impacts and costs of SE projects are best
assessed through an analysis of the basic inputs
already discussed--credit and technical assistance.
But one should also assess the role of four other
"participants" in this process, who also affect project
development.  These include, first, the targeted
entrepreneurs and the broader community in which they
live.  Second, are the actors and institutions making
up the political and administrative system in and
beyond the project locale.  Included here are
indigenous and transnational interest groups, which can
be sources of support for project activities.  Third
are the local, regional, national, and international
markets for goods and services.  Finally, there are the
relations among project staff members, and the internal
structure and processes of the field agency.  The
latter are important for facilitating effective
relations between external actors and small
enterprises--relations that are often critical to
enduring project success.  The advocates of
institutionalization argue that simultaneous attention
to these factors is fundamental to the success of SE
projects.

The following propositions summarize the key
institutional factors that can promote the success of
SE programs.

1.  Carefully structured project efforts to
    encourage backward and forward economic
    linkages, and to generate support for project
    activities from (i) associations of
    beneficiaries, (ii) public regulatory and
    policy bodies and (iii) other national and
    international development agencies will tend
    to:
    a.  reduce long-term project costs despite the
        expenses incurred in the development of
        autonomous organizations;
    b.  increase the sustainability and spread of
        project impacts to all sectors of the
        community, broadening the economic
        linkages of project activities and
        increasing the chances for a relatively
        equitable distribution of project benefits;
    c.  facilitate the development of mediating
        networks which can protect project

interests and influence social, economic,
and political elites toward behaviors
supportive of project goals;

d. create new human resources, including
managerial skills and solidarity, as well
as material resources; and

e. encourage a more plural, representative
political process (thus increasing the
potential for SE owners to exert
continuing influence on public policy).

2. These networking efforts work best where
project and associated institutions maintain
high levels of <u>independence</u> (autonomy) and
<u>coherence</u> in basic goals and strategy.

3. Autonomy and coherence for project and related
institutions depends a good deal on government
actions. Autonomy in particular is increased
where governments are basically democratic in
nature and strong supporters of SE projects.

4. Project autonomy and coherence can also be
enhanced through efforts to develop
beneficiary organizations to legitimize
project goals, and through:

a. efforts to increase the quality of
internal project management and the amount
of information available to that
management;

b. efforts to minimize the capacity of
powerful others to interfere with project
operations by making benefits as
unattractive to elites as possible (via
limits on loan size and on types of
activities supported) without destroying
their utility for targeted groups; and

c. efforts to expand linkages to indigenous
and external agencies beyond those
directly involved in project
activities--to generate a visible,
politically significant support community,
capable of checking elite interference.

## AID Evaluations and Institutionalization

The AID evaluations reviewed for this analysis
demonstrate that there is considerable interest in
questions of institutionalization. There is increased
sensitivity in these materials to such things as
solidarity groups and processes for accommodating
political elites. There are determined efforts to see
that benefits achieved by targeted entrepreneurs are
linked to other local businesses. Four examples are
discussed below. They illustrate how current SE
development projects can accommodate the broader

institutional and economic environment. This will
provide additional opportunity to deal with the
strategy and tactics of PVOs that have been evaluated
by AID. It will also suggest some of the successes and
problems with a systems approach to development.
Finally, it will reintroduce a major theme of this
chapter: when and where are PVOs most effective in SE
development activities?

The first example is that of the OICI, an
organization whose development programs feature efforts
to associate influential individuals with project
activities. The OICI enterprise development efforts
are centered in Africa, specifically in Liberia, Sierra
Leone, and Lesotho. They involve training programs of
six weeks duration and emphasize work with small
traders and manufacturers, many of whom are women. The
OICI programs are now being expanded into rural areas
of these countries. Training efforts in all cases are
coupled with a number of vocational programs directed
at school leavers. Thus, the training activities of
the organization tend to focus on the provision of a
range of skills to the least advantaged, and the
development of human resources capable of meeting a
wide range of economic needs in the nations served.

A particularly significant aspect of their
efforts in Africa, and in the United States where their
work began in the 1960s, has been their emphasis on
program institutionalization. The OICI sets up three
policy and advisory bodies for each of its country
programs--a board of directors and two advisory
committees to handle different questions concerning
training and the economy. These bodies involve
individuals from the public and private sector with
specific technical skills--especially educators and
business people--and those from policy-making levels of
government. They provide policy guidance, assistance
in the development and up-dating of curricula, and
assessments of economic opportunities for students.
They are also supposed to insure that the organization
gets a hearing in government circles. These
institutional mechanisms seem to have resulted in a
consolidation of the status of the training
organization and in closer ties with national training
efforts. But students have also benefited from the
training and have enjoyed wider commercial and
vocational opportunities at graduation. This is
reflected in the unusually positive evaluation of
course offerings by former students.[69]

The aspirations of OICI for this type of
institutional development differ from those of most
PVOs, given the range of activities that are covered,
and the effort made to work closely with government
elites. Close association with governments in volatile
societies can be risky. Nevertheless, other PVOs are

working more intensively to establish local boards of
directors. In the AID sample, for instance, both IIDI
and PfP report considerable interest in the development
of autonomous boards to support the credit and
extension programs they have set up.

The second example illustrates the process of
political participation and mobilization. Just as PVOs
are beginning to seek an effective means for
accommodating political and regulatory forces in the
society and for utilizing the sources of information
these sectors command, so too are they recognizing the
importance of drawing on the support which
beneficiaries themselves can provide. In the
discussions of credit and technical assistance
components of SE projects we have noted the reported
advantages of having well-organized associations of
beneficaries as partners in the development effort.
They can promote potential cost savings, as well as
improved means for reaching poorer sectors of society.

This second example is focused on the efforts of
ACCION/International AITEC, a PVO which works
extensively in Central and South America. ACCION was
one of the original sponsors of the UNO project in
Brazil. Its experiences there, and its work with
microsector enterprise in Colombia and Mexico, have
been marked by efforts to better reach the poor in the
informal sector economy. Opportunities provided by an
AID-sponsored informal sector project (PISCES) gave
ACCION the chance to further test means for doing
this. One result has been the adaptation of work done
in El Salvador and Madras, India, with "solidarity
groups" of microentrepreneurs. As a consequence of
these experiences, ACCION has become one of the more
active PVOs in promoting associations of beneficiaries
in SE projects. A recent evaluation of this work
suggests that solidarity groups can provide the
mobilizational and cost benefits expected, but also
clearly indicates that the process of creating and
working with these groups is complex.[70] Conclusions
reached on the development and maintenance of group
morale and commitment, particularly with respect to the
repayment of loans, are close to those reached in
theoretical studies on the mobilization of the
poor.[71] Where these groups "work" they are usually
the product of careful extension efforts that stress
the significance of associations. Demographic
characteristics, such as long-term familiarity of
members with each other, also contribute to success.
Also, smaller loans which leave ownership of
beneficiary property temporarily with the solidarity
group can be particularly helpful. Combined with
administrative changes which expedite subsequent loans
for fixed and working capital, this may not only reduce
the problems of late payments but increase the

spill-over effects of group activity as members stay
more active.[72]

Overall, there is a good deal of positive evidence
on the significance of solidary groups. A recent review
of successful PVO activities by the Netherlands
Institute of Social Studies concluded that having an
organized group of the poor to deal with was one of the
best guarantees of PVO success in reaching the
poor.[73] As one study of the impact of rural roads in
Liberia concluded, the political (organizational) base
for the poor must be built at approximately the same
time as the other infrastructure, if the poor are to
benefit from the introduction of new resources.[74] It
is not enough simply to set up an association of small
entrepreneurs and expect it to serve as a vehicle for
change. A study of small traders and manaufacturers in
India revealed that while the correlation between
membership in a business association and a range of
economic improvements in the enterprise was strong,
(these explained nearly 50 percent of the variation in
success), it was strong and positive only among small
businessmen and women who ranked highly on several
indicators of social status.[75] The conclusion drawn
in this case was that business associations (even those
for small business) generally were dominated by, and
worked for, the more established members of the
business community. Later studies in India of business
associations have offered additional evidence in
support of this conclusion.[76] This underscores the
notion that special efforts are required to see that
these bodies are responsive to the poor.

An even more broadly defined concern for grouping
beneficiaries can be seen in the efforts by
organizations such as the Sarvodaya Shramadana in Sri
Lanka. It was started in the late 1950s as a community
self-help movement in very poor villages. Programs in
each community were began with attempts to create a
sense of solidarity. Where possible they involved
Buddhist priests as leaders and symbolic sources of
unity. The community-building efforts were designed to
lead to community plans for a broad range of activity,
including the development of business enterprise.
Central to the efforts, however, was the goal of having
members of a village collectively define appropriate
business activity, and share together in the benefits
through the institution of a variety of public
programs. Enterprise development was therefore
considered as an adjunct to community development
activities. While such goals were not always realized
in practice, there were significant successes.[77]

A third example is provided by PfP International
which has begun to emphasize the creation of
complementary economic relationships in the communities
where it promotes SE development. PfP International

has been involved in enterprise promotion projects since the early 1970s, beginning in East Africa and now including eight countries in Africa and Asia. Its experiences have highlighted the need to assure that credit and technical assistance are provided in a manner that supports economic linkages within the target community.[78] Partly as a consequence of these concerns, its SE project in Upper Volta has evolved into an effort to assist both the urban and rural microsector, while at the same time working through demonstration farms to generate technologies helpful in improving agricultural production. A major goal of this project is to support rural enterprise through the generation of more purchasing power. But a more dynamic, commercial agricultural sector also provides intermediate and finished goods beneficial for area business. PfP attempted to go beyond this through its credit program and training operations. The goal is to provide loans and training which seem likely to stimulate various, complementary business lines. The evaluation of PfP Upper Volta found problems in carrying this out, but found reason for optimism in the plans PfP had for stage two of the project. Indeed, PfP appears to haved learned from earlier mistakes and seems to be on the verge of establishing workable complementary linkages.[79]

There are other means that PVOs can use to establish economic relationships. They could collaborate in assisting complementary economic sectors, with each of the organizations emphasizing those types and sizes of firms with which have had had the most experience. The effect would be similar to what PFP seeks: an assistance effort that builds upon and energizes the broader impacts that PVOs and developing nations desire. This issue will be considered in more detail below.

A final concern that PVOs involved in SE activities should emphasize is the quality and independence of indigenous field staffs. Among the PVOs that rank highly in this regard is the IIDI. IIDI begins the process of setting up a credit fund with field visits by volunteer representatives who search for appropriate project locales. Among the issues raised in the preliminary work is that IIDI's commitment will be limited in duration, and that the indigenous body will be required quite soon to secure funds from operations and other donors if it is to continue. IIDI project field staff find that the survival and potential for expansion of the credit body depends on the efficiency of their operations and the learning of skills, including fund raising. IIDI works to provide these skills, and calls on the support of local church networks to provide moral support and assistance in securing clients for the program. A

central concern is institutional autonomy. The
emphasis on the development of internal management
processes compatible with this goal is a well-developed
aspect of IIDI's efforts. Other PVOs certainly show
concern with management issues, and in some ways show a
greater awareness of relationships affecting
institutional autonomy than IIDI does. But IIDI's
program for staff development demonstrates in an
exemplary way the importance of this element of project
institutionalization.

The four examples discussed above illustrate
contemporary concerns for setting project operations
within a larger context of environmental constraints
and opportunities. Effective SE projects require an
effort to establish compatible relationships with
individuals and organizations. While the PVOs
discussed in these examples do try to account for
issues raised in more than one of the relationship
categories, it is rare to find anything approaching an
equivalent interest in more than one of them. OICI,
for instance, has recently worked to develop an alumni
association to give more representation to program
graduates--though probably the major reason for the
effort is to gather support for the Lesotho OICI's
fund-raising activities. Officials from ACCION might
well suggest to them the benefits of viewing the alumni
association as a solidarity group--perhaps using it to
help in finding new trainees or to express the needs of
the small business sector to the government. This
would be especially useful since there are few
functioning business associations in Lesotho responsive
to the small enterprise sector.[80] A successful
alumni association could also serve at some future time
to temper efforts by the government to control OICI--a
risk OICI runs with its efforts to involve political
elites closely in its activities.

Similarly, ACCION and its solidarity groups could
learn from PfP's concerns for facilitating linkages
among economic sectors. There is evidence from surveys
conducted as part of a recent evaluation that many
entrepreneurs would like to branch out into related
lines of activity--with delivery men and women also
starting fixed retail outlets or firms to supply the
goods for those involved in hauling operations.

Finally, all of these organizations might consider
the suggestions originating from the conference of the
Institute for Social Studies in the Hague. A common
theme there was that PVOs need to find the broadest
possible network of organizational supporters,
especially in the local and international private
sector. Just as beneficiary organizations can be
useful for countering demands by political elites, so
can the broader coalitions. The conference summary
refers to these as "umbrella organizations" protective

of project autonomy.[81]  We turn now to a discussion
of the benefits that can be gained from a more complete
systems level perspective.


SE DEVELOPMENT FROM A SYSTEM PERSPECTIVE

There are examples of PVO SE projects which show
unusual sensitivity to the need for simultaneous
accounting for a wide range of beneficiary, political,
and voluntary sector institutions.  It should be noted,
however, that more comprehensive programs are not
necessarily better than the more limited ones.  It is
even possible for more limited ones to be more
comprehensive in impact, or more effective in fitting
with system needs--a point which will be elaborated
upon momentarily.  The more immediate point is that
there are SE development efforts which show sensitivity
to the need for system-level thinking.
Three examples will be sufficient to illustrate
these arguments.  One of them, the UNO project, will be
dealt with in some detail here.  The other two
enterprise projects, those of the Manila Community
Services Incorporated (MCSI) and of Technoserve in
Kenya will be considered more briefly so as to
highlight additional issues.


Examples

The UNO Project.  Judith Tendler's evaluation of
the UNO project operations in Recife indicated the
strength of the institution-building thrust of this
operation.[82]  While she found numerous problems with
the management effort and the choice of beneficiaries,
she concluded that significant steps had been taken
toward the institutionalization of project activities.
There had been successful efforts to build alliances
with private sector interests and local political
officials who desired to see more assistance given to
the informal sector.  Local political officials also
wished to protect an important regional program from
any encroachment by higher officials.  These sources of
support, when coupled with a careful effort by project
managers to keep the project small and thus to maintain
a low profile (assisted ironically by the lack of money
available to them) tended to allow for the emergence of
an autonomous credit institution.  Indeed UNO's
reputation was enhanced by its frugal and long-standing
provision of credit to the poor.  UNO's success at the
regional level was important in bringing the project to
the attention of international donors--including the
World Bank which later became involved in the UNO
project.  UNO subsequently expanded its activities.

These changes caused some concern, since they seemed to
bring into question the continuation of some of the
things which had led to the success of UNO in the first
place. Some were concerned that the careful staff work
which had characterized relations between creditor and
borrower in the past might be threatened with the very
rapid increase in the size and scope of activities.
Additional money might well bring more intense effort
by elites to interfere with the lending process.

An evaluation of activities in the city of
Caruaru, one of the new sites begun during the expanded
effort, suggests that overall the UNO is in fact
building well on the base Judith Tendler
described.[83] One reason for this success appears to
be the effort to expand activities to encompass a
fuller range of the external and internal forces acting
on the project. This is supported by Jackelen's
analysis which points to an emerging strategic sense
within UNO regarding where its activities fit in the
overall development of the region. A clear indication
of this is in UNO's interest in the development of
cooperatives and enterprise associations as a regular
part of its project activities. Traditional patronage
relationships still dominate cooperative activities in
some ways, but in some settings these beneficiary
groups are emerging as worthy competitors, thereby
increasing the resources and the options of small
entrepreneurs.

One of the reasons it is possible for the UNO
project to create beneficiary institutions that are not
completely dominated by local elites, is that it has
maintained a high level of autonomy over the years.
While it has been generally supported by the national
government and defended by regional interests, its
acquisition of major international support enhances its
independence. If it can maintain distance from the
powerful influence of the World Bank through a
continued expansion of its financial support base, it
will at least approach the type of "umbrella of
support" mentioned at the Hague conference on NGOs and
development.[84] It will have significant relations
with a variety of supportive, but unrelated agencies,
in both the public and private sector, at the national
and international level. To the extent that it can
continue to build its beneficiary base it will add
perhaps an even more important component to this
umbrella coalition.

From the perspective of system-building efforts,
the UNO project is perhaps weakest in its concern for
the economic linkage effects of its credit activities.
Project lending continues to focus on helping those who
come in for assistance. Applicants are judged not on
their firm's potential for growth or the degree to
which they complement otherm firms that are already

aided, but rather mainly on their size.  However, we
have seen from other sources that microfirms may have
broad and positive economic effects through family
commercial activity which is hard to sort out and
document.  Anthropological case studies may be required
to determine what the potential linkage effects are in
these cases.

In any event, the UNO project has also expanded
efforts in recent years to provide systematic research
data on the commercial environment and on appropriate
technologies for local business activity.  The World
Bank has arranged for a local appropriate technology
research center to provide information.  Additional
assistance comes from neighboring academic institutions
which now provide regional economic analyses on which
selection efforts can be based.  These will be useful
for beneficiary firms.

There is little doubt that the recent changes in
UNO's mode of operations have improved the project's
operational efficiency.  While questions remain as to
how general and enduring this effect will be, overall
the project seems to be emerging as a significant
example of what a broader system-level perspective can
produce.

MCSI.  By way of comparison, brief reference can
be made to the microenterprise development effort of
the MCSI.  MCSI is similar to UNO in many ways.  For
instance, lending by both organizations to informal
sector enterprises is based more on size than linkage
potential.  But there are differences as well.

For one thing, MCSI, unlike UNO, depends on a
large number of volunteers as promoters and mediators
between the lending agency and beneficiaries.  These
volunteers (who in fact receive some modest benefits,
mainly priorities for small loans) are given limited
amounts of money which they can lend for short periods.
Most of them are also involved in business and know
both the local economy and the people requesting
assistance.  This approach would seem to encourage
considerable abuse by the volunteers who could easily
choose to use the money for patronage purposes.
However, the project evaluation done by Bear and Tiller
for Appropriate Technology International suggests that
this has not happened.[85]  Perhaps the prominence
gained from being part of this volunteer network, plus
the opportunity to be involved in decisions which can
be so important to the borrowers--when coupled with the
relatively small amounts of money involved--are
altogether a satisfactory check.  On the clearly
positive side, it is evident from the evaluation that
the volunteers have been motivated and active in their
promotional role, providing relatively low-cost
outreach for the project.  They have developed
effective systems of rapid assessment in finding and

judging potential borrowers. Moreover, their proximity
to these individuals and their business has helped to
generate good monitoring efforts and high levels of
loan repayment. The monitoring has been coupled with
effective technical advice: beneficiaries report
considerable satisfaction with the volunteer extension
effort.[86] There is also an interest in the possible
contributions of the volunteers to the development of
community-wide organizations of small entrepreneurs.

MCSI's most important institutional innovation is
its relationship with the Micro Industries Development
Center (MIDC). The MIDC is a nonprofit, nonstock
company with no paid staff or regular offices. Its
leadership comes, in turn, from individuals seconded
from sponsoring agencies. These agencies include MCSI
and other public and private small enterprise promotion
organizations. MIDC's purpose is to serve as catalyst
and facilitator, helping with the development of skills
in project design and implementation, and with the
diffusion of information on activities that support
enterprise development. It also serves as a vehicle
for liaison with government agencies. Liaison
activities can include arranging for subcontracting
opportunities within the context of the govenment's
development efforts, and consultation with bilateral
donors on the resources available for small enterprise
promotion. MIDC has also been involved directly in
lobbying for the interests of small business. In
short, it has the potential to fulfill many of the
"umbrella" and brokerage functions that students
believe are necessary to reach and assist small firms.
Together with the contributions of MCSI's voluntary
project associates, MIDC provides the type of external
support that is necessary for the development of
sustainable projects that benefit the poor.

Technoserve. Unlike the UNO and MCSI projects,
those of Technoserve in Kenya or of IIDI in Kenya or
Honduras emphasize assistance to the larger of the
small enterprises. Technoserve also assists
cooperative groups of rather large scale; often these
are substantial agribusinesses--such as cattle
ranches. However, Technoserve also provides
consultative services for a range of organizations
assisting the small business sector, and in this way
becomes an important source of advice, and for
brokerage with larger agencies. In this sense it
resembles the MIDC.

There is a significant role for PVOs working with
the larger of the small enterprises. Technoserve may
in this sense be "filling gaps" in the system in much
the same way as UNO and its associated indigenous and
international supporters. Technoserve and IIDI can
argue persuasively that there is a need for agencies to
handle "graduate" small firms, that are well beyond the

microsector in size. While the main emphasis of
Technoserve is, and probably should remain, on the
larger of the small firms, it is important that it
continue to provide technical advice to small
enterprises as well. This would encourage the broader
economic linkages we have been discussing. Technoserve
could also encourage broader economic linkages through
more aggressive efforts to link its firms with those in
the informal sector. It could then become portions of
the "umbrella" of support for smaller firms and their
donor organizations.

## Justifications for System Level Concerns in Enterprise Development Efforts

The evidence suggesting that the projects just
discussed are somehow superior to those that do not
attend to the same range of issues has been limited.
Most practitioners are well aware of projects which
have failed to meet their goals after governments
changed policies, or were overthrown in a coup. There
is ample opportunity to study SE programs aimed at
mobilizing the poor that have ended up bringing
unexpected benefits to the prosperous. Also common are
situations where the commercialization of a community's
economic processes contribute less to the stimulation
of local entrepreneurship, than to new patronage
relationships which retard creative potential.[87]
These add costs that most would judge intolerable in
light of project goals, if they were commonly
calculated in some form. The fact is that because they
have normally been perceived as outside the area of
control of project officials, they have not been
regarded as factors to be monitored and confronted. As
the examples cited above suggest, many enterprise
development projects are now dealing with a larger
range of previously external factors as integral to
project activity. These external factors are
increasingly seen as influencing not only the way a
project fits in its setting, but how well its managers
can handle the day-to-day activities associated with
the promotion of firms and entrepreneurs.

## THE ROLE OF PVOs IN THE PROMOTION OF SE DEVELOPMENT

What then can we conclude from the evaluations and
other materials about the role of PVOs in the
development of business enterprise? Is the evidence
sufficient to provide some insights into the
comparative advantages of PVOs? Are they likely to be
particularly helpful in meeting some of the dilemmas
sketched throughout this chapter? To a considerable

extent the conclusions offered here are suggested in
the previous discussion, but merit summary restatement.

First, efforts to find matches between types of
PVOs and types of enterprise projects may be in vain.
What is critical in a given situation is whether a
match is made between the inputs and the development
requirements of the project setting. Are the typical
"gaps" in the relations among, entrepreneurs, firms,
and the wider political economy filled? More
specifically, it is important to consider whether
project supports are geared to allow:

1. improved business operations, especially among
   the poor, as well as links to other local
   businesses;
2. entrepreneurs to gain new business skills;
3. the linking of SE to each other to facilitate
   effective bargaining coalitions, and for
   mutual support in project related activities;
   and
4. the establishment of supportive relations with
   political and administrative elites.

A second major conclusion is that this matchmaking
is in large measure synonymous with what well can be
called "entrepreneurial behavior" in the sense that it
places a premium on seeing what is missing in a
production function and filling it. It also requires
knowing and avoiding the unessential. PVOs are most
likely to be effective where they do this type of gap
filling.

This means, in part, that reputed PVO advantages
may or may not be important. Large, relatively
technical and nonparticipatory organizations may handle
the entrepreneurial function very well if they can
gather sufficient intelligence to find a place for
their activity in a larger project network. An effort
to reach the poor serves both the cause of justice and
the generation of an integrated economy. But it should
be noted that not all PVOs have to be associated with
the formation of solidarity groups to serve these ends.

Alternatively, the most commonly presumed (if not
proven) advantages of development-oriented PVOs--their
staying power--would seem to be quite helpful for the
type of entrepreneurial activity required in the
majority of development settings. For there is a need
not only to fit into a setting, but to assist in the
creation of agencies capable of sharing in development
activities. The availability of motivated PVO staff,
willing to spend long periods in a locale, would seem
to be particularly compatible with the creative
management of institutional relationships. Similarly,
the availability of relatively small amounts of money
encourages reliance on beneficiaries and their

organization for basic research and tactical
information. These are likely sources of meaningful
intelligence on "gaps" which organizations with staying
power can use. (The training of PVO staff in concepts
of development which stress interrelationships and
institutional concerns would seem likely to make it
possible for them to make the best use of these
development resources.)

Finally, these points also suggest that the
successes which PVOs have are not a function of a
particular characteristic or action. For instance,
while a concern for participation is necessary, the
amount and range of involvement depends very much on
the participatory "gaps" in the setting. Where little
or no opportunity exists for beneficiary firms to
express their policy concerns or work free of
inequitable patronage networks, a participatory
component needs to be stressed. Alternatively, when
the poor cannot be organized without generating
dangerous elite responses (a rarer event than most
would think), the focus should be on reducing the
incentives for elites to hijack project benefits. As
noted earlier, this can be accomplished by setting
stringent limits on size of loans, and by lending for
economic activities in traditionally low status
activities. In addition, there will be situations
where a base may have been built by others. Here PVOs
with special skills in working witn "graduate" firms
may contribute nicely to a more participatory political
economy by aiding those larger of the small firms to
serve as bridges between the microsector and the
industrial sector. Where such a situation obtains,
there would be less reason for PVOs to become involved
in organizing of beneficiaries, save perhaps to offer
some training for the professionals in business
associations representing them.

It has been argued by many that PVOs tend to
innovative because they have highly motivated staffs
and fewer bureaucratic constraints to deal with
compared to government programs. This may or may not
be true. The fact that this chapter has tried to
emphasize is that the replication of even a tired
project package can be innovative. The question is
whether the project fills a missing piece that makes it
possible to generate business and to adapt to its
beneficiaries and their environment. Totally new ideas
which produce excellent results in one limited area may
be less valuable.

It seems clear that the broadly social or
institution building approach described in this chapter
is increasingly important for many PVOs. Such activity
presents extraordinary opportunities for new "global
linkages" (e.g., more elaborate PVO networks,
PVO-multinational corporation collaborations, etc.).

These should further facilitate attempts to tie
enterprise promotion to more ambitious development
efforts.  Successes in these ventures will require some
of what psychologists call "tolerance for ambiguity".
Indeed, few answers will be clear or easily
quantifiable, though there will be every reason to
consider economic costs of alternative strategies.  But
the concept of costs and benefits would need to be
broadened so that it would encompass more than discrete
economic and social indicators, and point instead
toward a sense of how the larger system of human
relationships in a community of beneficiaries is
evolving.


NOTES


     1.  This chapter summarizes research supported in
part by Illinois State University and the U.S. Agency
for International Development.  The assistance of both
institutions was vital and is appreciated. Particular
thanks are due to Dr. Ross Bigelow, of AID for his
interest and his criticisms.  However, the views
expressed in the work are those of the author.
     2.  American Council of Voluntary Agencies for
Foreign Service, Inc.  Small Enterprise Development
Assistance Abroad (New York:  Technical Assistance
Information Clearing House, June, 1982).
     3.  Robert Hunt, A Review of Evaluations of Small
Enterprise Projects Designed and Implemented by Private
Voluntary Organizations (Washington, D.C.:  Bureau of
Food for Peace and Voluntary Assistance, AID, 1982); E.
Chuta and C. Liedholm, Rural Non-Farm Employment:  A
Review of the State of the Art (East Lansing,
Michigan:  Michigan State University, Dept. of
Agricultural Economics, 1979).
     4.  Chuta and Liedholm, Rural Non-Farm Employment.
     5.  World Bank, Rural Enterprises and Non-Farm
Employment (Washington, D.C.:  World Bank, 1978).
     6.  Robert W. Hunt, "Social Psychological Aspects
of Active Citizenship and Economic Development,"
(Unpublished doctoral dissertation, Princeton
University, 1974).
     7.  Devres and Co., Small Scale Enterprise
Development, (Washington, D.C.:  Devres and Co., 1981);
Eugene Staley and Richard Morse, Modern Small Industry
for Developing Countries (New York:  McGraw-Hill, 1965).
     8.  Michael Farbman, ed., The PISCES Studies:
Assisting the Smallest Economic Activity of the Urban
Poor (Washington, D.C.:  AID, Development Support
Bureau, 1981).

9.  Hunt, A Review of Evaluations of Small Enterprise Projects.

10.  Chuta and Liedholm, Rural Non-Farm Employment.

11.  Philip Neck, Small Enterprise Development Policies and Programmes (Geneva:  International Labor Office, 1977).

12.  Susan Goldmark, Timothy Mooney and Jay Rosengard, Aid to Entrepreneurs:  An Evaluation of the Partnership for Productivity Project in Upper Volta (Washington, D.C., Development Alternatives Inc., 1982); Lassen, "A Response to the DAI Evaluation of PFP/Upper Volta" (Washington, D.C.:  Partnership for Productivity International, typescript, 1982).

13.  Neck, Small Enterprise Development; Development Commissioner for Small Scale Industries, Report of a Census of Small Scale Industrial Units (New Delhi:  Government of India, 1977).

14.  Judith Tendler, Ventures in the Informal Sector and How They Worked Out in Brazil, Evaluation Study no. 12, (Washington, D.C.:  AID, 1983).

15.  Henry Jackelen, "The UNO Program of Assistance to Micro-Enterprises in Caruaru, Brazil," in M. Bear, H. Jackelen and M. Tiller, Microenterprise Development in the Urban Informal Sector (Washington, D.C.:  Appropriate Technology International, Working Paper, 1982), 19-93; Jeffrey Ashe, Memo to Director of the Office of Private and Voluntary Cooperation, AID, 1982.

16.  F. O'Regan, T. Schmidt and J. Sebstad, "Kenya Rural Private Enterprise Project: Social Soundness Analysis, NGO Assessment and Recommendations on Project Design," (Nairobi, Kenya:  Report to USAID/Kenya, Manuscript, 1983).

17.  Jeffrey Ashe, "Synthesis and Overall Findings," in M. Farbman, ed., Assisting the Smallest Economic Activities of the Urban Poor:  The PISCES Studies (Washington, D.C.:  AID, 1981), 1-56; Jackelen, "The UNO Program"; O'Regan, et. al., "Kenya Rural Private Enterprise".

18.  Jeffrey Ashe, Assisting the Survival Economy:  The Microenterprise and Solidarity Group Projects of the Dominican Development Foundation, PISCES, Phase II (Boston:  ACCION International/AITEC, 1983).

19.  Goldmark, et. al., Aid to Entrepreneurs.

20.  Peter Fraser and Bruce Tippett, Impact Evaluation:  IIDI/IDH Houduras (Washington, D.C.:  AID, Bureau of Food for Peace and Voluntary Assistance, Office of Private and Voluntary Cooperation, 1982).

21.  O'Regan, et. al., "Kenya Rural Private Enterprise".

22.  Marshall Bear and Michael Tiller, "The Micro-Industries Development Center of the Philippines," in M. Bear, H. Jackelen and M. Tiller,

198

eds., Microenterprise Development in the Urban Informal Sector (Washington, D.C.: Appropriate Technology International Working Paper, 1982), 95-153.

23. O'Regan, et. al., "Kenya Rural Private Enterprise".

24. Partnership for Productivity International, Annual Report, 1982 (Washington, D.C.: Partnership for Productivity International, 1983); Lassen, "A Response to the DAI Evaluation of PFP/Upper Volta".

25. V. G. Patel, "Innovations in Banking: The Gujarat Experiments," (Washington, D.C.: The World Bank, mimeographed, 1978); Judith Tendler, Turning Voluntary Organizations into Development Agencies: Questions for Evaluation, Program Evaluation Discussion Paper no. 12, (Washington, D.C.: AID, 1982); Jackelen, "The UNO Program of Assistance".

26. Tendler, Voluntary Organizations.

27. Jason Brown, "Case Studies: India," in M. Farbman ed., Assisting the Smallest Economic Activities of the Urban Poor (Washington, D.C.: AID, 1981), 337-378; Josh Beardsley, Report on Investment in the Small Capital Enterprise Sector: PISCES Phase II (Boston: ACCION International/AITEC, 1982); Ashe, "Synthesis and Overall Findings," in M. Farbman, Assisting the Smallest Economic Activities of the Urban Poor, 1-56.

28. Jackelen, "The UNO Program of Assistance"; Ashe, Assisting the Survival Economy.

29. Jackelen, "The UNO Program of Assistance".

30. Robert Gamer, The Developing Nations: A Comparative Perspective (Boston: Allyn and Bacon, 2nd Ed., 1982).

31. Doug Hill, "Overview," in M. Bear, et. al., Micro-Enterprise Development in the Urban Informal Sector (Washington, D.C.: Appropriate Technology International Working Paper, 1982), 1-17.

32. Fraser and Tippett, Impact Evaluation IIDI/IDH.

33. Hazel Henderson, Politics of the Solar Age: Alternatives to Economics (New York: McGraw-Hill, 1981).

34. Bear and Tiller, "The Micro-Industries".

35. O'Regan, et. al., "Kenya Rural Private Enterprise".

36. Goldmark, et. al., Aid to Entrepreneurs.

37. Bear and Tiller, "The Micro-Industries"; S.R. Daines et. al., Agribusiness and Rural Enterprise Project Manual (Washington, D.C.: AID, Office of Agriculture, 1979).

38. World Bank, Rural Enterprises.

39. See research cited in Chuta and Liedholm, Rural Non-Farm Employment.

40. Daines et. al., Agribusiness; Chuta and Liedholm, Rural Non-Farm Employment.

41. World Bank, Rural Enterprise; Chuta and Liedholm, Rural Non-Farm Employment; Neck, Small Enterprise Development.
42. Jason Brown, "Case Studies: India".
43. See discussion in Fraser and Tippett, Impact Evaluation.
44. Goldmark, et. al., Aid to Entrepreneurs.
45. See Chuta and Liedholm, Rural Non Farm Employment, for a list of some of these studies.
46. Devres, Small Scale Enterprise Development.
47. V. G. Patel, "Motivation and Small Business Training," (Ahmedabad, Indian Institute of Management, Guest lecture on management, 1976); Bear and Tiller, "The Micro Industries".
48. Ashe, Assisting the Survival Economy.
49. Malcolm Harper, "Selection and Training for Entrepreneurship Development," (Geneva: International Labor Office, Management Development Branch, 1983); Udai Pareek and T.V. Rao, Developing Entrepreneurship (Ahmedabad, India: Indian Institute of Management, 1978).
50. Jackelen, "The UNO Program of Assistance".
51. Chuta and Liedholm, Rural Non-farm Employment.
52. Bear and Tiller, "The Micro-Industries."; O'Regan, et. al., "Kenya Rural Private Enterprise".
53. Ashe, Assisting the Survival Economy.
54. O'Regan, et. al., "Kenya Rural Private Enterprise".
55. Tendler, Ventures in the Informal Sector.
56. S. Barnett, S. Druben, N. Engle and B. Ricci, An Assessment of the Institutional Capability of OIC International, Inc. (Philadelphia, PA: Opportunities Industrialization Centers International, Inc., 1982); Robert W. Hunt, The Evaluation of Small Enterprise Programs and Projects, Special Evaluation Study no. 13, (Washington, D.C.: AID, Office of Evaluation, 1983).
57. Harper, "Selection and Training for Entrepreneurship"; David C. McClelland and David Winter, Motivating Economic Achievement (New York: Free Press, 1969); V. G. Patel and Anil Trivedi, "Report of the Third Entrepreneurship Development Program," Ahmedabad, India:  Gujarat Industrial Development Corporation, 1972).
58. Jackelen, "The UNO Program of Assistance".
59. Pareek and Rao, Developing Entrepreneurship; Patel, "Lecture on Motivation".
60. Hunt, Evaluation of Small Enterprise.
61. Robert W. Hunt, "Business Association and the Small Manufacturing Sector in India," International Journal of Comparative Sociology 21 (July-December, 1981):  254-267.
62. David C. McClelland, The Achieving Society (New York: Free Press, 1967); Pareek and Rao, Developing Entrepreneurship; Harper, "Selection and

Training for Entrepreneurship".
    63.   Chuta and Liedholm, Rural Non-Farm Employment.
    64.   Patel, Innovations in Banking.
    65.   Chuta and Liedholm, Rural Non-Farm Employment.
    66.   Anwar Divechia, "The Management of Trade and
Industry Associations" Indian Management 14 (Sept.
1974): 4-9ff; Hunt, "Business Associations".
    67.   Chuta and Liedholm, Rural Non-Farm
Employment. Dr. Liedholm and his colleagues at
Michigan State University have since collected a great
deal of additional data that supports these
conclusions.
    68.   David Korten, "The Management of Social
Transformation," Public Administration Review 41
(November-December, 1981): 609-618; Henderson, Politics
of the Solar Age.
    69.   Robert W. Hunt, The Entrepreneurship Training
Program of the Lesotho Opportunities Industrialization
Center: An Evaluation of its Impact (Washington, D.C.:
AID, Office of Private and Voluntary Cooperation, June,
1983).
    70.   Ashe, Assisting the Survival Economy.
    71.   James Downton, Rebel Leadership: Commitment
and Charisma in the Revolutionary Process (New York:
Free Press, 1973); Coralie Bryant and Louise White,
Managing Development in the Third World (Boulder,
Colo.: Westview Press, 1982).
    72.   Ashe, Assisting the Survival Economy.
    73.   Jan van Heemst, The Role of NGOs in
Development (The Hague: Institute of Social Studies,
1981).
    74.   Richard Cobb, Robert Hunt, Carolyn Bledsoe,
Charles Vanderveen and Robert McClosky, Rural Roads in
Liberia, Impact Evaluation Study no. 6, (Washington,
D.C.: AID, 1980).
    75.   Hunt, "Social Psychological Aspects".
    76.   Hunt, "Business Associations".
    77.   Nandesena Ratnapala, "The Sarvodaya Movement:
Self-Help Rural Development in Sri Lanka," in P.
Coombes ed., Meeting the Basic Needs of the Rural Poor
(New York: Pergamon Press, 1980), 469-523; Denis
Goulet, "Development as Liberation: Policy Lessons from
Case Studies," World Development 7 (1980): 555-566.
    78.   PfP, Annual Report, 1982. (Washington, D.C.:
Partnership for Productivity International, 1983).
    79.   Goldmark, et. al., Aid to Entrepreneurs.
    80.   Hunt, The Evaluation of Small Enterprise.
    81.   van Heemst, Role of NGOs.
    82.   Tendler, Ventures in the Informal Sector.
    83.   Jackelen, "The UNO Program of Assistance".
    84.   van Heemst, Role of NGOs.
    85.   Bear and Tiller, "The Micro-Industries".
    86.   Ibid.
    87.   Gamer, The Developing Nations.

# 8
# Making PVOs Count More: A Proposal

*Gene Ellis*

In this chapter it is argued that private voluntary organizations (PVOs) whatever their other merits, often have poor projects in at least three senses--the benefit-cost ratios of the projects (either overall or from the point of view of needed factors) are poor, the projects are not sustainable without subsidies by the populace over the long run, and the projects are not highly replicable throughout the societies in question. There are several other criteria of interest in evaluating PVO projects--the extent of participation or the impact upon the distribution of income, for example--but the discussion will center on these three criteria in the belief that they make the difference in determining whether the PVOs function as <u>development</u> rather than <u>welfare</u> organizations.

It is further argued that ongoing attempts by donor agencies to siphon monies to PVOs and like organizations (e.g., the <u>Accelerated Impact Project</u> (AIP); the <u>Improved Rural Technology Project</u> (IRTP), the Peace Corps Small Project Assistance Program--all Agency for International Development (AID) supported projects), and to make small amounts of money available to them faster, have not dealt with the problems raised in the failure of PVOs to meet these three basic criteria.

In conclusion, a proposal for a feasible, low-cost method of identifying highly replicable, appropriate technologies for voluntary organizations that are feasible under <u>local</u> conditions is made.

POINT 1: MANY PVO PROJECTS MAY NOT BE SOUND.

Development Alternatives, Inc. (DAI), carried out (for the Office of Private and Voluntary Cooperation of AID) an evaluation of seventeen PVO development projects in Niger and Kenya in 1979. The aim of the team was to observe "what PVOs 'do best'."[1] The PVO community, both in the U.S. and in the field, helped pick the best projects. The impacts of the projects were studied and

201

(among other things) the net ratio of benefits to costs
in these projects was determined. From these estimates
of start-up costs and yearly increments of project
benefits and costs, it is possible to construct simple
benefit-cost analyses. One such set, which assumes that
all the projects will last ten years with no additional
costs, with a discount rate of 15 percent is shown
in Table 8.1. While not a good method of determining
the relative standing of projects--some would endure far
less than ten years--the generous assumption as to time
horizon allows us to assess the overall viability of the
projects. It is of considerable interest that eight of
these seventeen self-selected successes, in projects
designed as development projects with monetary benefits,
failed to return benefits equivalent to costs expended.

A study by Robert R. Nathan Associates, Inc., for
PACT and AID conducted site visits of nineteen PVO
projects, and found that the most frequent exceptions to
satisfactory performance came 'in terms of cost-effectiveness', where about 40 percent of the projects were
found to be borderline or unsatisfactory.[2] These findings are in accord with the author's findings of PVO
projects in seven African and Asian countries. In the
Philippines, for example, a review of some water
projects constructed by the San Carlos Foundation indicated a cost of sixty-eight pesos per family served
with hand pumps, whereas the simpler Amoeba Project
water supply had a cost of only thirteen pesos per
family.[3] In Liberia a PVO had helped put in water pumps
and close open wells, but the breakdown rate (and repair
rate) were such as to actually reduce the supply of potable water.[4] Over 95 percent of the time of a
PVO's training in the Philippines was spent on biogas, a
technology with, it turns out, a low benefit-cost ratio,
a high breakdown rate, and benefits concentrated on the
richest farmers.[5] And in a number of countries, PVOs
and governmental organizations thought themselves to be
disseminating 'virtually free' stoves (made of sand and
clay) because they had made no estimate of the overhead
costs involved in a dissemination program (which often
raised costs to U.S. $25 or more per stove).[6] As the
Robert Nathan study notes,

> ...PVO representatives seldom try to conduct
> a full cost-benefit analysis. ...The application
> of a full cost-benefit analysis is usually more
> demanding of funds, time, and technical
> expertise than available personnel at the
> project and sponsoring agency level can provide.[7]
> ...the basis of the problem seems to lie in
> choices of inappropriate and inefficient
> approaches to meeting needs.[8]

So it is perhaps understandable that PVOs cannot compare

TABLE 8.1
Direct Benefits of Private Voluntary Organizations: The
Development Alternatives Study

| PROJECT | NET RATIO BENEFIT TO COST | IMPLIED BENEFIT -COST RATIO |
|---|---|---|
| KENYA: | | |
| Bushiangala | 1.25 | 5.3 |
| Kandara | O.31 | 2.1 |
| Katothya | O.76 | 3.82 |
| Katyehoka | O.71 | 3.61 |
| Interchurch | O.78 | 2.19 |
| Maseno South | O.14 | .91 |
| Kyuso | 2.35 | 5.17 |
| REES/RMLS | --- | .25 |
| Kawangware | .05 | .64 |
| | | |
| NIGER: | | |
| Cdarma | .03 | .5 |
| Libore | .10 | .73 |
| Maggia | .05 | .29 |
| Talak | .08 | .44 |
| Oasis Air | .38 | 1.73 |
| SIM/Maradi | .72 | 2.64 |
| Tchin Tabisgine | .08 | .64 |
| Telemces | .67 | 1.6 |

SOURCE: Final Report: The Development Impact of Private
Voluntary Organizations: Kenya and Niger, by
Development Alternatives, Inc. (see Figures 3 and 4) for
the Office of Private and Voluntary Cooperation, AID,
Washington, D.C., 2 February, 1979. The implied
benefit-cost ratio was calculated assuming the variable
project costs and benefits remained constant, that no
additional fixed investments would be called for, that
the projects would last ten years, and that the discount
rate was 15 percent. These assumptions are highly
optimistic ones, yet eight of seventeen projects still
fail. On the positive side, assuming a five year
horizon would result in the same number of failed
projects.

the relative returns of projects, or may be unaware of
whether projects are in fact capable of returning more
in benefits than they cost.

As Judith Tendler cogently notes, part of the
difficulty is that the nature of the endeavor has
changed over time, as the focus of projects has changed
from relief efforts to development.  In addition,
whereas construction efforts often used outside (and
controllable) inputs, income-generation efforts require
much more of the community.  Not only do "income-earning
projects seem to be as difficult as construction
projects are easy," but construction projects lent themselves to a simplistic 'Is it there or isn't it?' form
of evaluation, whereas income-generation projects force
attention to be paid to outputs (and outputs over time)
as well as inputs.[9]

POINT 2:  MANY PVO PROJECTS MAY NOT BE
SUSTAINABLE OR REPLICABLE

In the DAI survey referred to above, six of the
seventeen projects were infrastructure projects requiring outside funding; of the eleven others which required
service or budget support, two provided services free,
seven had a formal subsidy arrangement and the remaining
two required contributions to partially cover costs.  As
DAI noted:

It is apparent...that none of the projects in
this category is presently 'paying for itself',
i.e., raising enough funds from participants
to cover all operations.[10]

In Bangladesh a 10 percent sample review of PVOs by AID
found that; "few if any show promise of being
Bangladeshi, self-sufficient, viable, continuing development activities"[11] and that;

few PVOs set as an objective, per se, reasonable
time frames for entrance and withdrawal from
a development project.  A dependency relationship develops (between the service population
and the PVO).[12]

The significance of sustainability and replicability for long-term development can be illustrated by
contrasting the development of the Eucalyptus forests
of Addis Ababa (begun at the turn of the century) with
present-day reforestation efforts of governmental donors
and with the Tin Aicha settlement project (a Malian
American Friends Service Committee project).[13]  By the
late 1890s, the forest surrounding the capital of Addis
Ababa were depleted, and there was pressure to move the

capital.  Foreign missions, not anxious to desert their
embassies, imported a large variety of seedlings, which
they provided freely.  Three varieties of eucalyptus
(of over a hundred varieties of trees) prospered, and by
the late 1920s, the energy problem had been resolved.
Until 1975, when the forests were nationalized, the
growth of these forests roughly kept pace with the
growth of the city, serving as a major source of household energy and building materials.  Yet the modest
initial foreign aid was not continued, nor did the
various ministries aid the endeavor.

By way of contrast, none of the donor aided forestry projects in Africa come close to paying their costs.
All are dependent upon continued heavy subsidization by
foreign donors, and the impact of their subsidization is
to make private, small-scale efforts unprofitable.[14]

The Tin Aicha project sought to rehabilitate (and
settle) nomadic families who had been greatly impacted
by the Sahelian drought.  Begun in 1975, the village
grew from two hundred original families in 1976 to more
than a thousand people in 1981, with a market, school,
dispensary, village government and a variety of provided
services.  Aside from the restocking of lost livestock
(which involved a revolving credit fund with only a
modest amount of subsidy), all other major areas of
investment--education, health, forestry and building
(for schools, clinics and cooperatives)--were heavily
subsidized.  In reforestation, ten workers were paid $10
per month plus a grain subsidy.  The dispensary received
more funds than all the rest of the cercle (district)
combined, giving 1000 people more care than 150,000.
With a dispensary, the village was entitled to regular
visits from the epidemic control service.  In education,
the American Friends Service Committee (AFSC) provided
the building, the students received a lunch program from
donors.  The World Food Program (WFP) provided animals
and implements for the school; the AFSC financed the
cooperative.

How sustainable were these efforts?  In 1977, when
responsibility for the dispensary was transferred from
AFSC to the cercle, the immediate result was a severe
cut in supplies and a rise in epidemic diseases.  The
forestry costs were not picked up, and without aid, it
appeared most of the trees planted would not survive.
(Costs of teachers for the school were picked up by the
government.)

Not only were the project components not sustainable, they were not replicable.  The major impact of
the project was to give some resources (and the
political power to call upon other resources) at the
expense of others.  It also redistributed available
resources, or subsidized one segment of the population
rather than laying the groundwork for a long-term
increase in resources.  As the Robert Nathan study

notes:

> Some PVO personnel provide a highly personalized
> service to a relatively small number of bene-
> ficiaries.

> When the costs of subsidized inputs and services
> are identified and the question is raised of
> beneficiary contribution towards these costs,
> some PVO personnel reply that poor people
> cannot afford to pay such costs; they fail to
> consider the implications of this response
> for the viability and replicability of the
> project.[15]

Even were projects like Tin Aicha to have higher
benefit-cost ratios than a forestry project like the
Addis Ababa one, the fact that the forestry project
might be replicable by contagion (i.e., by mere example
to others, without transfer of additional resources)
might make them preferable. For a given amount of
development organization input, a greater developmental
impact is achieved (and maintained) under such circumstances. If the resources used by the organization
(for example, skilled bureaucrats) are scarce, or if the
mechanisms by which savings might be drawn from the
citizenry are imperfect, or if public investment
programs for Less Developed Countries (LDCs) are less
efficient than their private counterparts--all of which
the author believes to be commonly true of LDC
conditions--then the overall benefit-cost ratios of
projects replicable by contagion might well be higher
than projects without such replication possibilities.
Projects easily emulated by entrepreneurs and
smaller entities (e.g., cooperatives, villages) might
also have better impacts on the distribution of income.
As Judith Tendler notes,

> ...it is not that PVOs work 'bottom-up' in
> contrast to the 'top-down' style of
> governments; rather, it is that the top-down
> style--where development projects are in-
> fluenced by national and regional elites--
> brings less benefits to the poor when
> practiced at higher as opposed to lower
> political levels.[16]

If the technologies are carefully selected to cater
to basic human needs and to have a mass appeal (and
affordability), if care is taken to develop competitive
markets for the products, such projects might serve to
better redistribute income to the poor.

POINT 3:   ATTEMPTS TO EASE FUNDING MECHANISMS
HAVE OVERLOOKED OTHER PROBLEMS IN PVO PERFORMANCE

Programs like the AIP or the Improved Rural Technology Project (ITRP)--both funded by AID--have attempted
to reduce the amount of preplanning and documentation
necessary for funding, and have tried to speed up the
funding process (with limited success). But the small
projects in which the PVOs so often specialize can only
be competitive with large-scale projects (which cost
proportionately less to plan, administer, and evaluate)
if in fact they work better, and if they can be replicated. Yet the ITRP, for example, cannot point to a
single example of a successful project concept which was
replicated. Rather, each project stood alone, and
proved expensive to plan, assess and implement. Whatever advantage smallness may bring, it appears to bring
none in planning. As Judith Tendler notes:

> ...the very smallness of PVOs in relation to
> the large donors means that they do not do
> the research, writing and information
> dissemination on their experience that large
> donors have done. Information on the state
> of the art in development projects, then,
> must be drawn mainly from the research and
> evaluation outputs of large donors and
> academic institutions.[17]

And, as she notes, the most innovative PVOs are
precisely the largest, most bureaucratized and
professionalized ones who can afford such speciali-
zation.[18] While fearing outside evaluation, seeing it
(perhaps rightly) as a potential instrument for imposing
outside control,[19]

> PVOs, particularly with relief and missionary
> backgrounds, have problems in designing a
> development strategy/plan, organizing their
> resources accordingly, providing adequate
> leadership...(and) monitoring and evaluating
> performance.[20]

POINT 4:   WHERE DO WE GO FROM HERE?   A PROPOSAL

Recognizing that conventional analyses of PVO
projects may result in disappointing results, there have
been a number of approaches taken. One is to argue that
the figures are wrong in some fundamental sense. In the
simplest form, refuge is taken in the argument that
'benefits cannot be quantified', and therefore that any
analysis has to yield to the predilections of others.
At a more sophisticated level, it is argued that the

introduction of technologies and institutions have complicated, unforeseeable, and fundamental impacts which are, at best, subject only to ex post facto analysis.

There is, to be sure, more than a little truth in this line of reasoning. Lynn White Jr.'s classic analysis of the impact of the introduction of the chimney into Europe--a technology which made possible separate living quarters for servants and elements of the family, and which has been said to have promoted concepts of individualism and romanticism, with great impacts upon Western philosophy and development--is a case in point.[21]

To admit the uncertainties of technological assessment should not lead us to forego analysis, however. The approach suggested here is one which would accept the inherent uncertainties while concentrating on the fact that projects thought worthwhile by communities and entrepreneurs (enough so to spread by contagion) are especially important for development. Granted that we see the effects and true costs of technologies and institutions only after the fact, but there is little in the way of even ex post facto analysis now being done. Tendler notes that:

> ...little information on government adoption
> of PVO successes is available and no studies
> of replication have been made for PVOs working
> in the Third World.[22]

The approach proposed here would start with ex post facto studies and seek to use the knowledge gained to replicate worthwhile technologies on a broader scale.

Another approach is to argue that most projects fail anyway, so that to insist that PVO projects succeed (in terms of benefits exceeding costs, sustainability, and replicability) is unfair. The DAI argues:

> Because development work is necessarily
> imperfect in the sense that a very limited
> number of interventions can be regarded as
> truly successful, PVO activities should be
> evaluated against the experience of others
> rather than against some absolute norm.[23]

Certainly there is some merit in this view, both because the projects attempted by the PVOs are filled with risk, and because it is difficult to know what measure to take of success. Most small businesses in even so benign an environment as the United States fail within a year, for example. Yet if we examine the histories of entrepreneurs who have undoubtedly made great contributions, we often find that they went through many earlier failures and misfortunes. Such spread effects and spillovers

are difficult to assess.  Both because of internal and
external idiosyncratic environments, the DAI report
hypothesized that:

> ...'Reproducing' numerous carbon copies of a
> successful small PVO project is not a realistic
> option, nor a defensible use of scarce human
> and material resources.  Equally important, it
> will not produce comparable impact in most of
> the new settings where it is attempted.[24]

The author, to the contrary, suggests that, whether
strictly optimal or not, there are numerous technologies
and enterprises which have spread widely across a
number of external environments, and which a number of
cultures have been able to undertake with some success.
While recognizing that factor prices and operating
environments vary widely across Third World countries,
it is argued that generalizations can in fact be made,
and that many of the factors which seem to make certain
technologies inappropriate in some settings can be
allowed for.
In sum, a system is needed which would:

1.  improve the flow of information to voluntary
    organizations,
2.  focus attention on replicable technologies and
    projects while weeding out less desirable ones,
3.  aid in overcoming the diseconomies of scale in
    project identification, feasibility analysis
    funding and evaluation inherent in small-scale
    projects.

There is a perception that PVOs, while often excellent
in organizing grass-roots organization and participation, are often poor in identifying appropriate,
highly replicable technologies and projects.  Feasibility studies, often required by donor agencies, often
are little more than wishful thinking  by those who
possess less than the necessary analytical skills.
Even when conducted by professionals, feasibility
studies do not reflect the quite real difficulties encountered in instituting technologies (especially as
these arise from nontechnical factors).  In the
Philippines, for example, feasibility studies of biogas
invariably counted on no maintenance breakdowns, full use
of side-products, and replacing relatively expensive
Liquid Propane Gas (LPG).  In practice, sludge and
effluents were seldom used, breakdown rates were high,
and the biogas usually replaced cheap wood rather than
expensive LPG.  Obviously, the only parameters which can
be attached are probability parameters--that is to say,
in a given case where side-products are utilized and
maintenance is carried out well, the technology could be

profitable and effective. But it is nevertheless
necessary in analyzing programs of technology transfer
to consider what in fact experience has been, and to
consider what the returns might be if failure rates
vary. If nothing else the analysis aids in focusing on
crucial aspects of the transfer.

It is obvious that there is a need for a simple
information system which would start with evaluations
of types of projects in the field, which could build up
prototypes of such project types, and which could determine the feasibility and replicability of the
projects. In conducting such an analysis, it is
essential to be able to adjust for local inputs and
local prices. Such a system could serve to inform PVOs
about possibilities in several generic areas of
projects (e.g., cookstoves, woodlots, charcoal conver-
sion), and thus would focus attention on areas in need
of replication. The system would allow neophytes to
conduct project analyses, and inform them of the role
of appropriate parameters (e.g., discount rates, time
horizons). The output--localized project analyses--
could be used as a means of preproject approval by
funding agencies.

Such a system would require the assistance of
expert evaluators who, rather than doing large numbers
of individual project evaluations, would concentrate
their efforts on generic types of projects, eventually
producing a 'catalogue' of project possibilities for
PVOs. The system could be computerized in order to
allow local PVO users to adjust for local prices and
materials, while still allowing the form of the
analysis to be set within a larger context. Such a
system, even if entirely permissive, would create norms
and expectations while informing PVOs of the opportunities afforded by some technologies and types of
projects. If such projects were given 'preapproval'
status by donors, PVOs would be all the more likely to
utilize such opportunities.

The Peace Corps and AID have recently agreed to
fund development of such a computerized catalog. The
proposed catalog would include:

1.  An Evaluation Section, describing who evalu-
    ated what technology when and where, as well
    as a description of the technology.
2.  A Bibliographic Section, containing a short
    bibliography of pertinent materials relevant
    to technical information, implementation and
    maintenance and/or previous evaluations, as
    well as addresses of sources of expertise.
3.  An Evaluation Guidelines/Key Issues/Critical
    Assumptions Section, containing answers to a
    short list of questions about the technology,
    what it replaced, maintenance and

dissemination, characteristics of adopters, etc. The critical assumptions and key issues affecting the feasibility and appropriateness of the technology are spelled out.

4. An Itemized Components Section, for which local users can insert local prices and substitute materials. A benefit-cost and sensitivity analysis is automatically produced from the result, which can be utilized in obtaining donor funding.

5. An Impacts Section, which explores linkage and spread effects.

6. An Evaluation Section, suggesting how to evaluate the project as it progresses.

7. A Forms Section, containing the standard forms used for small projects by the major donor groups.[25]

The research would also produce a standardized format which the Peace Corps, AID, and PVOs might use to produce their own contributions to the catalog.

The catalog of disks (each containing an analysis of a particular technology) provides PVOs with a framework for analysis, and spreads the costs of a thorough evaluation across a wide number of users. This would help to surmount two problems PVOs have: the lack of requisite skills for evaluation and the lack of large amounts of revenue for evaluation. It would allow PVOs and local users to compare and choose from a wide range of technologies. Donor agency expenditures on project design and evaluation could be reduced. Finally, by taking advantage of user input, the disks would encourage 'localized analysis', with expected returns adjusted for local factor prices. (If expertise were available, these could be 'shadow priced' to correct for imperfections in local market prices).

Although the cost at which such a catalog can be developed is an important consideration, the crucial factor is the degree to which projects (delineated in terms of the technologies employed) can be generalized across cultures. In a multicountry investigation of stoves, for example, it was found that in wealthier countries, a more expensive waist-high stove sold well, but in poorer countries, smaller, cheaper stoves were preferred. In addition the qualities of the soils used affected stove performance. Nevertheless, it was found that important generalizations could be made about stove performance, stove design and entrepreneurial production and dissemination systems, and that these generalizations held up across countries, across regions, and across diets. Just as with cars or agricultural inputs (e.g., seed, fertilizers), there is much to be gained from 'fine-tuning' technologies to their specific micro-environments.

The system proposed here, however crude in its
initial formulation, is an important first step in helping PVO development activities to count more--that is to
achieve sustainability and cost-benefit effectiveness.
In the end not only PVOs, but their beneficiaries, stand
to gain much from a keener awareness of benefit and cost
realities.


NOTES

1.   Development Alternatives, Inc., The Develop-
ment Impact of Private Voluntary Organizations: Kenya
and Niger: Final Report, Report to the Office of
Private and Voluntary Cooperation, (Washington, D.C.:
AID, 1979).
2.   Robert R. Nathan Associates, Inc., Assessing
the Cost-Effectiveness of PVO Projects: A Guide and
Discussion (draft) Prepared for the Office of Program
Management Support, Bureau of Food and Voluntary
Assistance, AID, (January, 1982) 2.  This discusses
points raised in Robert R. Nathan Associates, Inc., An
Evaluation of Private Agencies Collaborating Together,
prepared for PACT and AID Office of Private and Voluntary Cooperation, (June, 1982).
3.   Bruce Hanson and Gene Ellis, Report to PC/
Philippines A.T. Volunteers, unpublished mimeo, (August
1982).
4.   Gene Ellis, Trip Report: Reviewing and Evaluating Peace Corps Renewable Energy Technology Projects
(RETs) in Mali, Liberia, and Ghana (Feb.-March, 1981),
unpublished mimeo, (May, 1981).  A change to less
permanent caps was later made.
5.   Gene Ellis and Bruce Hanson, Evaluating
Appropriate Technology in Practice: Biogas and Lorena
Stoves in the Philippines, unpublished paper.
6.   Gene Ellis and Bruce Hanson, Stoves in West
Africa: Some Experience in Benin, Upper Volta and
Senegal, unpublished paper.
7.   Nathan, Assessing the Cost-Effectiveness of
PVO Projects: A Guide and Discussion, 15.
8.   Ibid., 3.
9.   Judith Tendler, Turning PVOs into Development
Agencies: Questions for Evaluation, AID Program Evaluation Paper No. 12, (Washington, D.C.: AID, 1982), 137
and 140.
10.  DAI, 34.
11.  I. Buxell, PVOs in Bangladesh and the PVO Co-
Financing Project Evaluation, mimeo, USAID/DACCA,
(April, 1977), 5.
12.  Ibid., 5
13.  These projects are analyzed in Gene Ellis, Two
Tales of a City: The Eucalyptus Forests of Addis Ababa,

unpublished paper, (September, 1982) and Gene Ellis,
Book Review of Tin Aicha: Nomad Village, in <u>Africa
Today</u>, forthcoming.

14. Data from a number of generally unpublished
sources are drawn together in Gene Ellis,"On Teaching
How to Fish"in <u>Proceedings</u> of Workshop on Energy,
Forestry, and Environment, Vol. II (Washington,D.C.: AID,
Bureau for Africa, April, 1982).

15. Nathan, 3.
16. Tendler, 31.
17. Ibid., 105.
18. Ibid., 89.
19. Ibid., 134.
20. Buxell, 7.
21. One is inclined to wonder what benefit-cost
ratio would be assigned to a small labor and community
organization center in East Tennessee (the Highland
Folk School, now of Knoxville, formerly of Monteagle,
Tennessee) which in the third decade of its precarious
existence taught the organizational techniques and provided the hymns by which a young Baptist minister was
able to mobilize the civil rights movement. Photos
of Dr. Martin Luther King attending this inaccurately
labelled 'communist training camp' decorated Southern
billboards in the early 1960s, and a former singing
director (now director), Guy Carawan, was responsible
for the hymn 'We Shall Overcome.'

22. Tendler, 87.
23. DAI, 93.
24. DAI, 91.
25. For details, write the designer, Dr. Gene
Ellis, Development Designs, 2421 So. High St., Denver,
CO 80210.

# 9
# Appropriate Administration: Creating A 'Space' Where Local Initiative and Voluntarism Can Grow

*Michael Calavan*

Creation of a "space" where voluntary organizations, autonomous local governments, cooperative ventures, and small-scale enterprises can thrive should be a major item on the development agenda.[1] If successful, this effort can release great amounts of human energy and creativity. Efforts to reform procedures, structures, and conceptual systems which currently limit movement toward this development goal can usefully be labeled "Appropriate Administration." Issues of Appropriate Administration can be considered from the vantage point of five distinct actors in the development process: central government (bureaucratic and elected leaders), external donors (bilateral and mutlilateral), external private voluntary organizations (PVOs), local leaders and organizations, and researchers and consultants.

Behavioral and perceptual changes are required of each group. Central officials must cease to regard instances of local initiative and assertion of autonomy (lobbying, demonstrations, noncooperation in central projects) as administrative failure. They must learn to deal with villagers in a frankly "political" manner. External donor officials must begin to question their own bureaucratic values, and to understand better the role of autonomous, democratic institutions in the history of First World development. External PVO workers must learn to balance parodoxical responsibilities as benevolent patrons and temporary activists in local politics. Local leaders must acquire sufficient confidence to be subtly (not excessively) self-assertive. Researchers and consultants must overcome conceptual, methodological, and professional limitations in order to provide other actors with a clearer notion of the problems they face.

Bureaucratic culture teaches officials to resist and overcome autonomous behavior through recourse to professional standards and myths. An example from

216

Thailand illustrates this (virtually unconscious)
strategy. Thai officials frequently characterize the
commodity marketing sector as inefficient and
exploitative, and propose significant administrative
reforms. Assertions regarding inflated transport
charges, manipulation of local markets, and unfair
practices are made, and seldom challenged. Yet, field
studies suggest that few of the charges are true.
Middleman, milling, and transport costs for paddy rice
account for about a fifth (21 percent) of the Bangkok
retail price, and are not unreasonable by any
standards.[2] What's happening, then? Are officials
stating true feelings? Yes, to some degree. Are they
engaging in convenient populist rhetoric? To some
degree, yes. But these denunciations are best
interpreted as an indirect assertion of bureaucratic
privilege and potency--"We can do it better than these
semi-literate, provincial Chinese businessmen" and
"Naive peasants need our protection". In this
instance, and many others, the unstated axiom is that
rural areas to be administered, and not politicized.
      External donor officials accept this principle,
since it is consistent with bureaucratic values which
are virtually universal. Research consultants,
especially public administration experts, may also
accept the principle. In any case, they work
temporarily for bureaucratic organizations where it is
seldom questioned. Local leaders and external PVOs are
(perhaps) confused by the democratic and populist
rhetoric of administrators. In any case they lack
power and must devote most of their limited energy to
manipulation of existing bureaucratic processes.
Creating a "space" for local autonomy is extremely
difficult.


SOME PROPOSITIONS FOR APPROPRIATE ADMINISTRATION

      All relevant actors need to move outside
established conceptual systems. To that end, several
provocative propositions are offered here. They will
not find ready acceptance. Most run directly "against
the bureaucratic grain", and conflict with conventional
notions of administrative propriety and
self-interest.[3] Some may be wrong, but there is
value in opening a dialogue with tentative
formulations. Bureaucrats seriously attempting to
reorient toward Appropriate Administration require some
compass points. Time will tell which ideas proposed
here define True North, and which miss it by 180
degrees.

217

## Consideration I: Be Aware of Local Management Capacities and Do Not Undercut Them Casually

It is bureaucratic commonplace that "villagers lack managerial skills". From this definition of the situation, solutions flow smoothly--management training for officials and village leaders, preparation of organization charts, local planning activities, etc. In the process, a basic fact is ignored; a lot of managing goes on in villages, and skills exist. A catalogue of activities which are widespread and locally managed in rural Thailand includes:

1. small-scale irrigation systems;
2. flood control efforts;
3. construction and maintenance of Buddhist; temple structures;
4. administration of temple fiscal matters;
5. support of monks and novices;
6. provision of "public welfare" benefits which pass through the Buddhist temple;
7. construction, maintenance, and regulation of wells and ponds;
8. administration of funeral insurance clubs;
9. cult activities, weddings, and funerals, and;
10. construction and maintenance of roads, paths, bridges, and cremation facilities.

In addition to activities in the public sector, villagers have long organized themselves into cooperative groups (often modeled on the Chinese hui). Such groups accumulate and extend credit; operate daily and periodic markets; engage in cattle trading; purchase land; contract to harvest crops, etc. They do not constitute "official" cooperatives since they lack bureaucratic patrons and do not conform to legal codes prescribing cooperative organization. In addition, a series of unofficial cooperative activities have been introduced quite recently. These include: medicine banks, rice banks, buffalo banks, and cooperative ventures for production of weaning foods. Several impressive examples of local management were encountered in a Northeastern Thai village in June, 1979.[4]

A village road system. In 1973, during a period when there was a great deal of interest in village development, a proposal for reorganizing village roads on a grid system was originated by the Abbot of the temple in Ban Kham Phaum, a village in Khon Kaen. The plan called for building five straight, north-south

and five straight, east-west roads in place of one
meandering road and several trails already in
existence. The kamnan (subdistrict headman) called a
public meeting, and in the course of it the plan was
accepted. It became apparent that itwould be necessary
to move 118 houses (out of a total of 300 in the
village) and villagers still accepted the plan.
Several substantial tasks were implied by this
decision, including, house removal, road construction,
paying for gravel, and maintenance.

House removal caused inconvenience to many
households. Some families discovered that they would
lose all their house land to the road right-of-way.
They were forced to buy new house land or to move to
already-owned garden plots at the edge of the village.
Other families lost only part of their house plots, but
still found it necessary to move their houses out of
the right-of-way. "Moving" a house ordinarily implies
tearing it down, board by board, and reconstructing it
elsewhere. It would have been impossible to fully
repay families for expenses incurred and effort
expended. However, an ingenious (and apparently
satisfactory) form of symbolic compensation was
devised. Each household that did not have to move was
asked for a voluntary contribution to a compensation
fund. This amount was divided equally among the 118
households that did have to move. The 130 baht
received by each family was said to be for nails.
Inconvenienced households were further compensated by
the assistance of kinsmen, neighbors, and friends in
the relocation process.

Road construction was carried out over a two-year
period. Tools used in preparing road beds were limited
to heavy hoes and bamboo carrying baskets. Necessary
tasks included digging, carrying, spreading, and
tamping of earth. The work was organized and
supervised by the nine members of the village
development committee. Straight segments through the
village were completed one at a time. Work days were
set during agricultural slack periods. They were
announced throughout the village, but most workers came
from houses located close to the right-of-way. All
households were expected to send representatives to "do
their share" over the two year period. Attendance was
recorded in an account book. No specific sanctions
were contemplated for nonparticipating households other
than gossip and ill will. The Abbot organized a
rotational system whereby families in each of the five
village khum (neighborhoods) were expected to feed the
workers.

A village electrical system. For more than six
years, from 1972 to 1978, residents enjoyed electrical
service from a system which was planned, paid for, and

maintained solely on local initiative.  Two nearby
villages had established generator-operated systems,
and the Abbot proposed that local residents do the
same.  Under the Abbot's direction, a total of 100,000
baht was raised.  Some funds were contributed by local
residents specifically for the electrical project;
others had been contributed to the general temple fund.
The Abbot and a local resident knowledgeable about
generators sought a used generator in Bangkok and at
several locations in Northeastern Thailand.  They
finally located one in a rock crushing plant in Buriram
Province and paid 40,000 baht for it.  The remaining
60,000 baht was sufficient to finance house wiring,
electrical poles, and installation.  Equipment and
installation materials were purchased from a single
shop in Khon Kaen.

Initially, slightly less than half of the village
households agreed to accept service.  There was no
hookup fee, but those families connected to the system
agreed to pay a monthly fee of five baht for each
twenty watt fluorescent bulb used, and twelve baht for
each forty watt bulb.  No additional charge was made
for radios, TV sets, fans, and other appliances.  Later
monthly charges were raised to seven baht and eighteen
baht.

Initially, the generator was operated from 6:00 to
11:00 or 11:30 p.m.  Later, as fuel became more
expensive, it was shut down at 9:00.  The cost of fuel
and lubricating oil was nearly one-hundred baht each
night.  The generator broke down frequently, and
monthly payments were insufficient to cover the high
cost (typically 4-5000 baht) of repairs.  Costs were
usually covered by an appeal to users, and by drawing
funds from temple revenues.

Those households not connected to the system
initially could be by making a request to the Abbot.
In such cases, wiring was done by local monks.  The
monks also acted as bill collectors, visiting customers
monthly.  One monk acted as bookkeeper for the system.

The system was closed down at the end of 1978,
after more than six years.  The decision to do so was
made in response to a government promise to connect the
village to the regional grid before the elections (of
April 22, 1979).  When we visited the village in late
June, piles of concrete electrical poles could be seen
along village roads.  A few poles had been raised, but
no wire had been attached.

The "big well".  The "big well" lies about one
kilometer beyond Ban Kham Paum's northern boundary.  It
lies near a village more than 130 years old, and was
originally dug soon after the village was established.
During the dry season, it supplies drinking water to
residents of a number of villages in the area.  A

recent problem is that some families residing as far as
ten kilometers away cooperate in renting a truck, fill
it with large barrels, and come to draw water in great
quantities. The kamnan would like to close the well to
all who reside outside the three or four nearest
villages. However, he feels constrained from doing so.

In about 1965, a famous monk who resides at Wat Po
(an equally famous temple) in Bangkok, but is native to
a nearby village came to "sponsor" improvement work on
the well. He lived at the site during the dry season,
and encouraged residents in the work of digging the
well deeper and wider, and in lining the walls with
boards. The well is approximately thirty feet in
diameter. Because the monk was present, all labor
done, and donations of cash and construction materials
could be interpreted as tham bun or "merit making".

Minor maintenance tasks--such as patching
boards--are carried out by residents of the nearest
village. Once a year the kamnan mobilizes workers from
three or four surrounding villages. On a specified day
in March (when the water level is low) 170-180 people
gather to remove mud that has been deposited in the
bottom of the well.

Tube wells. Ban Kham Paum has a total of seven
tube wells distributed rather evenly through its
territory. They were dug in 1971-72. These, too, were
built under the leadership of the local Abbot. When
people came to the temple to draw "use water" from the
temple ponds he would ask "Why don't you get a tube
well?" When they asked "Who's going to organize the
effort and pay for it?", he would reply "I am." He
would then give them one-hundred baht to initiate a
construction fund. Each of the local wells was
constructed, at a cost of about 1500 baht, by a local
man. Each is provided with a hand pump, a roof, and a
sign which lists all contributors. In each case the
Abbot's name leads the list.

Several types of projects which are currently
fashionable seek to establish or upgrade resources at
the local level, and imply significant expansion of
local management capability. These projects include:
small-scale irrigation, village woodlots, minihydro
power generation, fish ponds, and potable water
systems. Before such projects are initiated, officials
must ask: What role will central officials and local
residents have in managing these resources? Who will
take day-to-day responsibility for maintenance and
regulation? In most cases, high costs for personnel,
vehicles, and gasoline dictate a strong emphasis on
local management. If so, officials and residents must
focus jointly on institutions and skills which already
exist locally, and can be built upon. In addition,
which successful practices can be extended from nearby

or similar villages?  Officials must learn to identify
and understand the potential of existing institutions.
This can save much of the time and energy spent in
building completely new structures and procedures and
raise the probability of project success.  But
officials are wont to ignore this approach.  For
example, Thai fisheries officials often describe ponds
in Northeastern villages as low swampy places.  In
doing so, they ignore historical and contemporary
realities.  Such ponds may be up to two-hundred years
old, and their continued existence depends on regular
annual maintenance and careful regulation of use.
Officials are actually upgrading existing ponds, rather
than building new ones.  What bureaucratic motives
underlie this persistent fiction?:

1. Bureaucratic action (pond construction) is
   justified, and the impact of any positive
   benefits which flow from the project will be
   exaggerated (since no credit will accrue to
   construction efforts 100 years ago or
   maintenance activities each year since).
2. Expenditure of already-committed funds is
   permitted.
3. The need for learning anything about existing
   managerial practices is obviated.
4. The "threat" which local expert knowledge
   poses to rapid planning, contracting, and
   construction is neutralized.

**Consideration II:  Do Not Assume That Uniformity
of Arrangements Between Central Agencies and Local
Groups is Feasible or Desirable**

Existing local groups will have varied structures
and processes.  However, central officials are inclined
to ignore this.  For example, irrigation workers in
Northern Thailand envision a uniform system of local
irrigators' associations, each subscribing to standard
bylaws, and led by a centrally sanctioned Common
Irrigator.  In Chiang Mai, Royal Irrigation Department
officials occupy a system of "ex post centrality".
Their concrete dams and canals and metal watergates
deliver water to local systems which are generations
older than modern, central structures.  The local
irrigation societies are not uniform.  Each has its own
approach to selection of leaders, organization of
maintenance tasks, regulation of water use, punishment
of cheaters, flood protection, etc.  If notions of
bureaucratic "efficiency" dictate that all such
associations be reorganized to fit some externally
designed template, there is grave danger that local
skills will be blunted and irrigation water used less

efficiently.  (I am not aware that this danger exists in Chiang Mai at present.  Irrigation officials may be satisfied with the myth of uniformity.)  Any decision which imposes ex post local uniformity (e.g., by threatening to cut off resources) should be supported by evidence that local efficiency and production will be enhanced, and not by unspoken, aesthetic judgments regarding bureaucratic order.  The unsupported assumption that uniformity is efficient and necessary leads back to the previously discussed fiction that local institutions and management skills don't exist.

American experience suggests that uniformity in local government structure and federal/local relations is unnecessary.  Central agencies deal relatively smoothly with a bewildering array of state, county, municipal, township, regional, and other governmental units.  No two towns or states have uniform structures, laws, personnel systems, regulations, or contracting procedures.  Central agencies impose standards on interactions with themselves and, being bureaucratic organizations, would undoubtedly like to impose greater uniformity.  But local governments are in a position, through open political processes, to guard their autonomy and uniqueness.

## Consideration III:  In Attempting to Improve Operations of Centralized Service Agencies, Devote Substantial Time to "Working Back" from the Agency/Community "Interface"

Central agencies will do well to focus analytical skills and reformist energies on those specific situations in which agency officials directly interact with and serve a target population.  This can be termed the "interface".  Initial attention should focus on fundamental questions:

1.  Where and how are services delivered?
2.  By and for whom are they delivered?
3.  What are the minimum skills and education required to deliver the services?
4.  How are officials who serve in local areas selected and trained?
5.  Are educational standards set, for bureaucratic rather than administrative reasons, arbitrarily high?
6.  Will educated urbanites really serve in rural areas?
7.  Are university graduates sufficiently sophisticated in rural ways to analyze and meet problems of service delivery?
8.  Will village women really accept services from male officials?

9. Do agency representatives offer services at the right time of day?
10. Do officials speak the local language?
11. Do they understand and respect local standards of politeness?
12. Do their normal patterns of food consumption, dress, and interaction effectively remove them from ordinary patterns of intelligent discourse?
13. Are the services offered really appropriate to the local situation?
14. What can be done "in the field" to improve services and delivery?
15. What can be done within the agency to better support field workers?

Thai villages are served by: agricultural extention workers (Ministry of Agriculture and Cooperatives); elementary school teachers (Ministry of Education); Community Development and Accelerated Rural Development workers (Ministry of Interior); sanitarians and midwives (Ministry of Health); and loan officers representing the Bank for Agriculture and Agriculture Cooperatives. The services they offer are limited by the following problems:

1. Officials have Monday to Friday, daytime work schedules. During some parts of the annual cycle it is difficult for residents to take advantage of services offered.
2. Many of these workers commute to the job site from district or commercial towns. This narrows the range of interactions they can have with villagers and limits their personal effectiveness.
3. These workers are too often absent from their posts. Many are uncommitted and uncomfortable in rural areas and avail themselves of every excuse (filing reports, receiving paychecks, attendance at meetings and ceremonies, illness) to avoid their village responsibilities.
4. Patterns of employee rotation remove officials from a locality soon after they have come to know it well, and remove officials from areas where they speak the local language, understand patterns of politeness, etc.
5. Local representatives of central agencies serving in Northern and Northeastern Thailand often distinguish themselves from local residents on public occasions by refusing to consume locally popular food items--sticky rice, minced raw pork, rice beer, etc.

This behavior limits the effectiveness of central officials. Ministries and Departments in question could improve the situation by:

1. Lowering educational standards where necessary, in order to find and retain village-born workers.
2. Altering pay schedules and promotion policies so that village workers are rewarded for continuous service and given promotions without moving to provincial towns, Bangkok, or another region.
3. Requiring all professionals in the organization to serve initially in rural areas, and tying promotions to successful completion of this service.

Analysts should form a strong image of how the interface is presently constituted, and how it can be improved--i.e., how central officials can best perform their duties among the citizens. This image should be formalized (e.g., in the form of a written description of "The Effective Agricultural Extension Worker and His or Her Work") and widely disseminated among agency employees. The organization would then have a set of clearly defined goals around which to initiate bureaucratic reorientation. Ordinarily, bureaucratic reform is built around abstract notions of bureaucratic propriety--careful attention to organization charts, documentation, careful demarcation of responsibilities--and achieves (bureaucratic) efficiency without (field) effectiveness.

## Consideration IV: Elicit "Local Participation" in Projects by Giving Participants Control Over, and Responsibility for, Essential Resources

Much has been written about local participation in externally funded projects. Most of this work is hortatory, and has little effect on project planning and implementation. Only a few authors have been able to define participation clearly[5] or describe successful practices.[6] Only recently have case studies of successful reorientation (in which central agencies have learned to tolerate, and even nurture local participation) become available. Korten, for instance, reports on an ongoing process in the National Irrigation Association of the Philippines.[7]

National Irrigation Association (NIA) officials plan and construct (or upgrade) small-scale irrigation systems. In recent years they have dramatically

reoriented their style of working with farmers'
groups. New financial arrangements have forced NIA
engineers to collaborate with farmers. Previously, NIA
technicians identified promising projects, sought
agency construction funds, and proceeded to the
construction phase. At the end of the process, the
system was turned over to the local farmers' group.
The farmers' role was severely limited. They could say
"No" to a free good, but not "Yes" while specifying
conditions. As recipients of government largesse, they
had little control over design, contracting, or
construction.

The NIA (with outside consultation) made two major
changes. First, community development workers were
brought in to mobilize farmer groups and help them
articulate group preferences. Second, farmers were
asked to "buy in" to the process by jointly accepting a
construction loan, and providing unskilled labor during
construction. As a result of these innovations,
Filipino farmers are becoming involved in such issues
as: location and design of dams and canals; purchase
of construction materials; and supervision of
construction workers. Their knowledge and judgment is
not substituted for that of professional engineers, but
usefully supplements it.

Partial control over projects and processes not
only strengthens the position of villagers vis-a-vis
central agencies; it also provides a basis for
livelier, more open intravillage politics. When
individuals and households provide labor or materials,
or cosign a loan agreement, their concurrence in local
decisions is required more often, and in relationship
to more fundamental issues.

## Consideration V: Support Local Government and Local Initiative

Support for local government and local initiatives
can take two forms, one preferred the other
acceptable. The preferred way is to give local
governments the power to tax, and stand back! The
acceptable way is to share national resources by giving
block grants to local governments and broad-based local
groups. Both solutions seem obvious to American
readers, and not in the least bit radical. It must be
realized, though, that the preferred solution is highly
suspect among Third World bureaucrats, and that many
officials resist the acceptable solution. When local
revenue generation is coupled with local legislative
power and local police power, many Third World
officials are shocked! Careful listeners quickly learn

why: "This is an open invitation to subversive forces." "We haven't finished building the nation yet." "The peasants simply can't manage for themselves; they'll be exploited by local elites." Where necessary, each proposition can be embroidered with statements of historical and cultural fact. However, the converse hypothesis can be argued in each case. Strong local government (and open politics) is possible, and may be invaluable in building the nation and resisting subversion. Local participation in organizations and politics is a major way in which individuals can assert their role in support of a national policy.

If, however, local officials resist arguments for a direct solution, a gradual, evolutionary process can be envisioned:

1. Begin with block grants expendable within narrowly defined limits.
2. Gradually respond to demands for broader parameters.
3. As political demand for local revenue generation begins to build, set aside a few administrative units for a fiscal/political experiment.
4. Support the experiment with provisional laws and regulations.
5. When the time is right, revise provisional laws in response to the experiment, and create legislation on a national scale.[8]

Development-minded officials should respond cautiously to the assertion that "There's no base to x." This may be another myth, justifying central control. Coupled with the assertion that "Poverty is so great that _any_ program will help", it excuses officials from serious attention to local conditions. If the fiscal base is modest, clearly locally initiated projects must be modest too. But somewhere, somehow, the process must begin. Ellis offers an innovative approach to nurturing local initiative under conditions of extreme poverty.[9] The national government (or an international donor) creates "credit accounts" which can be drawn on by local governments. These groups are then presented with a catalogue of locally appropriate items of technology--pumps, well drilling equipment, solar collectors, minihydro generators, construction tools, etc. Decisions would be informed by village-based knowledge and experience, and we can readily envision how technological and administrative learning become cumulative and widespread. When technological decisions are under exclusively bureaucratic control this is seldom the case.

Consideration VI:  In Project Analysis, Do Not
Confuse Standards of Scientific Rigor with
those for Administrative Usefulness.  Recognize
the Operational Primacy of the Latter.

Most decisions regarding project termination,
continuation, or redesign require knowledge of a
"structural" kind--who is doing what to whom; major
factors affecting significant decisions; whether or not
innovations offered are broadly appropriate to local
circumstances.  Knowledge of major elements of a
situation is combined with inspired guesswork regarding
future probabilities to make significant operational
decisions.  There is seldom time for detailed
investigation of the frequency of events, opinions, and
actions.  It must be sufficient to know that they
exist.  Information of this type can be acquired
quickly, and used in improving project administration.
Proponents of "scientific" project analysis
envision a utopian process in which quantified impact
data are measured against quantified baseline
indicators.  Ideally, sound insights can be derived
which will guide future design efforts.  In fact, in a
causally complex, "real" world, baseline indicators
seldom successfully predict project realities.
Furthermore, in those few cases where ex ante data can
be meaningfully compared to ex post measurements, the
resulting knowledge is often trivial.  In any case, the
results of such studies come slowly and at great
expense.  They are seldom available for reshaping the
project from which they are derived.  Furthermore, it
is ordinarily assumed that the requirements of
"scientific rigor" rule out participatory approaches to
analysis.  The result is analytical processes and
results which are inaccessible and irrelevant to local
leaders, ordinary people, and bureaucratic generalists.
If we assume that project analysis is primarily a
process of discovering "basic issues and related
problems", there is much greater scope for local
participation in setting an agenda, gathering data,
analysis, and redesign.
Much can be gained by widespread dissemination of
techniques of the Rapid Appraisal approach to field
data collection.  This method is accessible to
development workers who are not social scientists, and
to intelligent people (in villages and elsewhere) who
are not development professionals.  Rapid Appraisal is
a rigorous approach to exploratory, cumulative research
which relies heavily on semistructured interview
techniques.  It has been described in articles by
Chambers and Honadle and on videotapes by Grandstaff
and Schmidt and Grandstaff and Calavan. [10]

228

Consideration VII:  Avoid Oversimple Assumptions
Regarding Modernization and Learn to Accept
Technological "Dissonance".  (Water Buffaloes and
Microcomputers May Be Appropriate Technologies
within a Single Environment.)

Unless challenged, most people (including Third
World officials and development workers) assume that
development is fundamentally a "unilinear" process.
That is, all nations must pass through the same basic
socioeconomic stages, and these must be accompanied by
standardized technologies and management techniques.
External consultants and officials of international
agencies sometimes exhibit this mindset by making
strikingly inappropriate judgments regarding the
fitness of technologies and processes.  Ellis describes
an AID project in Ethiopia in which public sector well
drilling (at $200/vertical foot) was selected over
private sector drilling (at $100/ vertical foot) and
traditional methods of hand digging (at $3/vertical
foot).[11]
Ellis adduces several explanations for this
behavior which are based in bureaucratic values and
self-interest.  In addition, it seems fair to assume
that certain perceptual habits (regarding "developed"
technologies and administrative practices) made it
relatively easy to propose and defend inappropriate
technologies.  First, there is a human tendency to
regard the unknown world as simpler than the known
one.  Since consultants and officials seldom know the
village world as well as its residents, they make the
wrong simplifying assumptions:  "Some farmers in this
village are using hand tractors, therefore water
buffaloes must be an uneconomic source of draft
power."  Or: "Most farmers are using water buffaloes to
plow before rice cultivation, therefore there will be
no demand for custom tractor plowing before garlic
production."[12]  Second, officials may be stricken
with the "obligation disease".  ("Modest, low cost
projects have heavy bureaucratic labor costs, confer
little prestige, and do little to justify higher
budgets in the coming fiscal year.")  There are many
bureaucratic bases for this line of reasoning.
Having obligated funds for expensive, inappropriate technologies, officials are all too willing to
buttress their initial poor judgment by manipulation of
subsidies, licensing requirements, and import/
export duties.  In the language of cost-benefit
analysis, even when such projects achieve "financial"
success (measured in returns to selected individuals)
they are likely to be "economic" failures (measured in
costs to society).
For instance, Auerbach reports a case from Tunisia
in the early 1970s in which handloom weavers

working in their homes earned twice as much as the
young men who operated power looms in modern textile
mills.  The latter had to be "brided" with elaborate
fringe benefits including subsidized home loans.  It is
not clear that Tunisian society could "afford" a modern
textile sector under those conditions.[13]

Similarly, Liedholm describes the circumstances
under which a large, modern brewery was established in
a small southern African country to sell native millet
beer to residents.  The brewery hired a few workers,
was given tax breaks and favorable duties on imported
equipment.  Eventually, 30,000 part-time village
brewers were driven out of business.  The modern
brewery achieved financial success at considerable
economic cost to the country.[14]

Even humane, well-intentioned initiatives can be
inappropriate or premature.  For example, in Thailand
strict imposition of existing public health regulations
(meat inspection, licensed slaughtering, strict use of
municipal slaughterhouses, restaurant licensing, etc.)
could drive tens of thousands of food processors,
street vendors, and small restaurant owners out of
business.  In addition, the cost of prepared food would
rise and government officials would face an enforcement
nightmare.

Consideration VIII:  Think Carefully Before
Transferring Management Skills from the First
World to the Third.  That Which is "Transferable"
May Be Only Some Elements of Management Technology,
Rather Than an Integrated, Prescriptive Science

If we focus again on the interface between central
agencies and local groups, the most appropriate
management skills may be those which are fundamentally
"ahierarchical" and generic.[15]  Yet, when officials
do take responsibility for village management skills,
there is a tendency to emphasize those routines
essential to smooth bureaucratic interaction.  In rural
Thailand, a significant portion of the skills
emphasized--speaking Central Thai, organizing
ceremonies and receptions, briefing officials,
bookkeeping and contracting according to government
regulations--are primarily useful in dealing with the
central bureaucracy.  There is little in this training
which enhances autonomous management of local
resources.  Ahierarchical, generic skills of particular
relevance in local management include:  meeting
leadership, articulating and hearing novel ideas,
group-process and self-analysis, synthesis of ideas,
nonthreatening presentation of strongly held ideas,
definition and acceptance of tasks.  To the extent that
these skills can be widely disseminated,[16] the

quality of interaction and management between officials and villagers and among villagers will be greatly enhanced.

Great care should be taken to avoid imposing unnecessary auditing, inspection, and documentation functions on small, informal groups. Where face-to-face relationships predominate, the best procedures are simple and widely understood. Where they are not, personnel and money costs are likely to be disproportionately large in relationship to actual resource flows. Efforts in procedural reform can be usefully guided by careful attention to the use to which records will be put, and how specific decisions will flow from them. Records and data which are not used should be eliminated.

Long range, integrated planning is a bureaucratic chimera. It has enjoyed very limited success in the United States (where it has enjoyed substantial support in recent years) and in the Soviet Union (where it is considered fundamental to the administrative system). Yet it is often presented as a major solution to Third World problems, and a logical first step in efforts to decentralize and develop local government.

The fact that the ideology of planning is transmitted from First World professors and Second World ideologues to Third World officials offers one basis for its bureaucratic attraction. Another lies in its utility as a "consolation prize" to villagers who are denied significant autonomy or control over resources. Unfortunately (or fortunately), most rural residents are unimpressed and few participate.[17] The Third World is rich in dusty, unused local development plans. Villagers will be impressed and responsive when they can manipulate resources rather than plans. The opportunity to do so will also contribute to establishment of serious, open, local politics, a process far more fundamental to development than planning.


Consideration IX: Beware of Thinking of Culture as a Monolithic Barrier, or as a Magical, Omnipotent Tool

In the professional world of development, "culture" sometimes becomes a mythic force. Project failures can be attributed to some custom widely practiced or some value deeply held. Simple reasons--family structure or religious norms--are adduced to explain conservative behavior, and "conservatism" becomes a cultural force, in and of itself. Values and customs are useful abstractions, but, by themselves, of limited value in predicting and interpreting behavior. Development professionals and Third World officials must learn to understand villagers in the same way they understand their colleagues and family members.

The behavior of all people reflects experience, learning, personal preferences, efforts to better one's lot, decisions made under incomplete information, "tradeoffs" among possible strategies, efforts to avoid embarassment, i.e., it is causally complex. The fact that people are foreign, rural, and poor does not make their behavior easy to explain. However, the assumption that this is true makes it easier to avoid listening to and understanding such people, providing them with significant resources, or allowing them significant autonomy.

Do not assume that all members of a society share its dominant values. In fact the values expressed most often may be dominant only in the sense that they belong to an elite minority.[18] In order to test the range of values and concepts in a society, it is necessary to interact with a range of people. Officials should limit time spent listening to men who tell them "Our women want..." or to elites explaining that "Peasants in this country prefer to..." Ideally, they should listen more often to rural residents and less often to other officials and so-called social science experts.

We need not assume that all groups and activities within a society are hierarchical or sectarian, simply because a society is caste ridden, class dominated, or divided by ethnic loyalties. For example, 19th Century Northern Thai society was divided into legal estates of aristocrats, commoners, and slaves. Nevertheless, all estates participated in the activities of the Buddhist temple; many individuals in each group took part in Buddhist cult activities, and there was wide scope for egalitarian participation in exchange labor groups [19]

It is axiomatic that all cultures are changing. It is seldom true that peasants farm (or marry, or think) in the same way as their great grandparents. But the assertion is often made. This is another "prophylactic" myth. Like those mentioned earlier ("There are no management skills in the village; The marketing system is inefficient, These people are too poor to tax themselves.") it protects officials against intellectual and social intimacy with villagers. Officials must be aware of contemporary trends and their significance, and be willing to act.

One trend in Thailand holds out great hope for the growth of local autonomy. Thai universities are beginning to produce graduates in excess of the labor demands of the bureaucracy and multinational firms. Educated young people are flowing back to the countryside. Because many are articulate and energetic, they have enormous potential for support of autonomous local politics.[20]

Another trend is a corollary of overall economic growth in Thailand, and holds out hope for a more "mature" relationship between central officials and local residents. District towns are becoming better places to live. Schools are improving. The accouterments of middle class life--movie houses, shops with ready made clothing and home appliances, restaurants, "respectable" night clubs--are increasing. The towns are more attractive places to live and central officials will be less inclined to leave. Their interests will become more closely identified with town and district. They will assess local needs and report them to their bureaucratic superiors with greater conviction. Much can be accomplished by recognizing such trends, and supporting policies (grants to municipalities of this type provide indirect incentives to officials who wish to "stay put") which enhance them.

## Consideration X: Recognize Some Administrative Dilemmas As Such. There is No Uniquely Appropriate, Trouble-Free Framework for Interaction Between Government Agencies and Local Groups

In administrative processes, some situations lead inevitably to anxiety, misunderstanding, friction, and conflict. Sensible people will attempt to anticipate these dilemmas and react with intelligence and flexibility. Since they ordinarily have structural advantages over the ordinary people they deal with, it is incumbent on officials to learn about these dilemmas and develop appropriate reactions.

The "lack of information" dilemma. Everyone would like more information before making crucial decisions. But there are costs in acquiring information, and these are seldom fully known. Some participants in virtually any process will feel inadequately informed, and will assume that the process can be rationalized if only they are better informed. Sometimes this is true, often it is not. In any case, officials should avoid the assumption that information is necessary for them, and a luxury for ordinary people. Conversely, they should be prepared to deal patiently with people who feel left out.

The "intermediary" dilemma. In any social process involving more then a handful of people, one or more participants will be thrust into the "intermediary" role. For example, in rural Thailand agricultural extension workers, members of the temple administrative committee, and representatives to the Subdistrict Council all occasionally fill this role. Often, it involves interpreting the opinions of those not present to those who are. In order to get results (which will advance the general good) it is often tempting (or necessary, or appropriate) to shade, soften, or contextualize the positions of others. As a result, even successful intermediaries must anticipate occasional accusations of lying or treason.

Scudder cites a case in which correct intermediary behavior is virtually impossible.[21] Leaders of local communities designated for resettlement invariably lose the confidence of their followers. If they choose to fight inexorable bureaucratic processes, they lose the battle and their credibility with followers. If they opt for compromise, followers accuse them of "selling out" and their credibility is lost. (Here is a dilemma which resettlement officials can anticipate and ameliorate, but not eliminate!)

The "steering and joining" dilemma.[22] In all sustained administrative processes, it is eventually necessary to "pass the ball". Tasks are passed from one individual or group to another, or new group members must be brought on board. Steerers inevitably question the competence of joiners to understand the situation and carry on. Joiners readily detect this lack of confidence, and suspect that important information is being withheld. Such situations are invariably rich in anxiety and mistrust. Sensible individuals will meet them with flexibility, focused listening skills, humor, and a strategy for working things out with the "other side".

Consideration XI:  Sometimes Outsiders Wish to Understand a Situation, Sometimes They Wish to Change It

We have noted some of the myths that officials rely on to excuse themselves from serious understanding of those with whom they deal. Ideally, though, development processes should involve frequent shifts between learning and action modes. Learning about local institutions, behavior, and preferences should predominate in early stages of conceptualization and planning. Officials should resist a tendency to move too quickly to prescription and action. However, this tendency is bolstered by at least two previously unexamined characteristics of bureaucratic culture. First, the technical training provided to many officials provides them with "solutions looking for a problem". Second, bureaucratic units are typically organized to operate within a specific sector or provide a narrow range of services. In most cases, it would be bureaucratically impolitic for such a unit to identify problems and offer solutions which lie primarily outside its area of responsibility.

The learning mode should not end with the planning phase. All who monitor project activities must learn to occasionally set aside (most of) their prejudices while attempting to understand fundamental implementation issues.

Officials who "know" the solution and feel no need to learn are particularly troublesome.[23] Self-confident ignorance in the planning stage can lead to wild misinterpretation later on. Peasants who reject a technological innovation are dismissed as conservative, or vague management problems are diagnosed in the extension system. All too often, the program, or technology, or opportunity offered is inappropriate--too expensive, too risky, aimed at the wrong audience, and offered at the wrong time of the year. Often, efforts to simply talk with members of the target group will lay these problems bare.

## Consideration XII: Think Creatively About Technical Assistance (TA)

Thinking about transfer of technical knowledge has become sterotyped: useful knowledge resides in the First World (perhaps the Second) and must be transferred by an "expert" from a suitable university, consulting firm, or government department. Alternatively, Third World officials are trained at First World universities. There is value in this but not exclusive value. A narrow view effectively denies the reality of hundreds of generations of diffusion of technologies and ideas from person to person and group to group. In fact, useful TA can be transmitted village to village, from one Third World nation to another, or from the Third World to the First.

Kunstadter[24] provides an illustrative case of village to village transfer of knowledge. Most members of the Lua ethnic group in Northern Thailand are upland swidden farmers. In the 1930s, farmers in one village were experimenting with wet rice agriculture. Initially, their efforts failed and they didn't know why. Their strategy was to seek "technical assistance". They paid a Northern Thai farmer from the lowlands to come to their upland valley, oversee construction of wet rice fields and simple irrigation facilities, and then cultivate rice for a year. After this successful demonstration, Lua farmers in the area became successful wet rice farmers!

This process can be, in its essentials, replicated

at present.  For instance, small-scale irrigation
systems are being constructed by the Royal Irrigation
Department at many locations in Northeastern Thailand.
Farmers in these areas are familiar with cultivation of
rainfed, wet rice, but know little about irrigation
management.  Yet, in other parts of Thailand (e.g., the
North and the lower Northeast), small systems have been
managed successfully for centuries.  Creative
irrigation officials may wish to consider engaging
experienced irrigation headmen from long-established
systems to advise farmers who are beginning to manage
new ones, or taking leaders of new systems on a "study
tour" of established systems.

Officials should consider the potential of a
catalogue of successful practices.  This suggestion was
offered in support of a village fishpond construction
project in Northeastern Thailand.[25]  A catalogue
of "successful practices in village fishpond management"
could be assembled and used in the following ways.

1.  Brief fieldwork by a competent social
    scientist would reveal essential management
    elements--organizing construction activity,
    establishing an annual maintenance cycle,
    mobilizing labor, regulation of fishing,
    regulation of water use, punishment of
    offenders, etc.--fundamental to management of
    a new or upgraded pond.
2.  The next step, requiring twenty to
    twenty-five days of field research, would
    require discovery and description of several
    existing solutions for these elements, each
    used in at least one village of the region.
3.  This information can then be recorded in a
    readable, Thai-language catalogue for use by
    officials and village residents.
4.  The catalogue can stimulate discussion and
    provide a reference point for discussions
    among villagers, and between villagers and
    officials regarding management practices for
    a new or upgraded pond.  It is unnecessary
    for any successful practice to be fully
    adopted.  If the catalogue stimulates
    creativity, synthesis, and locally
    appropriate solutions, it can be considered a
    success.

It is likely that the First World can learn
useful things from the Third.  One intriguing example
is found in the "public transport system" of Chiang
Mai Province, Northern Thailand.  This motley
collection of trucks, modified as buses, is entirely
in private hands.  Each day it moves large quantities
of people (market sellers, students, middlemen,

construction workers) and goods (fruits and vegetables,
snacks, pigs, poultry, farm implements, etc.) from
village to town, town to village, and town to town.  It
supplements and successfully competes with a
state-operated transport system and provides service
which is cheap, relatively swift, moderately unsafe and
uncomfortable.  It is unlikely that significantly
higher ton-miles/gallon or passenger-miles/gallon
ratios are achieved anywhere in the world.

The system operates without central authority or
regulation; and it works well!  In the face of energy
costs which will rise in the long term and the
inability of mass transit systems to provide service
outside high density areas, Western officials might
learn many useful insights from the Chiang Mai system.
An assessment could begin with the technologies, norms,
incentives, and social structures which constitute the
system.


Consideration XIII:  Given Sufficient Time and
Resources, The Right Centrally Sponsored Program Can Do
Much to Nurture Local Initiative.

At some point, central bureaucracies must learn to
forfeit power and rethink their responsibilities and
capabilities.  But this need not imply that the
countryside be abandoned, without resources.  Some
central programs can nurture autonomy.

Thailand's Department of Community Development
provides a cogent example.  Personal observation
suggests that this unit has made great strides in
competence and effectiveness during the past fifteen
years.  My first experience with Community Development
workers was in a village in Chiang Mai Province in
1969.  A group of workers visited the village for
several days, held public meetings, and organized an
inconsequential public works project.  (Roadside
drainage ditches were dug in sand soil and disappeared
in a matter of weeks).  The workers were personable and
energetic, but there were no significant impacts on the
village.  The workers moved on, and physical projects
had no lasting effect.

Thirteen years later (November, 1982) I had an
opportunity to observe Community Development workers in
Ubon Ratchatani and Yasothon Provinces in Northeastern
Thailand, and Narathiwat Province in the South.  I
found workers to be highly committed, comfortable in
interactions with villagers, and knowledgeable about
rural life.  They were supporting local residents in a
large number of projects--road repair; construction of
playgrounds, rest pavilions, and meeting halls;
operation of libraries and nursery schools; and
establishment of medicine banks and other modest

cooperative activities. Specifically, they assisted villagers by:

1. Providing expert advice on small-scale public works projects (road repair, wells, ponds, small dams, etc.)
2. Providing advice on successful practices for organizing village activities;
3. Establishing liaison with district and provincial officials;
4. Identifying special funding sources for local projects.

Organizations of this type are seldom effective in their early years. Appropriate modes of operation evolve over a period of years. A cadre of effective workers must be recruited, trained, and carefully introduced to their profession through an informal apprenticeship. Successful practices must be developed and effective strategies gradually evolved. In addition, it is essential that other, synergistic institutions be in place. In rural Thailand, the Tambon (Subdistrict) Council is one such institution.

In 1975, during a period of unusually open political activity, the central government (under the leadership of Kukrit Pramoj and the Social Action Party) initiated a program of block grants to local areas. The program was established quickly, in part to take advantage of a large revenue surplus generated in 1974-75 by the rice export tax. All Tambon Councils in Thailand were given identical grants of 500,000 baht ($25,000 at the time) to carry out locally controlled, locally selected infrastructure projects. No provisions were made for differences among tambons in wealth or population. Projects were limited to roads, irrigation systems, and water projects such as pond construction. Local labor was generally employed under the direct supervision of Tambon Council members.

This program was well regarded in the countryside, but aroused great distaste among central bureaucrats. Villagers regarded the program as the most significant rural initiative of the government in living memory. Seven years later, most villagers can still identify "Kukrit roads" and "Kukrit wells". Bureaucrats who disliked the program cite examples of local corruption and inefficiency, and imply that these were virtually universal. Recently published studies show that reality lies someplace between these perceptual extremes. Corruption and inefficiency were common, but hardly universal. Many worthwhile projects were completed.

Perhaps the most significant thing about the Tambon Council Fund Program was that it created a political precedent that was hard to break. Ordinary

villagers and Tambon leaders liked the program.  The
authoritarian, unpopular Thanin government discontinued
the program in 1977, but nevertheless felt impelled to
finance a large number of small-scale, centrally
managed projects in rural areas.  In 1978, the
military-supported government of General Kriangsak
reinstituted a block grant program.  This time, grants
varied with the wealth and population of the tambon.
The program is currently in its fourth year, and has
been accepted as part of normal
political/administrative process in the countryside.
     The program is currently called the Rural
Employment Generation Program, reflecting its
importance as a source of slack season employment for
villagers as well as a funding source for local
government.  Grants now vary according to a standard
"need" formula, reflecting level of population, income,
and equity.  In the current fiscal year they will vary
from 150,000 baht to approximately 400,000 baht
($6,700-17,400).  The program is administered by a
special national committee attached to the Prime
Minister's Office.  Annual allocations must be expended
by Tambon Councils within a period of a few months.
Central bureaucrats argue, and Council members
generally agree, that annual allocations are
predictable within relatively narrow limits.  It is
reasonable, therefore, for Councils to project
activities over a period of several years.  Long range
planning is further encouraged by officials of the
Community Development Department who lead Council
members through a Five Year planning exercise.
     Local strategies vary.  In some cases, part or all
of the funds are reallocated to villages for local
projects.  In other cases, political reality dictates
that a significant local minority needs to be "bought
off" (e.g., with a well) so that a major project which
will benefit the majority (e.g., an irrigation system)
can proceed.  A single project may exhaust funds for
the year, or may require funds over several years.
Annual decisions are subject to review (for technical
quality and consistency with Tambon Five Year Plans) at
District and Provincial levels.
     The Tambon Council has access to substantial
technical expertise from bureaucrats serving at the
tambon, district, or provincial level.  They can call
on engineers who work for the Accelerated Rural
Development Department, public health workers at the
District Office, Tambon and District Agricultural
Extension workers, and Community Development workers.
It is unclear how much influence these advisors have
over selection of Tambon Council projects, but there is
evidence that it is substantial in some areas.  In the
Muslim South (where most villagers are not literate in
Thai) Community Development workers usually fill out

project data sheets.

Much of the construction work is carried out by small- to medium-sized contractors. In Ubon and Yasothorn Provinces, road construction and pond excavation projects are ordinarily turned over to contractors. In Narathiwat, fewer projects are given to contractors. A contractor ordinarily provides trucks, dozers, and fifteen to twenty workers. These employees are drivers, equipment operators, foremen, and skilled workers. Unskilled labor is provided by Tambon residents. They are paid at a piece work rate (e.g. on road projects a specified volume of earth must be moved) roughly equivalent to the official minimum daily wage of fifty-two baht per day. The Tambon Council establishes criteria for hiring local labor. Workers are typically hired for periods of one to three months. Annual projects seldom last longer.

RECOMMENDATIONS:  WORKING TOWARD "APPROPRIATE ADMINISTRATION"

Building on the considerations that have been discussed above, several recommendations can be made which, if implemented, would go far in achieving Appropriate Administration. The recommendations are aimed at the five distinct categories of actors in the development process which were identified at the outset of this chapter: central government elites, external donors, external PVOs, local leaders and indigenous organizations, and researchers and consultants.

Politicians and high ranking central government bureaucrats can launch programs, mandate training, manipulate incentive structures, and legally alter structures and processes in order to facilitate greater local autonomy. Specifically, they can:

    1A. Establish short-term training programs for midlevel bureaucrats who control rural programs. Officials should be sensitized to the existence of local management skills and taught how to identify those skills through semistructured interviewing. They should be taken to rural areas where they are expected to identify existing practices and develop procedures for adapting central government structures and procedures to them.

    1B. Establish in all central agencies which serve the countryside, a professional hiring quota for individuals who were born and raised in rural areas. If necessary, waive ordinary hiring standards--education, test scores, age limits--in order to fill this quota. Then put these people into jobs where they work in rural areas, or supervise people who do so.

1C. Create the administrative basis for a new
legal/cultural approach to the countryside.
Instead of establishing broadly appropriate
regulations for dealing with local groups,
make locally appropriate contracts with them.
Let the contracts be short, simple, and in
everyday language.

1D. Encourage bureaucrats to take chances by
sometimes meting out rewards--promotions,
merit raises--for "brilliant failures". Call
attention to professional efforts, e.g.,
creative contracts, productive village
meetings, and semistructured interviewing
skills--which facilitate egalitarian
interaction with rural people.

1E. Relocate the bureaucratic "fast track" (away
from central ministry offices). Make certain
that the bulk of promotions and merit raises
are given to those serving "in the provinces"
and outside ministry offices in the national
capital.

1F. Reshape the work habits of government
bureaucrats. Minimize paper flows, but set
monthly goals for face-to-face time with local
people. Monitor the activities of teachers,
extension agents, and health workers. Demote
those who spend more than 10 percent of their
time away from their rural posts.

1G. Make provisions for central bureaucratic
"volunteers" to be furloughed in order to work
directly for local governments. They can
assist in establishing simple accounting and
procurement procedures; start libraries,
recreation centers, and locally financed
clinics, and establish local revenue codes.

1H. Elevate local autonomy to the level of a
national development goal, along with economic
growth and equity. Allow local government
units to tax themselves, and establish
parameters within which they can begin to
practice judicial, police, and regulatory
powers.

1I. Set national minimum standards for local
contributions to infrastructure projects.
Establish a value for skilled and unskilled
labor, and construction material, so that poor
localities can substitute labor and in- kind
payments for cash. Encourage local groups to
initiate proposals by assembling budgets which
include their in-kind and labor contributions.

1J. Avoid imposing central auditing, accounting,
and documentation standards on local
government. Provide assistance to help them

develop their own, but do not assume that
these must be uniform in all localities.

External donors can support innovative central
projects, encourage appropriate administrative reform,
and seek out more direct avenues to financial and
administrative support of local governments and local
groups. In many cases, this implies establishing
long-term links with right-thinking, external PVOs.
Specifically, external donors can:

2A. Support training programs of the type
described in 1A. Local scholars and
researchers should play the major role in
planning and implementing both classroom and
field portions of the training.
Scholar/trainers can be prepared for this work
by external support of descriptive research on
existing local management skills.

2B. Take seriously the notion of transferring
technical knowledge <u>within</u> the Third World.
For example, if farmers in country A have
skills in local irrigation management which
could be usefully applied in country B,
support scholar/consultants from A and B to
study existing practices in A and the setting
into which they will be introduced in B.
Encourage them to develop a <u>process</u> for
transferring knowledge. Futhermore, finance
the travel of farmer/consultants from A to B.

2C. Set aside a portion of overall project funds
for "unconventional technical assistance".
Make sure that these funds are used to tap the
knowledge of experts in other Third World
nations, and within the country being aided.

2D. Support "traditional management" training
programs for young bureaucrats. Let them
spend three to six months living in a rural
area, half of the time researching existing
local management activities, half of the time
in apprenticeship to a local leader.

2E. Rethink procedures for contracting with First
World institutions for management consulting
skills. Require all consultants to carry out
a rapid appraisal of existing management
practices in the project area. If consultants
propose research techniques which rely
excessively on sampling, formal surveys, and
computer analysis, require them to spend some
time in semistructured interviewing.

2F. Occasionally require professionals to set
aside day-to-day administrative
responsibilities and so that they can think
about development. Require them to produce

personal definitions of the development
process, and test their assumptions against
the realities of First World history and
contemporary successes and failures in the
Third World.  Build training and seminars into
each year of professional life.

2G. Commission inventories of existing, successful
local groups in areas where new projects are
contemplated.  Produce manuals which distill
local wisdom on management of irrigation
systems, road maintenance, pond and well
funeral insurance schemes, daily markets,
etc.  Be sure that the manuals are translated
into appropriate languages and widely
distributed to local leaders, extension
officers, etc.

2H. Ease up on auditing procedures for small local
projects.  For projects expending less than
$10,000, require no more than one page of
financial and administrative data.

2I. In planning activities in local areas, abolish
organization charts.  Instead, emphasize the
importance of seeking out existing leaders and
groups to work with.

2J. Make description of "interactions at the
interface" a major focus of evaluation
activity.  Support the activities of PVOs and
government agencies that have a successful
track record of putting effective workers into
villages.

External PVOs must adopt local autonomy as a
dominant end and appropriate administration as a
fundamental means.  Thoughtful PVO leaders must
discover and create innovative ways of working between
central governments and local groups.  Specifically,
they can:

3A. Seek out existing local leaders and groups.
Carefully avoid establishing new groups and
practices where roughly appropriate ones
already exist.  If a new organization is
required, make it an umbrella organization
with leaders drawn from already-existing
groups.  Where feasible, place significant
financial resources under their control and
encourage allocation and utilization according
to already-established practice.

3B. Take village workers out of the "do gooder"
mode from time to time.  Ask them to stop
their work as community developers, extension
agents, etc. and spend 5 to 10 percent of
their time as researchers and analysts.  Take
them to a different rural setting and set them

to work <u>describing</u> the situation, not
<u>prescribing</u> changes.  Reward them for the
richness and subtlety of their descriptions.
Ask them to spend thirty minutes each week
describing and analyzing the setting in which
they ordinarily work.  Build the analytical
skills of the PVO in this way, in addition to,
or instead of, hiring full-time analysts and
evaluators.

3C. Where village politics are elite dominated and
inequitable, don't work within inequitable
processes.  Nor is it appropriate to directly
challenge the power of local elites at the
outset.  Instead, seek out those few existing
groups--neighborhood, cooperative work groups,
cults--where the poor are not entirely
powerless.  Assist them to slowly expand their
range of activities.

3D. Set a good example for the central government
and official donors.  Learn the vocabulary of
indigenous administration, rather than
imposing a new one.  Pose administrative
issues from the standpoint of local efficiency
and convenience.

3E. Be self-conscious in building a model of
"interface interactions".  Be prepared to
propagate your model during demonstrations and
field visits, and in written and spoken
communications.  Attempt to identify essential
features of the model so it can be transferred
from country to country or sector to sector.
(E.g., which PVO practices that have been used
in working with established irrigators'
associations can be transferred to work with
new day care centers?)

3F. Set aside some funds to facilitate travel and
unhampered contact among participants in
projects in different areas.  Use additional
modest funds to prepare mimeographed
catalogues of "successful practices".  Be sure
these are available in locally appropriate
languages.

3G. At a minimum, approach new localities with a
shopping list of projects in which the PVO is
willing to cooperate.  Better yet, find and
support local initiatives which have already
begun.

Local leaders and groups have the hardest task and
the fewest resources.  They must be assertive without
seeming strident or dangerous.  They must mobilize
local resources, and not allow them to be hijacked.
They must be subtle, without appearing to be
dishonest.  They must work within the system while

trying to change it. Specifically, they can:

4A. Publicize the existence of local leaders, groups, and management practices. Post signs in front of the homes of leaders of local government, youth groups, women's groups, producers cooperatives, etc. Publish a mimeographed directory of local groups, their leaders, and their members. Post rules, regulations, maintenance schedules, etc., next to major public resources--e.g., village ponds and neighborhood wells.

4B. Acquire a piece of land for public use. If necessary, "lean" on local elites to donate it. Use voluntary labor and locally available materials to build at least one building for public use. If land is sufficient, set some aside for cooperative garden plots, an athletic field, a community playground, etc.

4C. Make a catalogue of locally available resources which the community can use in cooperation with central government or PVO projects. Include available voluntary labor assessed on a seasonal basis, individual technical and managerial skills, locally available construction materials, privately held tools and equipment which can be borrowed, and realistic estimates of cash which will be donated for various purposes.

4D. Jealously guard those police functions and mediation and arbitration activities which are currently carried out within the community. If the headman, village council, or traditional religious leaders are able to assess fines, mediate disputes, or regulate use of local resources (wells, fish ponds, common land, and small-scale irrigation systems) they should continue to do so. These responsibilities should not be casually passed over to centralized police forces or courts. Local leaders should take initiative in assuming autonomy over activities initiated from outside.

4E. Demand a role in evaluation of local projects. Be generous with interview time and support; but in exchange require that the report be translated into the local language. Offer local people as part-time translators and data analyzers. Ensure that major findings and recommendations are presented in a form readily understandable by local people.

4F. In place of religious pilgrimages, organize development delegations. Spend a week

visiting local leaders and groups in other
provinces and regions.

4G. Be aware of when, where, and how local people
interact with central bureaucrats. Audit
these interactions by occasionally discussing
problems and possible solutions at public
meetings. Relay oral and written suggestions
to appropriate agencies as, "Resolution X by
Village Y."

4H. Be prepared to exchange your "catalogue of
community resources" in (4C) with nearby and
distant communities. Use this as a basis for
initiating joint projects, or for exchanging
scarce expertise.

4I. Assume a mature partnership with central
government officials, PVO representatives, and
others. Then learn to identify problems
without casting needless personal aspersions.
If a health clinic worker is absent from her
job for an average of one day in three,
inquire what local people can do to assist her
with the problems that draw her away.

4J. Pay careful attention to establishing norms
for committee activities and public meetings.
Avoid inflammatory rhetoric, but evolve
procedures for maintaining open discussions
and agreeing to disagree.

4K. Establish regular discussion groups in which
local leaders get together with young people.
Leaders should discuss local politics in a
balanced fashion, including detailed
strategies and tactics in mounting local
projects. Allow young people to debate local
issues and make recommendations for
consideration by their elders.

Researchers and consultants will continue to
gather data and analyze development processes. But it
is equally necessary for them to question assumptions.
They must begin by adopting an external, iconoclastic
view of their own ideas, and then proceed to perform
the same service for others. Finally, they must air
their insights in a manner that captures the attention
and imagination of other actors. Specifically, they
can:

5A. Carry out research on local management
practices. Produce inventories of local
groups, descriptions of group practices, and
prescriptions for mutual adaption between
central/ bureaucratic and local/nonformal
administrative practices. These materials
will be of more immediate use to central
bureaucrats, PVO workers, and local leaders

than sophisticated analytical treatises.

5B. The researchers who ordinarily use universities, research center, etc.--must reorient themselves. They must give professional recognition--tenure, promotions, grants, merit raises--to work which expands our knowledge of local management skills.

5C. Avoid asserting the absence of local groups and management activities if they have not lived in the countryside for an extended period. Design research with a substantial component of participant observation and semistructured interviewing in rural areas.

5D. Be wary of arguments which justify data gathering or analytical procedures on the basis of "scientific rigor". Ask instead whether the results of a survey or tabulated data will be directly useful in deciding how to improve administrative arrangements. Master the techniques of rapid appraisal and semistructured interviewing, and consider these as alternative approaches in project planning, monitoring, and evaluation work.

5E. Do not make the assertion that survey research is quick and cheap. It is seldom either.

5F. Set out to do research which tests our most fundamental assumptions about good management. For example, test the assumption that effective organizations document all significant discussions. Test the assumption that elaborate accounting and auditing are necessary to prevent fraud. Look for organizations that do not do these things. What is the result? Are there other ways to achieve rigorous decision making and prevent fraud? Are there alternative models? Must Third World village organizations be identical to First World bureaucracies in order to be effective?

5G. In research, delineate administrative dilemmas. Label them clearly in writing, teaching, and in consultant reports. Present solutions for what they usually are--partial, temporary, and appropriate only in some portions of a developmental cycle.

5H. Seek out and systematically raise the status of research associates. These include both trained scholars and rural residents who are acute observers. Make special efforts to support, encourage, and recommend local scholars who are willing to work face to face in village settings. Locate rural residents who are willing to advise and train others on

such practical topics as "How to make a living
in periodic rural markets" or "Some approaches
to preventing overfishing of village fish
ponds."

5I. Observe and describe rural programs that
work. Explain why they work. In the real
world potential wrong approaches to a problem
probably outnumber right ones by a factor of
ten to one. Examining failed projects may
provide information on dozens of things not to
do, while identifying no solutions that will
work.

5J. Establish a new field of ethno-
administration, which examines successful
management practices outside of normal
bureaucratic boundaries.

Building local autonomy is essential for
socioeconomic development. Some of these
recommendations may be useful in achieving it.


NOTES

1. This chapter is rich in allusion to the
author's experience as a researcher a social analyst
for the Agency for International Development (AID) in
Thailand. No apology is offered, but readers are
encouraged to test general propositions against their
own experiences and identify discrepancies which can
enrich and accelerate understanding of Appropriate
Administration. The opinions expressed are those of
the author and should not be construed as AID policy.
2. Dan Usher, "The Thai Rice Trade", in T. H.
Silcock, ed., Thailand: Social and Economic Studies in
Development (Canberra: Australian National University
Press, 1967), 221.
3. Herbert Rubin, "Integrating Rural
Development: The Problem and a Solution," PASITAM
Design Study, International Development Institute,
(Bloomington: University of Indiana, 1978), 2-6.
4. Michael Calavan, "Social Analysis for the
Village Fishponds Project", Unpublished Report,
(Bangkok: AID, 1979).
5. John Cohen and Norman Uphoff,
"Participation's Place in Rural Development: Seeking
Clarity through Specificity," World Development 8
(1980).
6. Coralie Bryant and Louise White, Managing
Rural Development: Peasant Participation (West
Hartford, Connecticut: Kumarian Press, 1980). See
also, Norman Uphoff, series of unpublished field

248

reports on the Irrigation Rehabilitation Program in Sri
Lanka.  Titles include "The Institutional-
Organizer Program in the Field After Ten Months" and
others, various dates 1981-83.
      7.  David Korten, "Community Organizations and
Rural Development:  A Learning Process Approach",
Public Administration Review, Special Supplement,
(September-October 1980) and Stanley Staniski, "The Dam
at Laur", Videotape Produced for AID, 1978.
      8.  The Decentralized Development Management
Project sponsored by AID in Thailand is based on
(unwritten) assumptions equivalent to these.
      9.  Gene Ellis, "Development from Below:
Serve?:  the People?  Or Let the People Serve
Themselves?  Unpublished Paper, 1980.
      10.  Robert Chambers, "Rapid Rural Appraisal:
Rationale and Repertoire," Public Administration and
Development 1 (1981): 95-106; George Honadle, "Rapid
Reconnaissance for Development Administration:  Mapping
and Molding Organizational Landscapes," World
Development 10 (1982): 633-650; Terry Grandstaff and
Terry Schmidt, "Rapid Rural Appraisal and
Semi-Structured Interviewing," in Social Science in
USAID/Thailand, Videotape Series (Bangkok: 1982); Terry
Grandstaff and Michael Calavan, "Semi-Structured
Interviewing Techniques", Videotape Produced for AID,
1983.
      11.  Gene Ellis, Man or Machine?  Beast or
Burden?:  A Case Study of the Economics of Agricultural
Mechanizations in Ada District, Ethiopia, Ph.D.
Dissertation, University of Tennessee, Department of
Economics, 1972.
      12.  Both assumptions are wrong for Sansai village
in Northern Thailand.  For insights into the underlying
decision framework see Michael Calavan, Decisions
Against Nature:  An Anthropological Study of
Agriculture in Northern Thailand, Monograph Number 15,
Center for Southeast Asian Studies, Northern Illinois
University (Detroit:  Cellar Bookshop, 1977).
      13.  Steven Auerbach, Personal Communication, 1979.
      14.  Carl Liedholm, Personal Communication, 1981.
      15.  This formulation is etymologically equivalent
to "anarchist" and indeed development professionals and
Third World officials can derive useful insights from
the successful practices of social anarchist
enterprises in the United States.  See Howard Ehrlich,
"Anarchism and Formal Organizations," Research Group
One, Report Number 23 (Baltimore:  Vacant Lots Press,
1977).
      16.  The success of training programs offered by
the Coverdale Organisation in England, the United
States, Bangladesh, and Egypt suggests that this is not
impossible.

17.  In 1970, the author and his wife/colleague were doing dissertation research in a Northern Thai village.  A directive came down from the District level for Tambon leaders to prepare a plan which detailed infrastructure projects desired by villagers.  We assisted this effort by providing data supporting requests for construction of a village middle school and provision of electricity to village homes.  No reply to this local plan was ever received.  Later, in a chance meeting with a USAID official, I learned that this exercise took place in order to "test" the reporting system.  Two subdistricts out of hundreds that responded received project funding.

18.  Two myths can be refuted.  First, most Indians are <u>not</u> vegetarians (see C. Gopalan et. al., <u>Diet Atlas of India</u>, Hyderabad: National Institute of Nutrition, 1971).  Second, even in pre-Communist China most Chinese did <u>not</u> live in extended families.

19.  Kay Mitchell Calavan, <u>Aristocrats and Commoners in Rural Northern Thailand</u>, Ph.D. Dissertation, University of Illinois, Anthropology Department, 1974.

20.  Michael Calavan, "An Assessment of Conditions in Rural Thailand and Some Thoughts on a Future USAID Strategy," unpublished report, Bangkok, 1982.

21.  Thayer Scudder, "Social Analysis for Resettlement Projects," Videotape Produced for AID, 1976.

22.  I have borrowed this formulation of the problem from staff members of the Coverdale Organisation.

23.  One character in the development film, <u>A Simple Cup of Tea</u>, clearly displays the behavior associated with this approach.

24.  Peter Kunstadter, <u>Farmers in the Forest</u> (Honolulu:  East-West Center Press, 1978).

25.  Calavan, "Social Analysis for the Village Fishponds Project," 1979.

# 10
# Conclusion

*Robert F. Gorman*

The themes discussed and conclusions drawn in the preceding chapters are numerous. There is no need to recount them all here. However, some common elements can be discerned which merit brief recapitulation. First, it is a common belief that the programs of PVOs need to be subjected to greater evaluation and scrutiny, if they are to be further refined in the interest of promoting ever more effective progress toward development in the Third World. PVOs, themselves, will need to be more sensitive to the need for evaluation, whether conducted by internal or external means. The long-range effectiveness of PVOs can be gauged only by such efforts. Indeed, PVOs should be interested in evaluation of this sort in order to identify and, where possible, to replicate the most successful development programs. From a more general perspective, the academic and governmental communities also stand to learn much about the relative effectiveness of specific PVO programs and sectoral activities as a result of such evaluation. Where PVO performance is strong, efforts could be made to extend and broaden its impact. Where PVO initiatives are weak, alternative approaches might be identified to strengthen performance.

A second major theme that appears in many of the previous chapters focuses on the relationship between PVOs and the U.S. government, which, through AID, has become a major source of PVO funding. There is not complete agreement about whether the growing PVO/AID relationship is a healthy from the PVO standpoint. Some contributors, as well as many PVOs, see this development as a very problematic one. Others are more inclined to see it as a natural development which can be managed successfully and to the mutual benefit of both parties. Although optimism on this score may vary, there is general agreement that PVO/AID ties are likely to to continue to grow and deepen. Over the next several years, PVOs will be grappling with the consequences of this development, especially with regard to maintaining

an acceptable degree of organizational and program
autonomy.

Several contributors have noted that PVOs, in
pursuing development initiatives abroad, should be in a
position to focus their efforts on meeting the needs of
the very poor.  To accomplish this, PVOs will need to
maintain a commitment to BHN objectives.  But, in fact,
not all PVOs have such a commitment, nor is it necessary
that they should.  Some PVOs, such as those in small
enterprise development, can do extremely useful work
with the middle income range of a poor countries
population.  Successful enterprise development and
credit schemes can contribute to the overall development
of poor communities.  A slavish, or insincere,
commitment to BHN objectives is not desirable.  It is
wholly appropriate, then, that PVOs marshall their
resources to meet the development needs of those
segments of the Third World poor, and those sectors of
Third World economies, that they are most suited to
address.  They need not all, or always, focus on the
needs only of the poorest.

The role of indigenous PVOs as potential vehicles
for the internal development of Third World countries
has been mentioned often in this book.  Clearly, the
building of local initiatives will be a key to any
successful, long-term development effort.  Foreign-based
PVOs have a special role to play in nurturing the growth
of counterpart organizations and affiliates in Third
World countries.  The relationships formed between
indigenous and external PVOs may be very formal and
close, or less formal, and temporary.  Whatever the case
may be, PVOs and indigenous organizations stand to learn
and gain much from cooperation when their goals, program
approaches, and philosophical orientations are conducive
to collaboration.

For U.S.-based PVOs that do not already have ties
with indigenous PVOs, several steps might be taken to
identify suitable local organizations for the potential
collaborative activity.  It is important first to become
familiar with local private sector entrepreneurs and to
solicit information about indigenous associations from
governmental or private foreign aid organizations.  Some
of the most effective indigenous PVOs are in smaller
towns and rural areas, rather than in the major cities.
Hence a survey of the rural areas and not merely the
major cities is often in order.  Rural groups may be
harder to identify but also may be more genuinely
participatory in character and knowledgeable about local
problems.  Of course, the external PVO will also be
interested in finding indigenous PVOs that have
competent staffs and whose philosophical orientation is
compatible with its own.  Successful partnership is more
likely under such circumstances.  Many U.S.-based PVOs

are finding it useful to engage the partnership of
indigenous PVOs in this way. This is a development
which holds out some promise and is one that should be
encouraged. Of course, as Calavan has suggested, it is
important for PVOs in pursuing ties with indigenous
organizations to avoid stifling the creative energies
that allowed the local organization to emerge in the
first place. The trick is to consolidate and strengthen
rather than to control and dominate them.

Another theme identified in earlier chapters is
that PVOs need to examine more closely and expand their
roles as policy advocates and as development educators.
Development is obviously a hard concept to sell to the
peoples and legislatures of developed countries, but
PVOs could and should be making a greater effort to do
so. In this regard, the PVO sector and the academic
community share a special responsibility. Moreover, it
is in this area that these two communities could be
working closely together in order to advance our
knowledge about development and to disseminate that
knowledge more broadly. There is room for considerably
more contact between the academic and private voluntary
communities. Institutional networks should be developed
here to share information, insights, and learning on
development issues.

Although not the subject of major inquiry in the
preceeding chapters, it is worthwhile to explore a bit
more how university/PVO relations might be deepened and
broadened in the interests of both communities. The
notion that universities teach about development and
that PVOs do development is at once true and misleading. Many in the PVO community are quick to assert
that the theoretical prescriptions about development
advanced in university classrooms are often quite apart
from the realities encountered in the practical realm.
But theories are not the exclusive monopoly of
universities. Indeed, even the most practically minded
PVOs harbor pet notions about development that can be
disabused by real world experience. On the other hand,
to eschew theories--which after all are ultimately but
an effort to make sense of, explain, and understand the
practical realm--may encourage a limited, parochial, and
purely anecdotal understanding of the development
process. In truth, the academic and PVO communities are
both repositories of useful knowledge about development
and there is a crucial need for more dialogue between
them so that each can learn from the other.

There are two levels at which University/PVO ties
can be developed; the institutional and the personal.
It is fair to say that both are largely unexploited
today, but personal ties are more evident and more
easily established than institutional ones. In fact the
meager institutional ties that do exist are probably a
function of personal ones. Fortunately, once largely

ignored, PVOs have recently attracted the attention of a growing number of scholars. The interaction that will result from this newfound scholarly interest in PVOs may well lead to more systematic institutional linkages to the mutual benefit of both parties.

An obvious area in which institutional ties would be mutually beneficial is that of developing practitioner-oriented programs for students who may be interested careers in the PVO sector. But there are few university programs that focus on development training with special emphasis on the role of the voluntary sector. However, one pioneering program established at the University of California Polytechnic at San Luis Obispo suggests that programs of this nature are indeed possible. In developing such programs, universities should look to PVOs for advice on appropriate curriculum development.

Similarly, universities are a source of academic expertise on development issues and policy which could be more systematically tapped by PVOs in their preparation and evaluation of country specific programs and projects. Universities could encourage and facilitate this by creating offices devoted specifically to identifying those resources at its disposal which might be of value to PVOs. One such program at the University of California at Los Angeles has been well-received. In the same way PVOs can provide useful information about their own experience in implementation of development programs. Building on the rather disjointed and limited data-base regarding PVO development activities should be an important goal of the scholarly community and one in which PVOs could play an obviously invaluable role. Scholarship will continue to be an important aspect of the university's mission in advancing our knowledge of development and the role PVOs play in it. However, it is time for universities to consider the practical aspects of how that mission can be facilitated and how it can play a role with PVOs in actively promoting development.

While on the subject of universities and research, it should be noted that the questions addressed in this volume, although numerous, have only scratched the surface of potential questions that call for further study. For those interested in the study of PVOs as agents of development, there is yet much to be learned. This volume, for instance, has focused primarily on U.S. PVOs, which leaves a thousand or more of those headquartered in other countries unexamined. Indeed, if little has been written on the styles and approaches of U.S. PVOs in development, still less is readily available on PVOs in other countries. A comparative understanding of PVOs with varied origins would be a welcome addition to the literature. Similarly, in-depth studies of PVO/indigenous PVO relations, of PVO

involvement in local settlement activities which combine
both refugee- and development-related components, and of
the intra-organizational dynamics of PVOs would also
advance our knowledge in useful ways. These represent
but a few of the areas in which more research is needed.

Finally, perhaps the most recurrent theme of this
book is that PVOs are important agents of development.
In many respects, however, the potential for PVOs as
agents for development has been only partially
actualized. They do not as yet constitute a potent
alternative to traditional development assistance.
Their existing contribution is rather small and modest.
But there is room for an increasingly larger role for
PVOs, should they and governments, respectively, be
willing to pursue and permit one. As PVOs shift from a
welfare-dominated to a development-dominated focus, and
as they learn more about how they can promote
self-reliance, one might expect with a fair degree of
confidence, that the marks they make and the legacies
they leave in the developing world will be on the whole
positive ones.

# Contributors

ARTHUR W. BLASER is assistant professor of political
science at Chapman College.  His research has focused on
the role of nongovernmental organizations as proponents
of human rights and the on the varying perspectives of
countries and cultures toward the concept of human
rights.  His articles have appeared in a number of
edited works.

MICHAEL CALAVAN is an anthropologist/bureaucrat who
works for the Agency for International Development.  He
presently serves the AID Mission in Bangladesh as the
project development officer and social scientist.  From
1979 to 1983 he was Director of AID's Development
Studies Program.  From 1970 to 1979 he was an Assistant
and associate professor of anthropology at Illinois
State University.  His research in Thailand has been
supported by the Ford Foundation and the Midwestern
Universities Consortium for International Activities.

GENE ELLIS is associate professor of economics at the
University of Denver.  He served in Ethiopia as a Peace
Corps volunteer from 1964-66.  He has had a long
association with AID, initially as its first
dissertation fellow and later as a member of its
Development Studies Program faculty in 1980-81.  He has
been a consultant to AID and the Peace Corps on
appropriate technology and small-scale
entrepreneurship.  His research on development-related
topics has been published in such journals as World
Development, Journal of Modern African Studies, Journal
of Developing Areas, and Economic Development and
Cultural Change.  He is currently developing an
appropriate technology assessments package for the Peace
Corps.

ROBERT W. HUNT is associate professor of political
science at Illinois State University.  He has done
research in several nations of Africa and Asia, and has

257

written widely on small enterprise and participatory
issues in development. He is the author of a number of
AID Special Studies and Evaluation Papers, and is
currently completing a longer study on the role of the
private voluntary sector in development. He has held
consultancies with a several international donor
agencies in both the public and private sectors.

LARRY MINEAR has headed the Office of Development Policy
of Church World Service and Lutheran World Relief in
Washington, D.C. He has also been active in Interfaith
Action for Economic Justice (formerly the Interreligious
Taskforce on U.S. Food Policy). He has testified
frequently before congressional committees on
development policy issues. He has served as advisor to
a number of U.S. and U.N. commissions and agencies
dealing with world hunger, food aid, and international
development. His book, New Hope for the Hungry? The
Challenge of the World Food Crisis, was published
shortly after the 1974 World Food Conference.

HIBBERT R. ROBERTS is professor of political science and
Chairperson of the Political Science Department at
Illinois State University. His publications include an
article "Meals for Millions Foundation: Limits and
Potential for International Aid," in the International
Journal of Comparative Sociology and book reviews that
have appeared in the Journal of Politics and the
Political Science Quarterly.

BRIAN SMITH is associate professor of political science
at the Massachusetts Institute of Technology. His
research focuses on comparative development issues in
the Third World, especially in Latin America. His book,
The Church and Politics in Chile: Challenges to Modern
Catholicism (Princeton University Press) was awarded the
Best Book Prize in 1982 by the New England Council of
Latin American Studies. He is the author of several
articles and is currently writing a book on U.S.,
Canadian, and West European PVO development activities
in Colombia and Chile. His research has been supported
by grants from the Social Science Research Council, the
Fulbright Program, the National Endowment for Humanities
and the Institute for the Study of World Politics.

# Index